Studies in Theology and Sexuality, 4

Series Editors
Elizabeth Stuart   Alison R Webster   Gerard Loughlin

Editorial Board
Marcella Althaus Reid, Robert Beckford, J Michael Clark, Gillian Cloke,
Beverly Harrison, Renee Hill, Alison Millbank, Ann Pellegrini,
Kwok Pui Lan, Virginia Ramey Mollenkott, Peter Selby

Is There a
Future for
Feminist Theology?

Edited by Deborah F. Sawyer and Diane M. Collier

Sheffield
Academic Press

Copyright © 1999 Sheffield Academic Press

Published by Sheffield Academic Press Ltd
Mansion House
19 Kingfield Road
Sheffield S11 9AS
England

Printed on acid-free paper in Great Britain
by Bookcraft Ltd
Midsomer Norton, Bath

British Library Cataloguing in Publication Data

A catalogue record for this book is available
from the British Library

ISBN   1-85075-963-4
1-85075-979-0 pbk

CONTENTS

PART I
TEXT AND HER-STORY REVISITED

PART II
NEW DIRECTIONS FOR THE NEW MILLENNIUM

ACKNOWLEDGMENTS

The editors would like to thank the Goethe Institute, Manchester, UK, and in particular Richard Schneider, for generously supporting the colloquium from which this volume has evolved. We would also like to thank our colleagues in the Department of Religious Studies at Lancaster University and all those who participated in the colloquium for helping to make it such a successful and stimulating venture.

CONTRIBUTORS

Sally Alsford, School of Humanities, Philosophy and Theology, University of Greenwich, UK.

Tina Beattie, Department of Theology and Religious Studies, University of Bristol, UK.

Beverley Clack, Department of Theology and Religious Studies, Roehampton Institute, UK.

Diane M. Collier, Department of Religious Studies, Lancaster University, UK.

Sean Gill, Department of Theology and Religious Studies, University of Bristol, UK.

Elisabeth Gössmann, University of Munich, Germany, and University of Tokyo, Japan.

Brigitte Kahl, Union Theological Seminary, New York, USA.

Ursula King, Department of Theology and Religious Studies, University of Bristol, UK.

Gerard Loughlin, Department of Religious Studies, University of Newcastle upon Tyne, UK.

Sue Morgan, School of Religion and Theology, Chichester Institute, UK.

Ruth Page, Faculty of Divinity, University of Edinburgh, UK.

Melissa Raphael, Centre for the Study of Religion, Cheltenham and Gloucester College, UK.

Deborah F. Sawyer, Department of Religious Studies, Lancaster University, UK.

Natalie Watson, Cuddesdon Theological College, Oxford, UK.

Linda Woodhead, Department of Religious Studies, Lancaster University, UK.

FROM ISOLATION TO INTEGRATION?
NEW DIRECTIONS IN GENDER AND RELIGION

Diane M. Collier and Deborah F. Sawyer

> Twenty years of feminist study of religion demonstrates that feminist scholars of religion focus on a wide variety of topics—gender, sexuality, women, men, social structures, cultural regimes of knowledge, modes of knowing, and the contours of disciplines—within multiple religious traditions.[1]

This comment by Miriam Peskowitz highlights the diversity that has emerged in the years since traditional religion was first confronted by a feminist agenda. The once single voice has fragmented into a cacophony. Nevertheless the search continues for the elusive centre ground. Twentieth-century feminism can be seen to have been one logical development to appear in the tide of modernity's enlightenment project, albeit as this tide was beginning to ebb. The focus on the rights of man, the importance of the individual, broadens naturally, if uncomfortably, in a patriarchal world, into the feminist agenda: the demand for equality between the sexes. As we move into a postmodern world we experience the fragmentation of the foundational meta-truths of Western colonial society and culture. Within this transition inevitably we can observe the shift away from a feminist common ground.

There is no clear line dividing modernity and postmodernity, both co-exist in our world: in art, architecture, value-systems and, of course, the academy. Likewise, when we turn to feminist encounters with religion, examples of both modern and postmodern stances can be discerned. The diversity of experience that has emerged in recent years in studies of religion and gender has brought vitality and richness to this field of study. Such an observation does not, however, devalue the continuation

---

1. Miriam Peskowitz *et al.*, 'Roundtable Discussion: What's in a Name? Exploring the Dimensions of What "Feminist Studies in Religion" Means', *Journal of Feminist Studies in Religion* 1.1 (1995), pp.111-12.

of the challenge to traditional religion. The aim of this present volume is to encapsulate the branching out of gender issues as they relate to religion, while still acknowledging the original root of the problem. This is the place where those of us who are engaged with gender and religion find ourselves at the close of the twentieth century.

The colloquium upon which this edited collection is based was conceived at a time of apparent crisis within the academy of feminist theology. During the last two decades feminist theology has gained a foothold in many university departments of theology and religious studies; providing a critique of religious—and in particular Christian—institutions, scriptures, symbols and rituals. But as we reach the new millennium, the question needs to be asked, has this project of analysis and reconstruction based upon feminist principles run its natural course? The colloquium provided a forum for a reappraisal of feminist theology's achievements as well as space for self-reflection as to its possible future within the broader category of gender and religion. As Ursula King points out in her contribution to this volume, 'there is now sufficient material of enough substance and variety to do this in a spirit of openness and critical reflexivity',[2] which is the intent of this enterprise.

The foundational work of feminist theologians such as Mary Daly, Daphne Hampson, Elisabeth Schüssler Fiorenza, Rosemary Radford Ruether, Phyllis Trible, and in this present volume Elisabeth Gössmann and Ursula King, set the agenda for the critique of Western traditional religion, in particular Christianity, based on second wave feminist ideology. Their work uncovered the names and voices of women which had lain hidden and silenced for centuries. The methods they applied to their material identified conventional scholarship to be subjective in affirming patriarchal values, and not the objective, scientific exercise it had purported to be. In particular, these 'fore-mothers' enabled scholars of the next generation to intensify this critique with confidence and credibility.

However, a comparison of the situation in universities within the United Kingdom with that of Germany reveals the real difficulties encountered by some women scholars trying to work within the parameters of traditional, church and male-dominated institutions. In Britain universities have either shed their early closer associations with

2.   See below, p.101.

the established church or have been founded as secular institutions. Furthermore, for the past 30 years there has been a radical shift from religion being studied within faculties of Christian theology to the founding of departments of religious studies where Christianity is studied as one of many religious traditions. The Department at Lancaster University was at the vanguard of this development with its pluralistic approach to religious traditions and to the analytical methodologies applied to them.

German universities, for the main part, remain closely associated to either the Roman Catholic or Protestant traditions. Particularly in the case of Roman Catholic faculties, the Church hierarchy has continued to exercise control over academic appointments. This has had dire consequences for the professional careers of women theologians who, without the ecclesiastical licence of 'nihil obstat', have been disqualified as candidates for academic positions within the theological faculties. Elisabeth Gössmann's career bears testimony to this practice. Despite the depth and quality of her research over a lifetime of scholarship, she has been consistently overlooked in academic appointments in her home country. The Church's fears and suspicions about feminist theology have not only affected the lives of many women academics, but have also meant that both the German universities and, by relation, the Catholic Church have lost valuable contributions to theological scholarship. The work produced by German feminist theologians, particularly those of the Catholic tradition, inevitably reflects their embattled context as they are prompted by their situation to argue for a revision of the status of women within the tradition.

British scholarship in this area maintains a keen interest in revising and reforming traditional religion regarding the position of women, but it has also developed in a variety of other directions. Although we can account for this on the more abstract level of the modernity/postmodernity debate, on a more concrete level this diversity could well reflect the slow but sure progress of women academics within the disciplines of theology and religious studies in the United Kingdom. In gaining more security within the profession, they are freer to develop ideas and areas beyond the boundaries of traditional religion.

Text and Her-Story Revisited

With the assistance of the Goethe Institute the colloquium provided a welcome and refreshing opportunity to hear the voices of British and

German feminist scholarship and to debate with those views. Elisabeth Gössmann's chapter, the first in the volume, in our context could be categorized as reformist/traditional feminist theology. The critique and the solution—the equal integration of men and women within the Church—remain firmly within the context of traditional religion. In her contribution, 'The Image of God and the Human Being in Women's Counter-Tradition', she takes a reformist position in identifying a consistent strand of counter-tradition that runs throughout the history of Western Christianity. Her work is punctuated with rich and captivating illustrations of women's voices which tested the boundaries of patriarchal restrictions down the ages. These women might have been working with the masters' tools, yet they showed that the buildings that those masters' built lacked balance and proportion.

Elisabeth Gössmann presents a chain of tradition to feminist theologians, which provides authenticity and confirmation of their work within contemporary Christianity. The well-known publications of Elisabeth Schüssler Fiorenza on New Testament texts uncovered an early type of Christianity, which was characterized by gender inclusivity in its egalitarian anticipation of the Kingdom of God.[3] Gössmann's research on subsequent Christianity, particularly in the medieval period, uncovers the continued articulation of this theme. While the Catholic hierarchy might rest on two thousand years of apostolic tradition, the reformist theology of Gössmann shows that women's experience, women's counter-tradition, is a significant part of Christianity's history of divine revelation.

This convincing research answers criticisms that have been levelled at feminist theology's insistence on the 'golden age' of the Jesus movement and early Pauline urban Christianity. In particular Daphne Hampson has attacked Fiorenza's reclamation of primitive Christianity as irrelevant to the lives of women, and men, in our own era.[4] In her critique Hampson does not take account of the concept of revelation as a continuous phenomenon in Christian experience. It is not a marginal belief in Christianity that the sum of divine revelation does not rest

3.   See in particular her most influential work, *In Memory of Her: A Feminist Theological Reconstruction of Christian Origins* (London: SCM Press, 2nd edn, 1995).

4.   Daphne Hampson, *Theology and Feminism* (Oxford: Basil Blackwell, 1990), pp. 33-37; and *idem, After Christianity* (London: SCM Press, 1996), pp. 69-76.

solely in the single first century 'moment' of the Incarnation. Gössmann's work shows that women's voices and theological reflection are
part of the on-going revelation in history.

Perhaps what is most remarkable about the type of reformist feminist
theology evidenced by Gössmann's work is its energy and determination
in the face of a door that remains firmly shut. Recent papal statements,
argued to be infallible, have not only reiterated the impossibility of
ordaining women in the Catholic Church, the key development that
would affirm once and for all the fullness of female humanity, but have
also forbidden even its discussion. In the light of such close-minded-
ness with its implicit, if these days unspoken, insistence on Aristotelian
and Thomist notions of defective female nature, it is tempting to conclude with radical feminism that Christianity is irreformable in terms of
any feminist agenda.

Although we might categorize reformist feminist theology itself as a
feature of traditional religion simply because it continues to engage
with a particular tradition, we should not lose sight of its radical
impetus. Nor should we be judgmental of those who wish to remain
within a tradition even though its structures and theology are overtly
repressive to women. The continuation of a reform movement can be
understood if a religion is believed to contain a consistent, liberating
and affirming strand of tradition.

The work of reformist feminist theologians is undoubtedly radical
when set beside the type of teaching and practice found in the Roman
Catholic Church. Another reformist example contained in this volume
is Brigitte Kahl's exegesis of Galatians. The new and penetrating questions this scholar takes to the text clearly illustrate the positive contribution feminist analysis can continue to make in the field of biblical
studies. Moving beyond the well-trodden and tedious discussion of
whether St Paul can be assessed as 'good' or 'bad' in feminist eyes,
Kahl opens up the wider issues of gender and difference by approaching the text without traditional Christian presuppositions. In their place
is an open inquisitiveness prompted by contemporary analysis of
identity and gender construction. Kahl discovers in Paul a radical
thinker who is driven by the conviction that he is living in the messianic
age and who is acutely aware of the cosmological and ontological
implications of this 'new age'. In this unique context he can radically
test the given boundaries of race, gender and class.

In stark contrast to emerging, anarchic, urban Christianity in the time of Paul we encounter in Natalie Watson's contribution the fully-fledged hierarchy of the Roman Catholic Church in the twentieth century. Once more, in engaging with traditional religion, albeit in a critical sense, this contribution can be categorized as 'traditional' feminist theology. We can place this work within the context of the long diagnostic process to uncover the 'illness' of Christianity. In particular, Watson underlines the primary importance of identifying the full extent and depth of patriarchy within the structures and thought of the Catholic Church. Unless these foundational faults are exposed, any reconstruction would be a façade without substance. Watson's paper undertakes a thorough-going exercise of feminist deconstruction of the text of the Vatican II document 'Lumen Gentium' and examines women's interaction with it. She ends with the question of whether, after this process, a feminist reconstruction of ecclesiology on the lines of 'Lumen Gentium' would still be possible. A negative reply seems inevitable. Watson's paper reminds us that patriarchal Christianity does not reside among the relics of premodern times, but is alive and thriving at the end of the second millennium.

We might be tempted to jump uncritically in the direction of post-modernity, and regard our past as irrelevant; tempted instead to either construct ourselves anew as stark individuals in each generation or even perform a new identity daily, as some theorists might suggest. It might be liberating for postmodern man to unlock the shackles of the past and be 'him-self', but for women the past remains largely unknown and un-recorded. Before they are privileged to discard their past, women must first experience their past and evaluate it. As a consequence we do need to listen to those feminist theologians, and feminist historians, who are reluctant to abandon the past and who offer insights into 'her-stories'.

Taking up Ursula King's argument that historical investigation, 'is not simply a matter of setting the record straight ... it is also an issue of ... personal and corporate identity',[5] Sue Morgan examines new directions in the study of women's history and assesses their plaus-ibility. Feminist theology has employed a number of methodologies in its attempt to uncover the hidden voices of women in the past and in doing so to retrieve a useable past for women today. She discusses, for

---

5.   Ursula King (ed.), *Religion and Gender* (Oxford: Basil Blackwell, 1995), p. 222.

example, the extension of the subject to include broader questions raised by gender studies and postmodern critique. This contribution shows that historical research should not be rigid in following one particular methodological or theoretical line of inquiry, but that the most credible historical analyses are those produced by an integrated variety of approaches. Scholars engaged in history writing contribute significantly to the challenges posed by contemporary religion and gender scholarship and by so doing are redressing the balance so that a more adequate picture of the Christian narrative can be drawn.

New Directions for the New Millennium

In many respects feminist theology has isolated itself as a discipline within a discipline. As Linda Woodhead argues in the epilogue to this volume, it has become 'ghettoized'. This process can be discerned in a number of contexts. In this country, for example, there is the British and Irish School of Feminist Theology which has a journal, *Feminist Theology*, dedicated to its particular concerns. The aims and objectives of the journal confirm traditional feminist theology's continued engagement with established religion, 'to empower women who feel marginalized within their religious tradition'. Although these aims are not only necessary but laudable, it is questionable as to whether they facilitate feminist theology to negotiate new territory in the wider academy. One of the major theoretical problems rests on feminist theology's grounding in women's experiences; a relatively unchallenged and under-theorized concept. By defending the primacy of women's experiences above all other norms of theology, there is a real danger that the distinctiveness of the tradition, the essence that gives it its identity is subsumed. This is a danger, which has been highlighted by Linda Hogan,[6] and also by Linda Woodhead[7] who complains that feminist theology has failed to be sufficiently theological through its lack of engagement with, 'the realities of Christian faith and tradition'. Here we should note Ursula King's observation that, 'the isolation of feminists from other people can in practice lead to insularity and

---

6.   Linda Hogan, *From Women's Experiences to Feminist Theology* (Sheffield: Sheffield Academic Press, 1995).

7.   'Spiritualising the Sacred: a Critique of Feminist Theology', *Modern Theology* 13.2 (1997), pp. 191-212.

separatism when in theory relationality is so much stressed as a desideratum'.[8]

As a consequence of this isolationist tendency, we would argue that feminist theology has had little impact on its 'parent' discipline, and remains for many an exotic form of alternative Christianity. Although plenty of research is published on gender issues and religion, it remains more often than not within the 'ghetto'. Its place within 'mainstream' publications in the field of theology and religious studies is certainly not centre-stage. This point can be illustrated by taking as an example Alister McGrath's best selling general introduction to Christian theology, published in 1994,[9] where the subject of feminism and theology was granted only two pages out of five hundred and ten. In terms of its contribution to Christian thought, McGrath cites only three areas as being especially significant: the maleness of God, the nature of sin and the person of Christ. Indeed, we suggest that by remaining 'ghetto-bound' feminist theology has had less impact on theology and established religion than secular feminism has had on it indirectly through wider society.

The ghetto-mentality of feminist theology might also account for the lack of dialogue with women in non-Western religious contexts. Working within the framework of feminist theology it seems impossible to get away from Christian/Western centredness, and even the contemporary goddess movement is Western centred. As organizers of the colloquium we were keen to address this bias, and scholars from a variety of religious traditions were invited to participate. Consequently, we were disappointed by the limited response from non-Western/Christian-based colleagues, and by the fact that there is no paper from this perspective to include in our volume. In Ursula King's provisional assessment of feminist theologies she makes explicit the now direct and exclusive correlational between feminist theology and Western religious tradition. This observation becomes a challenge to feminist theology to look outwards and to learn from and share in the empowerment being experienced by women in so-called 'third world' contexts. Perhaps more than any other Western scholar, King is well placed to reflect critically on feminist theologies in contemporary contexts as her extensive and illuminating collection of works testify.[10] In this paper she emphasizes

8.   See below, p. 110.
9.   *Christian Theology: An Introduction* (Oxford: Basil Blackwell, 1994).
10. Of most significance in regard to this volume are, Ursula King, *Women and*

the pluralistic nature of feminist theologies as well as the plurality of contexts in which these theologies are formulated and experienced. Numerous challenges emerge as corollaries of this diversity; to do with terminology and definitions, as well as boundaries. She argues that it is important to address the challenge of a move away from a perception exclusively focused on struggle to, 'emphasize the richness, the depth, the commitment, the power of vision and spiritual energy that form the heart and blood of feminist theologizing'.[11]

The challenge for feminist theology is to positively channel this 'power of vision', and move out of the rut of repetitive critique and lack of momentum. Despite the re-engagement evident between contemporary gender theory and feminist spirituality, there is a sense that feminist theology has had to struggle to keep abreast of theoretical developments in secular feminism. This is not surprising since, as a body of knowledge, secular feminism has undergone seismic shifts in the 1980s and 1990s. Terms such as 'radical', 'Marxist' or 'liberal', which have been previously applied to categorize the diversity within the movement, are no longer appropriate. The meanings and ownership of feminist theory are now being contested; not only by black women or non-Western women, but also by men. The effect on feminism has been to broaden its perspective and force it out of the white, Western, woman-only ghetto. The ideology of the women's movement in the 1970s and 1980s has become the gender theories of the 1990s, and the effect of this on feminism has been disturbing. Gender studies is involved in a process of self-reflection that shows its theoretical maturity. Nevertheless, at the same time, the self-reflection exposes a tendency to become embroiled in inner debate which may detract from the original focus of study.

Another concern for gender studies is that unlike the early years of second wave feminism, feminist theory is now a recognized area of academic discourse. A consequence of this institutional acceptance is the inevitable vying between the various theoretical positions. In a postmodern context such variety or fragmentation is to be welcomed, but it has also led to the privileging of 'high' theory and the belittling of

Spirituality: Voices of Protest and Promise (London: Macmillan, 2nd edn, 1993); and two of her edited works, *Feminist Theology from the Third World: A Reader* (London: SPCK, 1994), *Religion and Gender* (Oxford: Basil Blackwell, 1995).

11. See below, p. 109.

the universal values of the second wave movement. Despite this apparent acceptance in the wider academe of the social sciences and humanities, there is still a tendency for gender issues to remain, or to be put, on the margins.

Engagement with secular gender theory is one of three categories we have identified as feminist theology moves forward and gains a new momentum in the 1990s. It is joined by significant developments in non-traditional feminist spirituality and the advent of men's studies. Each of these categories is represented in this volume. Many feminists who engage with postmodernity have found previous accounts of female subjectivity too limiting, and have argued against universalizing tendencies. But it is interesting that secular feminism does not recognize that by continuing to exclude the voices of religious women this situation is being perpetuated. In 'Global Sisterhood or Wicked Stepsisters' Tina Beattie argues that secular feminism has a 'patriarchal blind spot' regarding the significance of Christianity in many women's lives and in the theological heritage to Western thought. In her view our secular sisters consistently silence women's theological voices. Mary Daly is often regarded as the 'politically correct' face of theology—but of course, she cannot be considered representative, and more traditional views are rarely given space in feminist compendiums. The worrying hostility towards the Vatican delegation at the United Nations Fourth World Conference on Women in Beijing is an example of a dismissal of all things religious. Beattie examines Luce Irigaray's work and the problems she poses for secular feminists who are determined not to recognize her Christian heritage and faith. Irigaray's project, which attempts to bridge the gap between the sacred and profane, is a challenge to both secular and theological ideas. The question remains whether Christianity is always to be the poor relation of secular theory. Not so in Beattie's view. Christianity should not understand itself as yet one more voice in the postmodern wilderness. Feminist theology can and should take the lead by exercising a more critical level of engagement with secular feminist theory. Beattie's comments signal a clearly discernible new direction for feminist theology—a courageous step out of the ghetto.

In relation to gender theory, Tina Beattie's contribution identifies the problem for feminist theology in negotiating a respected place beside our secular sisters. Sally Alsford's chapter draws our attention to another concern that secular theory has addressed and found problematic, but with which feminist theology has had to deal from the outset. This is the question of 'nature', of difference and essentialism. Such concepts lie at the heart of traditional religion, with beliefs ranging from tame complementarity to brazen sexual hierarchy and misogyny. Familiarity with this concern, however, has not resulted in an articulate response from feminist theology; a point underlined by Alsford. As an example she considers the theme of inter-connectedness, a prominent characteristic of recent Christian feminism. Aware of the danger of reverting to a stance of difference, Alsford argues that this relational approach can signal a constructive contribution from feminist thought to theology. It can mark a feminization of theology; rather than offering a distinct exclusive theology for women, the relational approach can offer an inclusive theology for humanity.

The second category of non-traditional feminist spirituality takes us from theory to experience. Melissa Raphael and Beverley Clack's contributions exemplify the productive debate which was a feature of the colloquium, and which particularly epitomizes the exciting and constructive energy of thealogy. The focus of these papers is thealogy's non-realist dimension; in other words, the goddess as symbol of the sacred power of the self. Raphael contends that the non-realist emphasis is a reflection of its associations with 1970s radical feminism, and she sees a more realist and monotheist picture emerging in the 1990s. However, there are significant differences between this form of realism and the traditional theological model; such as the goddess as inseparable from nature. For Clack the non-realist perspective offers exciting possibilities for feminist theology, especially in the realm of religious language. Clack and Raphael differ on this point, and Clack suggests that Raphael is over-simplifying the realist case by not acknowledging the expressive nature of religious language. Both these contributions articulate the need to remain open to conceptual changes in all forms of feminist theologies.

Our third category, the inclusion of men's studies, signifies the importance of recognizing the full spectrum of gender to ensure informed and credible critique. The inclusion of men within gender studies alters the nature of the debate, and perhaps the subject area itself. Although widening the debate, it brings men 'back' to the centre stage. The trespassing of men into feminist territory has challenged the ownership of patriarchal oppression. Women have been forced to listen to male voices naming the pains of patriarchy, and understandably, some women are concerned about sharing their own ground with the 'enemy'. In the two papers from this category included here, one, from Sean Gill, is presenting a historical perspective, while the other, from Gerard Loughlin, rethinks the issue of complementarity. Both contributions clearly illustrate that male experiences are not uniform, or universally acclaimed in Christian tradition.

Sean Gill's work explores the inter-relationships between religion and masculinity through a study of the muscular Christianity movement at the end of the nineteenth century. The same troublesome implications of universalism and essentialism exist in this field also, and Gill addresses these issues through a conceptualized and relational approach to the ideal of Christian manliness. Gill likens the fears about the feminization of Christianity at the end of the nineteenth century, provoked in part by the rise of first wave feminism, to those at the end of our own century, this time prompted by unresolved gender debates within the churches.

In an innovative and provoking contribution Gerard Loughlin revisits and rethinks complementarity through the vivid imagery of the gay underworld. He examines the Pauline usage of the term 'slave' in 1 Cor. 7.3-4, and explores the notions of gift of self, mutuality and being male and female. In emphasizing the centrality of the relationship itself, over and above the differences between the individuals involved, Loughlin begins to offer an idea of gender-free relationality. This contribution represents not only the broadening out of gender studies to include complex issues of maleness and sexuality, but also a postmodern approach to sacred text, and one with which we are familiar from his recent book, *Telling God's Story: Bible, Church and Narrative Theology*.[12] Loughlin approaches the text of 1 Corinthians unfettered by the constraints of modernity's meta-truths of 'scientific' biblical scholarship, and discovers new possibilities for meaning and application.

This contribution can be considered beside Brigitte Kahl's essay in this volume, which also has the Pauline text as its focus. Although in many respects her work resembles more familiar biblical scholarship, particularly in its meticulous and close examination of the text, Kahl does allow questions to be asked of the text that are radical in gender terms. In bringing to light the fluidity of gender roles in Pauline

12. *Telling God's Story: Bible, Church and Narrative Theology* (Cambridge: Cambridge University Press, 1996).

imagery, Kahl allows challenging concepts from the realms of post-modernity gender theory to meet with the biblical text, and, like Lough-lin, opens the way for new meanings for sacred text. These two papers represent how scripture remains an important resource for theology, and is not restricted to traditional scholarship, but is central in the most radical contexts, including those that explore gender and sexuality.

Our volume concludes, in the fashion of postmodernity, with two possible scenarios for gender studies and religion. Ruth Page suggests that the agenda set out for feminist theology has a natural ending. Once the point of synthesis between it and established theology has been reached, it should be working towards its demise as a distinct discipline. To describe this scenario, Page applies the Hegelian progression of thesis, antithesis and synthesis to the problematic of feminist theology. This application of an overtly masculinist model to a feminist enterprise is incongruous to many students of gender matters, but helps to underline the diversity of possibilities under the broad umbrella of contemporary feminist theology. The positive picture Page paints of women's theology being fully integrated into an inclusive model of doing theology, does resonate with other new directions we have noted.

Our other ending, offered by Linda Woodhead, also maps out an integrated future for feminist theology, but one that maintains its identity. Woodhead is concerned that feminist theology should move out of the ghetto, where it has often been inaccessible to both women and men within the churches, and come of age within the existing disciplines of the academy, and the academy of Christian theology in particular. This begins to produce a wider canvas for us, where integration involves the faith community, which exists firmly within traditional religion, and not just in the comparatively marginal woman-church, or the ivory towers of the theologians.

Our colloquium and this volume testify to the new integration of gender theory and feminist theology, and the diverse application of this integration within contexts such as thealogy and men's studies, as well as the more familiar territory of feminist theology. Whilst the allure of these new directions is powerful, and provides satisfying intellectual theorizing, the process of reclaiming the past to inform the present will continue to be a vital component of feminist theology for the foreseeable future, or as long as traditional religion remains untouched at the core.

Modernity meeting with postmodernity produced a dynamic for the colloquium—and made explicit the implicit tensions within the various methodologies of gender and religion. Traditional feminist theology can be understood as part of the project of modernity. Its agenda calls for equality of status for men and women in the sight of God and in the institutions of religion. In theological terms it shares an agenda with liberation theology with calls for inclusivity, and for change in the structures of institutionalized Christianity. Capitalism and patriarchy are common enemies for both movements in varying degrees. In political terms, feminist theology shares the concerns and ideals of second wave feminism, with human rights encompassing those of women as well as men. In stark contrast, postmodernity asks who *is* a man or a woman? What is 'male' and 'female'? And the reflection we see in the mirror can be what we will it to be, and in that vision, there also, perhaps, is the sight of 'God'.

Although we include diversity in terms of theoretical and methodological issues, what this volume lacks—as we noted earlier—is any dialogue with non-Western contexts. This on-going lack of engagement by feminist theology, and gender theory itself, with experience outside Western culture artificially limits the issues of gender and religion. From our perspective, this is the major task for the next millennium. The traditional dichotomy between East and West, a meta-narrative of a past age, needs to be dissolved to allow the vast plurality of global experiences to take centre stage.

This diversity should be regarded as a positive development in gender and religion. It testifies to its coming of age as a dynamic dimension, both continuing to challenge the absurdities of traditional religion, and looking outside theology to be informed and to inform current gender debate. We need to resist any temptation there might be to search for some middle ground, since the tensions inherent within this diversity will ensure its vitality and plurality for the future; a future not characterized by insularity and separatism but by integration and integrity.

Part I

TEXT AND HER-STORY REVISITED

THE IMAGE OF GOD AND THE HUMAN BEING IN WOMEN'S COUNTER-TRADITION

Elisabeth Gössmann

Introduction

Since we, as feminist theologians, are interested in the question whether women and their theological works are acknowledged as representative of Christian tradition, first of all, I have to explain the meaning of the term 'tradition' according to Catholic understanding since the nineteenth century.

According to the far reaching influence of Johann Adam Möhler (Tübingen) who had defined Christian tradition as the 'continually living word in the hearts of the believers' and that of Cardinal John Henry Newman who had laid emphasis on the testimony of lay people in questions of faith,[1] a new Catholic consciousness of tradition arose. The efficiency of the Holy Spirit was experienced by believers from the laity and acknowledged gradually by theologians and bishops. Consequently, all the members of the Church, and not only the magisterium of the pope and the bishops, were regarded as persons bearing testimony to the Christian tradition. Since that time, lay people—including women—were no longer regarded as only passive hearers in questions of faith and tradition. But nevertheless, the function of control remained in the hands of the magisterium of the pope with the bishops. Only they had, and have even today, the competence to distinguish between the Catholic faith and heretic opinions.

In the middle of the twentieth century, the German theologian Mannes Dominicus Koster stressed the obligation of the bishops to explore the faith of the members of their diocese when a new dogma is

---

1. For this and for the following passages cf. Michael Schmaus, *Katholische Dogmatik*. III,1. *Die Lehre von der Kirche* (5 vols.; Munich: Max Hueber 1958), pp. 758-77.

going to be prepared. Cardinal Newman had already asked the bishops to do so, but he did not think it was an obligation for the bishops. Koster distinguished not only between the so-called simple members of the church and the magisterium; according to him there is an intermediate group of those fathers and teachers of the church who were not bishops, even so they enjoyed teaching authority throughout the centuries and do so even today.

Here there is a question: What does it mean that the Vatican in our day acknowledges some very few women as teachers of the church? Should we all cry 'Hallelujah' gratefully, asking for the next woman to be elevated to such a high degree? I do not think we should. It is not useful or meaningful if only very few women writers of former centuries are liberated from the limitations imposed on all of them by the pseudo-Pauline prohibition against women teaching (1 Tim 2.9-15) and the order to keep silence in the ecclesiastical community (1 Cor. 14.34-35.) which were received into the ecclesiastical law from very early times. If only very few women writers in history are liberated from these handicaps and all the other female theological writers in past, present and future times remain under these restrictions, there will be nothing liberating for Christian tradition.

During the centuries of ecclesiastical history, women lacked teaching authority in the public and general meaning of this word. They were only acknowledged as prophetesses and regarded as the successors of Deborah, Hannah and other female prophets in the Bible, legitimated by God's special calling, not as normally educated women doing theology.

What must be claimed is teaching authority for all the women writers of Christian tradition and not an exceptional legitimation of only very few of them. Women writers in the Christian tradition did not regard themselves as an exception but as touched by the grace of God that is open to all who are willing to receive it.

According to an article written by Joseph Ratzinger during the Second Vatican Council, the theory of Scripture and tradition as two different sources of Christian faith was replaced by the teaching of the Council.[2] The Bible is no longer regarded as different from tradition, but as one element in tradition. Those who testify Christian tradition, 'are not allowed to add something, but they have to announce and to interpret very much'. Ratzinger adds that this testimony can only be

2. Joseph Ratzinger, 'Tradition', *Lexikon für Theologie und Kirche* 10 (1965), cols. 293-99 (293).

given by the members of the Catholic church in harmony with the magisterium.

After the Council, my teacher Michael Schmaus wrote: 'The Holy Scripture is the expression of an oral tradition, and the oral tradition is the presupposition of the Bible and its subsequent interpretation.'[3]

It seems to me that the situation of women is still ambivalent. On the one hand we are regarded as active members of the Catholic church, able to transmit Christian tradition to the next generation, but on the other hand we are subordinated to the magisterium of the Catholic church in which women as women are not represented.

Now let me specify the question a little more. There was a tradition before there was a magisterium, and there are problems in the Catholic Church of today that many members of the laity, and even priests and some bishops, want to solve in a way different from the magisterium. What about the women in tradition before the Gospels were written down, the women following Jesus as his disciples, the female coopera-tors of St Paul, some of whom were in place in the first Christian com-munities before they met him? What about the women called 'diakonos' or 'apostolos' in the New Testament and those of later cen-turies who wrote theology even if they were not regarded as theologians but as mystical writers or poetesses? Is it still true that teaching is officially allowed for women only in the private environment of trans-mitting the Christian faith to children and their domestic surroundings, as most of the mediaeval scholastics believed?

Is this model of thinking the deeper reason for the scandals in Austria and Germany, caused by the fact that women theologians, called to a professorship in theological faculties by the ministry of education, could not take up their work because the Vatican refused or delayed the 'Nihil obstat' (permission to teach) despite the decisions of Vatican II concerning women in theology?[4]

To ask more precisely: How can we exist as women theologians in the Catholic Church, if we are not able to agree to the Pope's Pastoral Letter 'Ordinatio sacerdotalis' (Pentecost 1994) forbidding women's ordination for ever? To agree to this text would mean that women agreed to their exclusion from the power of definition, the power of

3.   Michael Schmaus, *Der Glaube der Kirche*, I, 1 (6 vols.; Sankt Ottilien: Eos, 2nd edn, 1979), pp. 215, 229.

4.   Cf. the chapter on Vatican II in my book *Das Bild der Frau heute* (Düsseldorf: Haus der katholischen Frauen, 2nd edn, 1967), pp. 41-50.

decision making and the power to standardize ethical norms. This means nothing else but the continuation of the hierarchy of the male over the female sex in spite of all lip service concerning the dignity of women or the equality of the two sexes by ecclesiastical authorities.

In 1996, in consequence of the Austrian and the German referendum of the members of the Catholic Church (*Kirchenvolksbegehren*), some essays concerning Christian tradition were published in the Jesuit periodical *Stimmen der Zeit*. Here the possibility was discussed that 'good traditions' in history could be blocked or buried later on and that 'harmful traditions' could be established and deeply rooted in the Christian community. Of course, what I want to call women's counter-tradition was not mentioned in this discussion, but in fact it is a tradition which was blocked and which existed without influencing the mainstream (mostly male) tradition of the Catholic Church. However, women's counter-tradition was not lost.

In the article of Wolfgang Beinert,[5] the case of non-agreement to a Vatican document is discussed. According to this author, a Vatican document without a positive echo from the Christian communities is devoid of any spiritual fertility and therefore remains dead. He gives examples of such cases from history. That not only 'male' decisions are agreed to can be the case today if we succeed in resuscitating women's counter-tradition by bringing it to the consciousness of all the members of the Catholic Church as a phenomenon that breaks the male monopoly of interpreting the Bible and doing theology. From at least the mediaeval centuries onward, the women's tradition can be recognized as a counterbalance to traditions that are of questionable origin.

It is necessary to say that we need a special method of research on the history of women's philosophical and theological writing. Without knowing the (mostly male) mainstream of Christian tradition, readers are unable to understand the nuances of women's writing. Until recently, although there was some research on female authors such as Hildegard of Bingen, Mechthild of Magdeburg or Teresa of Avila concerning the influences from church fathers upon their writing, the influence from earlier women writers upon later ones was neglected. However, the continuities that can be found in women's traditions are most interesting and meaningful.[6] There is a continuity of female

---

5. W. Beinert, 'Das Rezeptionsgeschehen in der Kirche', *Stimmen der Zeit* 121 (1996), pp. 381-92.

6. Cf. for instance Elisabeth Gössmann, 'Theologiegeschichtliche Frauenfor-

agreement to male traditions as well as disagreement that shows a difference of thinking on certain subject-matters, allowing us to speak about women's tradition as a counter-tradition.

Reading the ancient texts of women with a certain hermeneutics of suspicion, continuities can be discovered showing us that women writers did not accept certain foundations of the androcentric tradition and tried to create different foundations on which they could build up their own interpretation of Christian faith, according to their wisdom derived from their experience of life. Women writers from the Middle Ages reveal their wide reading, and even if some of them (because of their visionary style of writing) do not give the names of the male authorities to whom they refer, it would be naive to think they did not know them. Their reaction to male writing can very often be discovered. This is the reason why the method of research on women's tradition has to take into consideration the special situation of female writing.

Concerning the genre of women's writing, it must be mentioned here that most of the genres open to men were not open to women, because of their exclusion from teaching. So they could not write a *Summa Theologiae* or a commentary on the four books of *Sententiae* by Peter Lombard or a commentary on Aristotle or on biblical books. Only in their letters, when asked a certain question by a male theologian or monk, could they answer in a treatise-like style. The genre of writing conceded to them was that of description of visions and auditory experiences, regarded as prophetical writing, not teaching.

Nevertheless, within the context of prophetical writing women could and did comment on biblical passages, including their experiences of life. So there is a certain paradox in women's writing. Being conscious of their prohibition to teach, they surrounded their teaching by a language of mysticism and prophecy. Consequently, visions and auditory experiences and the interpretations of such experiences are the ways of theological utterance in female writing during the Middle Ages and the early modern world.

Even Christine de Pizan used visionary writing turned into a dialogue to verify her experiences. Questioning the authenticity of visions is a waste of time once we accept that women did not have other means of theological expression. Their seeing of visions and their auditory experiences functioned as an answer to their burning theological questions.

schung als Veränderungspotential theologischer Ethik', *Jahrbuch für christliche Sozialwissenschaften* 34 (1993), pp. 190-213.

A characteristic mark of women's writing is the expression of female modesty, as was expected from them by male authorities. These expressions of modesty are found continually in women's writing until the eighteenth century and sometimes even later, with the exception of some very self-confident Renaissance women writers. Introducing themselves as members of the subordinate sex, but at the same time alluding to 1 Cor. 1.27, most of the women writers express modesty together with a strong consciousness of God's calling. Hildegard of Bingen, for instance, writes: 'ego paupercula et indocta feminea forma' ('I, who am a little, poor, and uneducated female creature'), but also: 'ego paupercula forma, per veram sapientiam cogebar ut haec verba ipsius proferrem' ('I, who am a poor little woman, was overwhelmed by the true wisdom to bring forth these words of Her'). Like the prophet Jeremiah, who cited his youthfulness as evidence of weakness, Hildegard and many women writers used womanhood as an equivalent of weakness. So they filled up their modesty topos with the traits of the scholastic image of woman.

It took a long time for scholars to learn that an expression such as 'indocta feminea forma' does not mean that a woman writer using this formula could not be well educated. The same Hildegard says: 'intus in anima mea sum docta' ('in the interior of my soul I am educated'). The word 'indocta' is explained as 'not educated by any doctrine of fleshly teachers, but only touched by the divine light' which is a spiritual one.[7] In Mary's 'Magnificat' to which many women writers allude, exaltation is the complementary pole of humiliation. Both poles together form the consciousness of women writers, and, in addition, they were widely read.

Feminist literary criticism found the helpful concept of a 'double-voiced discourse' in the texts of women.[8] This concept can be discovered in theological writing of women even more than in their literary writing. At the beginning of their books or chapters, women demonstrate their orthodoxy by 'quoting' from the official interpretations of biblical texts or opinions of authorities, but in less conspicuous passages their counter-traditional biblical interpretations and theological reflections appear. This means that one of the text-immanent voices

---

7. Cf. Elisabeth Gössmann, *Hildegard of Bingen: Four Papers* (Toronto: Peregrina Publishing, 1995), pp. 5-16.

8. Elaine Showalter, 'Feminist Criticism in the Wilderness', *Critical Inquiry* 8 (1981), pp. 179-205.

refers to the main (mostly male) tradition, and the other one undermines and transforms it. This way of writing in a double-voiced discourse was a kind of shelter for women and at the same time a way of agreement between women writers. It seems to have functioned very well in their time and to be effective even today, since (mostly male) scholars still tend to regard mediaeval women writers as man-identified or ambivalent.[9]

Tradition and Counter-Tradition: The Human Being as God's Image according to the Male Tradition

Today feminist theologions deplore the misogyny in Patristic and scholastic anthropologies, mostly justified by a gradation of the image of God in the two sexes, that is to say, a very clear *imago Dei* in the male and a weaker one or even a total absence in the female. This gradation was generally legitimated by 1 Cor. 11.7, where woman is named man's glory, while he is God's image. Her inability to represent God or Christ was regarded as a consequence of the imperfection or weakness of woman's *imago Dei*. According to a very strong tradition of mediaeval canon law (Decretum Gratiani), 'woman must cover her head, since she is not the image of God'.[10] Such a negation of woman's *imago Dei* belongs to the arguments for her exclusion from ecclesiastical functions.

In summary, then, scholastic theology conceded a reduced or diminished kind of *imago Dei* to female human beings, but one strong enough to be a starting point for God's grace working also in women and leading them to salvation. Even Abaelard who was nearly a 'feminist' in his time, attributed the *imago Dei* in its full meaning only

9.   Cf. Peter Dinzelbacher, 'Das politische Wirken der Mystikerinnen in Kirche und Staat: Hildegard, Birgitta, Katharina', in P. Dinzelbacher and D.R. Bauer (eds.), *Religiöse Frauenbewegung und mystische Frömmigkeit im Mittelalter* (Cologne, Vienna: Böhlau, 1988), pp. 265-302 (290), where he maintains that mediaeval women writers had 'weitgehend internalisiert' the patriarchal ideology of their time.

10.   Cf. Ida Raming, *The Exclusion of Women from the Priesthood: Divine Law or Sex Discrimination?* (Metuchen, NJ: Scarecrow Press, 1976). Kari Elisabeth Børresen, *Subordination and Equivalence* (Kampen: Kok, 1995; Original French edition 1968). Index of Latin terms: imago dei, imago viri, imago et gloria viri; *eadem, Image of God and Gender Models* (Oslo: Solum Forlag, 1991).

to man, calling woman God's similitude,[11] since only Adam originated immediately from God the Father. Generally it was said that man was created 'principaliter' in God's image, because the rational faculty of his soul was regarded as stronger. Woman was compared to 'sensualitas' (sensuality or voluptuousness) which has to be subordinated to reason like woman to man. Because of Adam's similarity to Christ, it was said, only a man can represent God or Christ.

Of course, scholastic theologians conceded women's equal vocation to a life in God's grace, including eschatological perfection. This was a consequence of the contemporary interpretation of Gal. 3.28. So a first element or meaning of God's image in the human being was distinguished from a second one, and only the first one was regarded as equal in both sexes. In the tradition of Augustine, this means that the three faculties of memory, intelligence and will ('memoria', 'intelligentia', 'voluntas') in the unity of every individual soul are regarded as analogous to the Trinity of persons in the divine unity. The three faculties of the soul are also regarded as the starting point of God's grace working in human beings.

But concerning the so-called second element, women were not regarded as equal. Similar to many of his forerunners and followers, Thomas Aquinas described this in the following way:

> Sed quantum ad aliquid secundarium, imago Dei invenitur in viro, secundum quod non invenitur in muliere. Nam vir est principium mulieris et finis, sicut Deus est principium et finis totius creaturae.[12]
>
> But concerning something that is secondary, God's image is found in man and not in woman, since man is the origin of woman and her goal, just as God is the origin and goal of the whole of creation.

Thomas agreed with Augustine that woman was created as a help for man only because he needs her for generating his offspring, but that in every other kind of work a man would be a better help for a man than a woman. As a follower of Aristotle, he believed that by nature man's intellect was analytically stronger.[13] So the Christian doctrine of

---

11. Cf. Marie-Thérèse d'Alverny, 'Comment les théologiens et les philosophes voient la femme', in *La femme dans les civilisations des Xe—XIIIe siècles: Actes du colloque tenu à Poitiers 1976* (Poitiers: Université de Poitiers 1977), pp. 15-31 (26-27).

12. Thomas Aquinas, *Summa Theol.* I q. 93 a. 4 ad 2.

13. *Summa Theol.* I q. 92 a. 1 ad 2.: 'Naturaliter mulier est subiecta viro, quia naturaliter in homine magis abundat discretio rationis.'

God's image in the human being is intermingled with the pre-Christian anthropology of Aristotle, one of the reasons why everything seems to be deduced very logically by Thomas Aquinas.

The sentence of Aquinas I quoted above, reflects perfectly the empowerment of men in political societies and ecclesiastical communities, as well as women's deprivation of power. It is not so astonishing that the same sentiment, of course without the name of the original author, can still be found in early protestantism. At the end of the seventeenth century a member of the school of Jacob Thomasius in Germany wrote the following: 'Vir enim est origo et principium ex quo mulier, et est finis propter quem producta est mulier.'[14] (Man is the origin and principle from which, as well as the goal for whom, woman was created.) The reflection of God's creativity and government only in man and not in woman legitimized and justified the fact that the superior positions in the world should be male. Correspondingly, the few women in royal positions in European countries were regarded as holding this position not 'by nature' but only 'by law' and as an exception from the rule of male inheritance of power.

In questions of theological anthropology, there is hardly any change in post-mediaeval university teaching. In spite of the reservations towards Thomas Aquinas and Aristotle in early Protestant theology, the gradation of man's and woman's *imago Dei* is the same as before. In contradiction to the biblical text of Gen. 1.28, the dominion over the earth was referred generally only to the male and not to the female sex.[15] This interpretation continued to appear in Protestant as well as Catholic writers. The same model of thinking can still be found in the Pastoral letter of Pope John Paul II about the dignity of woman (Mulieris Dignitatem) of 1988. We should not forget this.

In scholastic thinking we also can find an ardent opposition against currents of gnostic and manichean concepts, distinguishing between a good God and creator of spiritual beings, and a 'demiourgos' as a creator of matter and material beings. Because of the identification of masculinity with 'spirit' or 'mind' and femininity with 'body', 'flesh' or 'sensuality', this dualistic way of thinking was dangerous for women.

14. Quoted in Elisabeth Gössmann (ed.), *Archiv für philosophie- und theologiegeschichtliche Frauenforschung*, I (8 vols. so far; Munich: iudicium, 2nd edn, 1998), p. 216 n. 46.

15. Cf. Ian Maclean, *The Renaissance Notion of Woman* (Cambridge: Cambridge University Press, 1980), pp. 6-27.

Stressing the oneness and goodness of God the creator of material as well as spiritual beings, scholastic thinkers were convinced that this concept of God had to be reflected in the world by one unique principle, which they found in man with his capacity of begetting children, since for them—according to Aristotle—only man is active and woman is passive. All this is reflected in Thomas Aquinas's sentence quoted above.

The reduction and diminution of women's *imago Dei* according to the mainstream (mostly male) tradition of Christianity corresponds to a strict limitation of female metaphors for divinity. As is known from the research of Caroline Walker Bynum, such metaphors appear in mystical writings of male as well as female authorship, but not in scholastic or later genres of theological writing, as far as they are regarded as scientia (science). Anselm of Canterbury gave the reason: male superiority and female inferiority as well as the more important role of the father in begetting a child. But the same Anselm as a writer of prayers used symbols of motherly care for Christ.[16]

The Human Being as God's Image in Women's Counter-Tradition

Women writers in the theological tradition from the Middle Ages generally did not mention the discriminations of the mainstream tradition concerning the female *imago Dei*. They passed over them with an eloquent silence. We often find that their concept of divinity includes male and female, motherly and fatherly features. Hildegard of Bingen named divine justice reflected in human beings as 'quasi virile' (so to speak something male), and divine mercifulness, reflected in human beings, she called 'quasi feminineum' (so to speak something female).[17] Using the word 'quasi', she was always conscious of the analogy (more dissimilitude than similitude) of human God-talk. In her interpretation of Genesis 1, Hildegard corrected the scholastic concept of God's creativity as only reflected in man with his generative power.

She did this by maintaining that God had conveyed the power of begetting neither to man alone nor to woman alone, but to the human couple. Against the phallocratic consciousness of her time, she simply

---

16. Cf. Caroline Walker Bynum, *Jesus as Mother: Studies in the Spirituality of the High Middle Ages* (Berkeley: University of California Press, 1982), pp. 113-115.

17. Hildegard of Bingen, *De operatione Dei* II.5; cf. Elisabeth Gössmann, *Hildegard von Bingen: Versuche einer Annäherung* (Munich: iudicium, 1995), pp. 63-64.

stated that not a single human being will be born if a man is alone or a woman is alone, but that human beings are born from the couple of father and mother. According to her, the couple of man and woman is the unique principle, reflecting in this world God's unity and creativity.

As a fighter against dualism, she agreed with male scholasticism's refutal of dualistic concepts in mediaeval heretical thinking, but in the different way of insisting on the unity of the human couple. 'Unde etiam vir et femina unum sunt' (Therefore man and woman are one), which means that she—well versed as she was in the gnostic-manichean concepts—'raised' woman's *imago Dei* to the level of man's power to reflect divine creativity and to represent divinity.[18] In her letter to Cologne where she had preached before, Hildegard warned the women against the Cathars who were attributed with such dualistic thinking.[19]

Correspondingly, Hildegard's male-female God-language is pervasive in her works. According to her, Christ is the incarnation of divine wisdom (divina sapientia). Paraphrasing Isa. 42.14, where God is revealed as a woman in childbirth, she enjoyed using the female gender of the Latin language. The 'daughters of Zion' can also be male in Hildegard's texts, since it is possible for her to symbolize the whole of humankind by help of female as well as male metaphors.

As a matter of course, the woman in Lk. 15.8-10 means divinity (divinitas) for Hildegard. 'Holy divinity had 10 drachmas', she wrote enthusiastically, and in *Scivias* I.4 she composed her own parable, inspired by those of Luke 15. In her parable, humankind as well as divinity are symbolized in female metaphors, according to Hildegard's concept of mutual reflection of God and the human being.

The starting point of her parable of the Mother of Zion and her daughter is a vision of the animation of an embryo in a mother's womb. The daughter has a multifold identity; she is the individual human soul sent into the flesh by the creator God, but she is also the people of Israel in the Old Testament. Later on, she becomes the 'lost daughter', found by and reunited with her Mother in heaven, the maternal divine Wisdom.

In Hildegard's parable, the daughter describes herself as a 'peregrina' 'female pilgrim', wandering in the shadow of death (Ps. 23). Without consolation, deprived of the joy of cognition, expelled from her home,

18. Cf. Gössmann, *Hildegard von Bingen*, p. 205.
19. Cf. 'Der Brief Hildegards von Bingen an den Kölner Klerus zum Problem der Katharer', in Gössmann, *Hildegard von Bingen*, pp. 163-73.

in prison and slavery, eating with the pigs, deluded, tormented and even raped, this pilgrim remembers her original vocation as a daughter of the Mother of Zion who should have lived in a tent, ornamented with stars and precious stones, a companion of angels, enjoying the tender love of her Mother. From her Babylonian prison, she cries to her now, shedding tears of repentance. Suddenly, the daughter is surrounded by a sweet odour, the 'odor sapientiae' which her Mother from heaven has sent to her. By this smell of wisdom (sapere and sapientia in Latin are derived from the same root) the daughter is paradoxically strengthened with tenderness and enabled to flee from her captivity and to fight her demonical enemies who use the sea and the mountains to impede her on her way. But sustained by the vigour of her Mother's sweet odour of wisdom, the daughter is able to reach the peak of the mountain, only to be terrified by scorpions and dragons on the other side. Now the daughter addresses her Mother again, challenging her: 'O Mother, where are you? My pain would be less if I had not felt the pleasantness of your presence earlier. I am going to fall back into that captivity... Where is your help now?'

After this cry of despair, the daughter hears the voice of her Mother: 'O daughter, hurry, wings for flying are given to you by the highest giver... Therefore, fly over these obstacles quickly!' The wings are explained by Hildegard as the power of faith. But it is important to notice that the daughter in this parable does not fly to her Mother like an immature child, but overcomes her obstacles and builds a new tent to live in. Her Mother's consolation enables her to lead a new life in this world as a woman of full age, tender and strong.[20]

One century later, Gertrud the Great in the convent of Helfta, living under the Cistercian rule, defended the dignity of woman as God's image without any restriction. In her 'Legatus divinae pietatis' she described an experience of meditation when, in dialogue with Christ, she perceived his words: 'As I am the image of God the Father in divinity, you will be the image of my essence towards humankind, since you received in your God-created soul the efficiency of my divinity, just like the air which receives the rays of sunshine.' For the Christ of this meditative audition, femininity is not an impediment to represent him.

We also learn from Gertrud's book that God was addressed in Helfta as Father and Mother and that Christ revealed his love as motherly care.

---

20. Cf. Gössmann, *Hildegard of Bingen*, pp. 29-37.

However, in the visions of Gertrud and other nuns of Helfta, Christ not only appears as a tender mother but also as a strict one, teaching the daughter according to his eternal Wisdom. Female work, like spreading the linen on the meadow to be purified by the sun, is a symbol of cooperation between God and the human being, which leads to salvation.

The grace of mystical unity is symbolized in Gertrud's text by Christ bestowing a crown on her, saying: 'Like a girl who receives from her mother a crown to be adorned for a feast, you may expect the crown from me.' Christ as the incarnation of eternal Wisdom is always present in the consciousness of the Helfta nuns.

Whereas Hildegard had reinterpreted the parable of Lk. 15.11-32 by exchanging the son for the lost daughter of Zion, Gertrud interpreted this parable in a different way; the son who stays at home with his father appears as a daughter. After an experience of alienation, caused by God's absence, she heard the words of Lk. 15.31, spoken to her: 'My daughter, you are always with me…'[21] This consciousness of being God's image and Christ's representative, had decisive consequences for Gertrud's and other Helfta nuns' legitimation to do pastoral work.

Omitting other mediaeval women writers, let us examine the continuity of women's tradition in Christine de Pizan, a woman living in the world and generally not regarded as a theologian. In her 'Epistre au Dieu d'Amours' of 1399, she wrote that God created woman in the dignity of being similar to him: 'Dieu la forma a sa digne semblance', a dignity explained by Christine in the following way: God conveyed wisdom, intelligence and cognition ('savoir', 'cognoiscence', 'entendement') to the first woman. So Christine regards woman's *imago Dei* before all as a guarantee for the equal participation of female human beings in reason or intelligence, which means the cognitive faculty of the human mind.[22]

Renate Blumenfeld Kosinski has studied this faculty given to holy women in the third book of Christine's *Livre de la cité des dames* of 1404–1405, including the reversal of many a misogynistic topos. From the hagiographic cross-dressing stories in Christine's time, she selected those of St Maryne (Marina) and St Effrosine. Religious cross-dressing

21. For the sources, cf. Elisabeth Gössmann, 'History of Biblical Interpretation by European Women', in Elisabeth Schüssler Fiorenza (ed.), *Searching The Scriptures. I. A Feminist Introduction* (New York: Crossroad, 1993–94), pp. 27-39.

22. Cf. Andrea Echtermann, 'Christine de Pizan und ihre Hauptwerke zur Frauenthematik', in E. Gössmann (ed.), *Archiv*, VI (Munich: iudicium, 1994), pp. 1-75.

such as the putting on of male clothes by women was regarded as a kind of 'imitatio Christi' or putting on Christ, which conceals the female sex in order to show its strength, representing a symbolic inversion of the topos of female weakness. Abandoning the prescribed female roles and rejecting the male-female hierarchy, these women saints were used by Christine to show the constancy and mental strength of women, the ability of women to suffer hardships and to be victims of false accusations (for instance of paternity). With the help of holy women like these, Christine showed that a woman can be like a man in everything but dress; however, by adopting male dress she becomes indistinguishable from a man. In Christine's cross-dressing stories, which are quite different from those in the works of male authors, such as Vincent of Beauvais in his *Speculum historiale*, it is important that the female body persists under the male cover and is triumphantly revealed after death.[23]

Consequently, it is not astonishing that Christine in her *Livre des trois vertus* tried to expand the margin of activity for women. As Doris Ruhe has shown in a recent work, a woman in the position of replacing her husband in his governmental duties during his absence or in widowhood, has to be educated in law, financial affairs and even military strategy. Christine's meaningful use of words concerning learning and knowledge like 'sage', 'savoir', 'cognoistre', 'apprendre', 'enseigner' is also mentioned here, as well as her conviction that a woman always has to be a 'moyenne de paix et concorde', a peace maker and creator of concord.[24]

Christine did not forget to mention that a well educated woman when widowed, will be able to manage her own affairs without remarrying. So her work differs completely from contemporary treatises on women's education written by male authors.[25]

Christine's counselling of women to live an independent life (and consequently her contempt for those who neglected their endowments) was founded on her conviction of the equal participation of both sexes

---

23. Cf. Renate Blumenfeld-Kosinski, "Femme de corps et femme par sens': Christine de Pizan's saintly women', *Romanic Review* 87 (1996), pp. 157-75.

24. Cf. Doris Ruhe, 'Von Frau zu Frau: Christine de Pizans Ratschläge für die weibliche Lebenspraxis', *Das Mittelalter: Zeitschrift des Mediävistenverbandes* 1 (1996), pp. 55-72.

25. Ruhe mentions the 'Livre du Chevalier de la Tour Landry pour l'enseignement de ses filles' of 1372, and the 'Ménagier de Paris' of 1394, as containing only rules according to which women have to live. Ruhe, 'Von Frau', pp. 7-20.

in reason, which is for her the deepest meaning of the *imago Dei* in both sexes. This theological basis of her thinking generally remains undiscovered, since Christine is regarded as a writer of literary works, or a chronicler, and neglected in her theological and philosophical concepts. Christine's attempt to reconstruct women's history in her main work is also quite different from male authors' way of writing about famous women from mythology, the Bible and history, which is very often ambivalent or misogynist; Boccaccio is no exception.[26]

Marie de Jars de Gournay is another important contributor to women's tradition concerning the female *imago Dei*. In 1622, she published her pamphlet 'Egalité des hommes et des femmes', dedicated to Anne d'Autriche, mother of King Louis XIV, for whom she took over the regency in 1643. Marie is one of the first authors to use sociological arguments in the modern meaning of the word, when she maintained that the difference of education and learning between women and women can be greater than that between women and men, because it depends on the country where a human being grows up, the circumstances of the family living in a big city or in the countryside and so on. She also noticed that in the society of his time Jesus could not have announced his message if he had been born a woman.

Following scholastic authorities and anticipating Descartes, she regarded sexuality as belonging to the body and not to the mind or soul. Alluding to Gen. 1.26, she wrote that the Bible counts the human being, created male and female, as one, and that Jesus is called 'son of man' because of his mother, and finally she attacked those theologians who reduced or even denied the female 'image de Dieu'. Very sarcastically, she wrote that these squabblers mistook their beard for the image of God and denied it to those who did not possess a beard. According to Marie de Gournay, this had far reaching consequences concerning the male usurpation of power and authority. Indirectly, the male concept of God as an old man with a beard is criticized here too by Marie's ironical style.[27]

These comments of women writers on the human image of God in

---

26. Concerning Boccaccio's misogyny cf. E. Gössmann, *Mulier papa: Der Skandal eines weiblichen Papstes. Zur Rezeptionsgeschichte der Päpstin Johanna* (Munich: iudicium, 1994), pp. 66-69.

27. Marie de Jars de Gournay is documented in Gössmann (ed.), *Archiv*, I (Munich: iudicium, 2nd edn, 1998), pp. 33-53.

both sexes and their explanations of Gen. 1.26-28 throughout the centuries show a continuity of biblical interpretation different from that of male theologians. For women theologians, the *imago Dei* warrants the equality of both sexes in nature as well as in the capacity of cooperating with God's grace. Neither the reduction and diminution of God's image in women is accepted by them, nor the discrimination against their mental talents. Women's writing on this subject intended mutual encouragement and empowerment and criticized women who tended to neglect their God-given endowments. To be created in God's image is the basis of women's self-confidence and self-regard as God's good creatures.

Creation, the Fall and its Consequences according to the Male Tradition

Until at least the eighteenth century, male as well as female interpreters of the Bible regarded the verbal meaning of biblical texts as 'sensus historicus' ('the historical meaning'). Consequently, the different way in which God created the human being as male and female according to Genesis 2, was most important as a basis of different anthropologies.

In the scholastic tradition, the interpretation of Genesis 2 was connected with that of Genesis 3 by the question of woman's subordination to man. Was it by nature, which means from the very beginning of creation, or was it a consequence of woman's participation in the original sin? Already within the Bible (for Catholics), in Sirach 25.24, the origin of sin and death was projected on woman, and in 1 Tim. 2.9-15, priority in a positive meaning was conceded to man as the first-created one, and priority in a negative meaning was appropriated to woman as the first one to be seduced.

In the biblical interpretation of the church fathers, like the first woman, all women are regarded more or less as the seducers of man. Augustine wrote that only Eve, because of the inferior capacity of her mind, believed in the snake's promise that they would be like God, and that Adam only sinned because Eve had sinned before him and he did not want her to be lost alone.[28] So man's sin was minimalized and

---

28. Augustine, *De genesi ad lit.* XI, 42, 58-60. Cf. Monika Leisch-Kiesl, *Eva als Andere: Eine exemplarische Untersuchung zu Frühchristentum und Mittelalter* (Cologne: Böhlau, 1992), pp. 58-98. Børresen, *Subordination and Equivalence*, pp. 54-55.

woman's sin was maximized. Adam was excused and Eve was accused. Because of Augustine's authority, this kind of interpretation was continued in the Middle Ages. For instance, in the twelfth century Peter Lombard wrote about the tumour of pride in Eve's bosom.[29] It is not surprising that through the sermons preached in churches, many mediaeval women were caused to internalize a negative image of woman as a sinner from the beginning, a view that intellectual women and women writers tried to refute.

Some of the ancient Christian writers and the scholastics claimed equality of the two sexes before the fall, without any subordination. According to Marie Thérèse d'Alverny, in the twelfth century it was not only Andreas of St Victor (who knew Hebrew), but also Rupertus of Liège and Gilbert de la Porrée who claimed woman's original freedom from subordination as well as the equality of God's image in both sexes. In 1 Cor. 11.7, where woman is named man's glory, these theologians saw nothing but a reference to her creation from man's flesh.[30]

But it is particularly these theologians with an egalitarian concept who do not hesitate to stress the fall of Eve. The more they are partisans of original equality, the more they burden Eve, the paradise creature, with responsibility for all kinds of evil in the world. Rupertus, for instance, accused Eve not only of having seduced Adam, but also of having offended God by infringing his commandment. He used examples from Roman law to demonstrate women's lifelong subordination before, in, and after marriage. These 'three obediences of woman' can also be found in Indian as well as Chinese sources, especially in Confucianism, where woman's subordination is also justified by her sinfulness. So it is not a problem of the Judaeo-Christian tradition alone. Only an intensive comparative study of religions can help scholars to overcome androcentrism in the world religions and societies.

The use of symbolism was also very influential in justifying woman's subordination. It was Philo of Alexandria in the first century who identified νοῦς with man and αἴσθησις with woman,[31] those Greek terms which appear in the writings of Ambrosius and other Latin Church

---

29. *Magistri Petri Lombardi Sententiae in IV libris distinctae*, Tom. I pars II (Grottaferrata, 1971), p. 443.

30. d'Alverny, 'Comment les théologiens,' pp. 30-35.

31. Cf. Philo, *Op. mund.* 134-172. Elisabeth Gössmann, 'Anthropologie', in Elisabeth Gössmann, *et al.* (eds.), *Wörterbuch der feministischen Theologie* (Gütersloh: Gütersloher Verlagshaus Gerd Mohn, 1991), pp. 16-22.

Fathers as 'ratio' and 'sensualitas'. Church fathers as well as the scholastics teach us that man has to govern woman just as reason has to govern sensuality.[32] Of course, it is not forgotten by these writers that 'ratio' and 'sensualitas' can be found in all the individuals of both sexes, and it is also said that women, like men, have to govern their 'sensualitas' by help of their reason. But as, according to this concept, sin arises from sensuality, woman once again is identified with the seducer.

Concerning the creation of the two sexes, there was a very favourable opinion, written down by Hugh of St Victor (twelfth century) who probably was influenced by Jewish writing. He maintained that woman was created from man, but not from his head, because she should not be his 'domina' (ruler), nor from his feet, because she should not be his 'ancilla' (maid). Created from his side, she should be his 'socia' (partner). But there was not much response to this concept, and Thomas Aquinas did not agree with it, since he believed in the Aristotelian anthropology of (only) male activity and female passivity.

Aquinas was convinced of a double kind of woman's subordination, a softer one from creation and 'by nature', and a more oppressive one as a consequence of sin. The Aristotelian terms of activity and passivity, form and matter as applied to the male and female sex, can be found in Dominican anthropologies more intensively than in those of Franciscan origin. Even if Bonaventure used Aristotelian terms and the definition of woman as a defective male, he followed Hippocrates and Galenus much more than Aristotle. Therefore according to him, men can also be passive and women active.[33]

Woman's subordination to man by nature and from creation is founded by Thomas on the 'bonum ordinis' ('good of [social] order') which means that the wiser ones (for him automatically males) have to guide those who are not so wise. In the following sentence of Thomas Aquinas, 'man' is identified with 'human being': 'Naturaliter femina subjecta est viro, quia naturaliter in homine magis abundat discretio rationis' ('By nature, woman is subjected to man, since by nature the human being has a more analytical mind').[34] Read maliciously, this

---

32. Cf. Elisabeth Gössmann, 'Anthropologie und soziale Stellung der Frau nach einigen Summen und Sentenzenkommentaren des 13. Jahrhunderts', *Miscellanea Mediaevalia* 12 (1979), pp. 281-97.

33. Cf. Emma Thérèse Healy, *Woman According to Saint Bonaventure* (Erie, PN: The Georgian Press, 1955), p. 11.

34. *Summa Theol.* I q. 92 a. 1 ad 2.

sentence would mean that woman is not a human being. But this is not Aquinas's conviction, since for him the difference of sex is not essential but accidental for the human being.[35] However, since Aquinas agreed with Augustine that woman was created as a help for man only in one respect, because he needs her for begetting his offspring, such an androcentric and patriarchal view was not able to regard woman as a partner in anything else.

Already before the thirteenth century the mediaeval philosophy of nature came under Aristotelian influence. Even in a Platonic school like that of Chartres, Guillaume de Conches believed that when he created man, God had mixed the elements in a better way than later on, when he created woman.[36] Other theologians identified fire and air, as the two so-called higher elements of the cosmos, with masculinity, and water and earth, as the two so-called lower elements, with femininity.[37] So the man-woman hierarchy was legitimated by cosmic proportions, and since, according to this concept, the temperaments depend on the mixture of elements in the male and female bodies, men are 'hot and dry', qualities regarded as very advantageous for higher talents, whereas women are 'cold and wet' with lower talents.

In summary, in continuation of their diminution of the female *imago Dei* in their interpretation of Genesis 1, the church fathers as well as the scholastics generally (with very few exceptions) used the text of Genesis 2 and 3 to confirm the priority of man as God's first-created human being and the superiority of the male sex, describing woman as a human being of a lower level of mind in intellectual as well as ethical regard.

Creation, the Fall and its Consequences in Women's Counter-Tradition

One of the women writers who were conscious that woman's dignity was part of the beauty of God's creation is Hildegard of Bingen. Her

35. Cf. Catharine Capelle, *Thomas d'Aquin Féministe?* (Paris: Librairie Philosophique J. Vrin, 1982), p. 44.

36. Cf. Hans Liebeschütz, 'Kosmische Motive in der Bildungswelt der Frühscholastik', in Fritz Saxl (ed.), *Vorträge der Bibliothek Warburg 1923/24* (Leipzig Berlin: Teubner, 1926), pp. 83-128.

37. Cf. Prudence Allen, *The Concept of Woman: The Aristotelian Revolution* (Montreal: Eden Press, 1985); *eadem*, 'Two Medieval Views on Woman's Identity: Hildegard of Bingen and Thomas Aquinas', *Studies in Religion: A Canadian Journal* 16 (1987), pp. 21-36.

anthropology is founded on her exegesis of Genesis 2: man was created from the loam (de limo) and had to be changed into flesh. His privilege, derived from the earth as the material of his creation, is physical strength, enabling him to do his hard work in an agricultural society. But woman was created from the human flesh and therefore did not need to be transformed. 'Caro de carne, in aliud non mutanda permansit.' 'De carne sumpta, caro permansit, et ideo datum est ei artificiosum opus manuum.'[38] (Taken from the flesh, she remained flesh, and therefore a skillful work of her hands is committed to her.) This is her privilege. Her hands are skilled for textile work 'to cover man' who would be 'naked' without her labour, and her body is skilled 'to cover the child' with the human flesh to be born from her.

Hildegard's theory of woman's better qualification for skilled work because of the special way she was created is also a kind of compensation and consolation for women living in a patriarchal culture under juridical obligation to be obedient to husbands and to work for them. But for Hildegard, this obligation is a mutual one. Man nurtures woman, and she dresses him. So both sexes, from the 'privileges' of their creation, are qualified for social cooperation. (According to modern concepts, Hildegard is speaking here much more about 'gender' than 'sex'.) It seems that Hildegard, with the help of Genesis 2, intended to raise esteem for women's work.

In one of her variations of the patriarchal opinion concerning man's strength and woman's weakness, Hildegard wrote: 'Deus creavit hominem, masculum scilicet maioris fortitudinis, feminam vero mollioris roboris.'[39] (God created the human being: the male of more strength, the female of a softer kind of power.) Accordingly, man's strength needs 'mildness' (mansuetudo). Man's strength in mildness and woman's softer kind of power indicate her anthropology of equality, even if she was not able to abolish the patriarchal matrimonial law of her time. But she tried to soften it. Concerning monks and nuns living in virginity, she used expressions of equality. They are 'idem inter angelicos ordines' ('the same among the angelic orders').[40]

It is necessary to mention here that Hildegard's macro-microcosmic concept of creation is different from the male interpretation, according

---

38. Hildegard of Bingen, *De operatione Dei* III.7, *PL* 197, col. 963. Cf. Gössmann, *Hildegard von Bingen*, pp. 101-104.

39. *De operatione dei* II.5, *PL* 197, col. 945.

40. Hildegard of Bingen, *Solutiones quaestionum* 38, PL 197, col. 1039.

to which the mixture of elements in the male and female body confirms the hierarchy of the two sexes. According to Hildegard, air and water as the two intermediate elements are prevailing in the female body, while fire and earth as the two extreme elements prevail in the male body. So Hildegard dissolved the cosmic fixation of the man-woman hierarchy, and consequently, she dissolved the hierarchy of talents of the two sexes. Nevertheless, women had to continue the fight against the misogynist doctrine of elements and temperaments, at least until the eighteenth century (for example, Moderata Fonte, Lucretia Marinella, Dorothea Christiane Leporin).[41]

In her interpretation of woman's 'subjection' to man according to Gen. 3.16, Hildegard used biological terms, probably in order to undermine its patriarchal connotation. She mentioned that a woman as a receiver of her husband's semen is 'placed under' his potency.[42] So the legal term of subjection is reinterpreted by its biological use. The biological act of generating a human being with the cooperating woman as 'subiecta' symbolizes for Hildegard a creature's subordination to God.

Hildegard distinguished between the newly created Eve as the splendid 'feminea forma' and model of virginity on one hand and the fallen Eve on the other. But according to the persuasive argument of Barbara Newman, Hildegard, in contrast to male theologians, magnified the role of Satan. Disregarding the question of Eve's motivation, Hildegard held that Eve was 'more sinned against than sinning, not so much tempted as deceived'.[43] Eve's frailty as a sinner calls up God's mercy. Consequently, Hildegard is not far from interpreting Eve's guilt as 'felix culpa' ('a happy fault').

Since in scholastic theology woman's subordination was regarded as making her dissimilar to God, Hildegard connected subordination with reverence and wisdom as gifts of the Holy Spirit. According to Hildegard's allegorical interpretation of the expression 'house of wisdom' in Prov 9.1, woman is, so to speak, a house of wisdom ('quasi domus sapientiae') in her reverence towards God and her husband.[44] Here, in a

41. These women writers are documented in vols. II and IV of Gössmann (ed.), *Archiv* (Munich: iudicium, 1985).

42. Cf. Gössmann, *Hildegard von Bingen*, pp. 101-103.

43. Barbara Newman, *Sister of Wisdom: St Hildegard's Theology of the Feminine* (Berkeley: University of California Press, 1987), p. 112.

44. Hildegard of Bingen, *Liber vitae meritorum* I.82.961.

spirit of solidarity, Hildegard equated married women bearing children and nuns delivering works of charity. All of them are the 'house of wisdom'. The only difference is that nuns show reverence, (*Ehrfurcht*) as the prevalent meaning of 'timor Dei', towards God directly, while married women do it indirectly through their reverence towards their husbands.

The 'house of wisdom' in Prov 9.1 was interpreted by most of the male exegetes of that time as the body of Christ. For Hildegard, it means womanhood, as we have seen. So it is not surprising that she discovered a parallel between woman and Christ or Eve and Christ. Christ (according to Lk. 1.26-38) and Eve (according to Gen. 2.21-22) have the same origin: 'not from semen but from human flesh'.[45] Christ's and woman's work are similar: humankind was born from woman's 'weakness', not from man's 'strength', and reborn from the 'weakness' of Christ's human nature, not from the 'strength' of his divine nature.[46]

In her interpretation of the prologue of the Fourth Gospel, Hildegard mentioned both sexes as being given the 'power' to become God's children: 'omnibus hominibus utriusque sexus qui eum receperunt' ('to all human beings of both sexes who received him').[47] The addition of 'utriusque sexus' (also in other women's texts) shows that Hildegard who read 'filii' (sons) in her Latin Bible, is very near to the Greek original (τέκνα θεοῦ) which, of course, she could not read. Mediaeval women realized that male writers often used the word 'homo' ('human being') only in the sense of 'male'.

The prophecy of Joel, quoted in Peter's sermon on Pentecost (Acts 2.17), which mentions the prophesying sons and daughters, was one of Hildegard's favourite texts of the Bible. It was important not only for her self-understanding but for that of other writing women as well. Quoting St Paul's text of 1 Cor. 11.9, she completed it: 'Woman was created because of man, and man because of woman.'[48] Against the contemporary dualistic concept of woman becoming man in eschatological perfection, Hildegard, in a context alluding to 1 Cor. 15.52, stressed the eschatological integrity of the female human being: 'All human beings will rise from the dead in body and soul... with integrity

---

45. Hildegard of Bingen, *De operatione Dei*, PL 197, col. 974.
46. Cf. Gössmann, *Hildegard von Bingen*, p. 57.
47. Hildegard of Bingen, *De operatione Dei* I.4, PL 197, col. 896.
48. Cf. Gössmann, *Hildegard von Bingen*, p. 98.

of their sex.'[49] But in this regard, she is in harmony with Augustine and most of the scholastic theologians such as Thomas Aquinas and Bonaventure, who were fighting against 'haeresim illam quod nulla mulier salvatur' ('the heresy that no woman can be redeemed').[50]

In the early modern period Christine de Pizan offers us one of the best examples of a positive understanding of the creation of woman. In her 'Epitre' of 1399 she mentioned that woman was created by God in a noble form. She continued that Eve was created from a 'better' material and not from the loam. But contrasting with Hildegard's concept of equal privileges of both sexes by their special way of creation, according to Christine, Eve's body is 'le plus noble des choses terriennes' ('the noblest of all beings on the earth'), created in paradise.[51]

The interpretation that privileges Eve's place in creation must be very old. Looking back to male authors fighting against this 'feminist' biblical interpretation, we find that Ambrose in his treatise 'De Paradiso' wrote several sentences of polemics against the interpretation of the Genesis text on the creation of woman in paradise as a privileging of the female sex. He concluded with the words: 'May other people see what they believe. For my part it seems that sin and falsehood originate from woman.'[52]

Ambrose did not say who these other people were who claimed woman's creation in paradise was privileged. But if they had been heretics, he would have told us. It is conceivable that some female biblical scholars, such as the women cooperators of Jerome, developed this type of interpretation of Genesis 2 and succeeded in finding some men to promulgate their way of reading the Bible. This is only a hypothesis. But by refuting it, Ambrose testified that such a biblical interpretation existed in his time.

It is interesting to see how Thomas Aquinas converted or better perverted Eve's creation in paradise to a privilege of Adam: 'Mulier facta fuit in paradiso non propter dignitatem suam, sed propter dignitatem principii ex quo corpus eius formabatur ('Woman was created in paradise not because of her own dignity, but because of the dignity of the

---

49. Hildegard of Bingen, *Scivias* III.12, PL 197, col. 743. *Corpus Christianorum Continuatio Mediaevalis* (CC CM) 43A, 608.

50. *Comm. in Eccli*, c. 8, ed. Quaracchi Tom. VI, 64.

51. Cf. Gössmann (ed.), *Archiv*, VI, p. 22.

52. PL 14, col. 320: 'Viderint alii quid sentiant; mihi tamen videtur a muliere coepisse vitium, inchoasse mendacium.'

principle from whose body her body was formed').[53] Only the *Summa Theologica* redacted by Alexander of Hales who was a Franciscan (and perhaps an English gentleman) did not refute completely the 'feminist' interpretation of Eve's creation in paradise. According to this *Summa*, Eve's creation does not mean a privilege for the female sex, since Eve was not created from paradise, but only in paradise. Rather it means a kind of compensation for her lower intellectual and moral talents. In other words, the 'defectus naturae' ('defect of nature') in the female sex was lessened by the favour of the exterior circumstances of Eve's creation.[54]

Christine de Pizan used this very old argument together with that of the 'better' material from which Eve's body was taken, and that of woman's noble form making her God's masterpiece, in which the mind can develop its talents perfectly without any impediment. This is perhaps an argument against those male authors who, acknowledging the equality of souls in male and female individuals, pretended that the soul in a 'weak' female body was not able to develop mental faculties perfectly. But as we have seen already, Christine claimed, by help of Genesis 1, the equal participation of female human beings in reason, and in Genesis 2 she discovered the favourable conditions for women to develop their talents.

Concerning Genesis 3, Christine as a defender of her sex against misogynist writers of her time and preceding ages, went further in expiating Eve than Hildegard did. This tendency was to be continued in women's tradition of the following centuries. The more woman was decried as man's seducer, the more women writers tried to declare Eve as innocent. Christine took the Bible as a testimony against all those who blamed Eve for deceiving Adam. She claimed that Eve, without any evil intention, believed what 'the enemy' had told her, and that a person who neither intends to deceive nor to betray, cannot be blamed for such faults.[55]

In the early modern world male writers who were not or not so much connected with philosophical or theological schools and university teaching, took over the main points of biblical interpretation in women's

---

53. *Summa theol.* I q. 102 a. 4 ad 3.

54. Cf. Elisabeth Gössmann, *Metaphysik und Heilsgeschichte: Eine theologische Untersuchung der Summa Halensis* (Munich: Max Hueber, 1964), p. 219.

55. Cf. Gössmann (ed.), *Archiv*, VI, p. 23.

tradition from the Middle Ages. Ignorant of this continuity, recent
works on the history of French literature maintain that the first feminists
were men and not women. These male scholars have to be blamed for
expropriating women of their tradition.

In fact, the first of the so-called 'male feminists', such as Henricus
Cornelius Agrippa von Nettesheim who published his praise of women
in 1529,[56] and François de Billon with his *Le fort inexpugnable de
l'honneur du sexe féminin* from 1555, are not simply 'feminists', but
also ambivalent writers, placing misogynist and feminist arguments
side by side. The readers are asked by Billon to make their own decision whether his praise of woman is honest or ironical. However, it
could be helpful for women, and especially for women writers, that
male writers published arguments for the abolishment of the limitations
of women's activities.

The self-aware Renaissance writer Lucretia Marinella who did not
even employ the humility topos generally expected from women
writers, published her *Le nobiltà et eccellenze delle donne et i diffetti e
mancamenti de gli huomini* ('The nobility and excellence of ladies and
the defects and imperfections of men') for the first time in 1600. This
was a counter-representation against the misogynist work of Giuseppe
Passi: *I donneschi diffetti* ('The defects of women'), published for the
fourth time in 1599. Re-evaluating or rather transvaluating the different
names and markings for 'woman' and for 'Eve' in the misogynist tradition, Lucretia, as a neo-Platonist of the Renaissance, described woman's
beauty of body and soul as a subject for man's meditation in order to
recognize God and to find the way back to unification with the divine.

Like her forerunner Moderata Fonte, she re-evaluated the doctrine of
the temperaments, maintaining that the mixture of elements in a
woman's body is the reason for her moderate temperament, while the
hot temperament of men leads them into immoderate sensuality and
other negative activities. Lucretia Marinella was even keen enough to
criticize Aristotle for his bad image of woman. She refused any contribution of Eve to the original sin, using arguments from moral
philosophy:

> If men say that Eve was the cause of Adam's sin and in consequence of
> our misery, I answer: 'She ... did nothing but propose that he might eat
> from the fruit of the tree believing that it was good for them... But we do

56. E. Gössmann, (ed.), *Archiv*, IV, pp. 9-100.

not read in the Bible that she urged him with requests, complaints, or angry words... As she did not know... that the snake... was the devil... how can we say that she sinned, since the presupposition of sin is a preceding cognition?'[57]

In a similar way, Marguerite de Valois or Reine Margot called God as a witness to the perfection of his last creature:

> God proceeds in his works by such a succession that he creates the lowest things first and the most excellent, most perfect and most dignified last, which he has shown in the creation of the world when he created the human being last of all—the human being for whom he had made all the other creatures. Therefore it is necessary to admit that the supreme degree of dignity must be attributed to woman, who was created after man as God's last creature. The highest perfections can be found in her as well, emerged as she is from God's hands just like man, but from a material as much more elaborated in its degree of excellence as the rib of man is in the way in which it surpasses the mud.[58]

Like Lucretia Marinella, Marguerite de Valois regarded the beauty of woman's body as a reflection of her beautiful soul, enabling her for beautiful actions. According to her, 'la plus vive image de Dieu' ('the most vivid image of God') can be found in woman. That woman's dignity is not lost by the subordination to her husband, according to Genesis 3, is evident for Marguerite by the election of a woman as God's mother. Consequently, the male sex continues to owe reverence to the female. This is possibly a reaction against the *Lex salica* in France which prevented women from the succession to the throne.

Because in seventeenth-century France moral philosophy was open to women, Suzanne de Nervèze could publish in her *Oeuvres spirituelles et morales* of 1642 an 'Apologie en faveur des Femmes', in which she complained of male arrogance in despising women's intellectual faculties. Her refutation of this anti-feminist position is a demonstration of the strength and wisdom of women in the Bible, daughters of Eve, the 'chef d'oeuvre' of God's works of creation. According to Suzanne, it is meaningful that God called his work of creation 'very good' (Gen. 1.31) only after finishing the creation of Eve.[59]

---

57. For Marinella and Moderata, cf. Gössmann (ed.), *Archiv*, II and IV.

58. 'Discours docte et subtil fait par la feue Reyne Marguerite et envoyé à l'autheur des secrets Moraux', in *Réponse des femmes à l'Autheur de l'Alphabet* (Paris, 1618), p. 11.

59. Suzanne de Nervèze will be documented very soon in my *Archiv*.

In addition to self-defence, women writers used their biblical interpretation with a didactic intention. In her *Nouvelles observations de la
langue Française* of 1668, Marguerite Buffet wanted to teach women
how to speak and how to write. As a means of encouragement, she
maintained that the human soul is sexless and therefore equal in both
sexes. But against the very old argument that a soul could develop its
faculties much better in a male than in a female body, Marguerite
stressed the bodily prevalence of women:

> ...since the body of man was formed from the loamy soil of the earth,
> which is a material not at all comparable to that from which the body of
> woman was formed; since we know that everything that is stronger in the
> body of man was used to form that of woman. In whom, however, can
> we trust with more submission than in the God of truth who assures us
> that the perfection of the universe depended on the creation of woman
> who was the last of his works as well as their crowning?[60]

As we can see, the *Sitz im Leben* of women writers' biblical interpretation can be quite different, but always they try to encourage and
empower women and to expand the field of their activity.

The last example of this continuity in women's tradition concerning
Genesis 3 will be taken from the youngest of the three women writers
who are known as the three stars of Venice. After Moderata Fonte and
Lucretia Marinella, it is the nun Archangela Tarabotti who, like
Hildegard and other nuns, showed solidarity between nuns and married
women. She paraphrased God's word addressing Eve in Genesis 3 in
the following way to make it applicable to every individual married
woman:

> Since you are too credulous, 'I shall multiply your labours and pregnan-
> cies, and you will bear children in pain.' Because man is a human being
> full of ingratitude, he will be thankless towards his own mother...who
> suffered deadly pains when she bore him. But I predict...that you will
> be drunk with matrimonial love so much...that you allow him to deprive
> you of all your authority, and since you believe him too much and yield
> to him, it can be said about you: 'You will be under the power of man,
> and he will govern you'; not as a punishment earned by yourself, but
> defeated by his promise or threats or urgent requests, you will fall into
> the traps which this ungrateful creature has set for you.[61]

---

60. Marguerite Buffet, *Nouvelles observations de la langue Française* (Paris,
1668), p. 201.

61. Cf. Gössmann (ed.), *Archiv*, VI, p. 115.

The 'feminist' as well as the misogynist exegesis are antiquated today as a consequence of modern methods of biblical research. But this does not mean that women's counter-tradition is meaningless. We can learn from it that women continually defended themselves against patriarchal and androcentric concepts, in order to encourage each other. It is a great pity that this counter-tradition is nearly completely forgotten even by women theologians of today. We should cooperate in resuscitating these women's works that have been passed down throughout the centuries and that can give us support in our problems of today.

Women and Priesthood according to the Male Tradition

In mediaeval theology, the ancient Christian deaconesses were not forgotten. It was well known that they had received a kind of consecration, but according to the contemporary Canon law, it was mostly assumed that the deaconesses of the ancient church had received only a benediction (which is not a sacrament according to mediaeval distinctions) and not a consecration or ordination. Even if some of the scholastics used women's capability for pastoral care as well as their strength in confessing their faith and suffering martyrdom as an argument in favour of their suitability for ordination, the negative arguments, taken from the (pseudo)Pauline prohibition against women teaching and the commandment to keep silence in ecclesiastical communities, were decisive.

Thomas Aquinas, in his commentary on Peter Lombard, maintained additionally, according to Aristotelian anthropology, that the 'defectus naturae' ('defect of nature') in women prevented them from representing the degree of excellence which a priest, by help of his masculinity, receives through ordination. Opposing this, Franciscan theologians— following Hippocrates and Galenos—acknowledged a certain amount of female (and not only male) activity. Consequently, Bonaventure testified to the opinion that women were forbidden to be ordained but that possibly they were able to receive the sacrament of ordination.[62]

Later on, most of the theologians maintained that women's ordination was not only forbidden but also invalid according to divine law, along

---

62. Cf. E. Gössmann, 'Äußerungen zum Frauenpriestertum in der christlichen Tradition', in Dietmar Bader (ed.), *Freiburger Akademiearbeiten 1979–1989* (Munich: Schnell & Steiner, 1989), pp. 304-321.

with that of heretics, Jews, hermaphrodites, 'monsters' (handicapped) and insane persons. A woman in ecclesiastical functions was regarded as a perversion of Christian tradition and doctrine.[63]

Women and Priesthood in Women's Counter-Tradition

Hildegard of Bingen found three reasons compensating for the exclusion of women from priesthood: (1) She discovered a parallel or analogy between the annunciation to St Mary and the liturgy of the Holy Mass in which the Holy Spirit was called down upon the gifts of bread and wine. In both cases, the Word becomes flesh. So the priest acts according to a Marian pattern; (2) Hildegard placed the nuns side by side with their 'sponsus Christus'; As brides of Christ, they participate in his original and ideal priesthood, being placed on a higher level than any human priest; (3) A priest saying Mass in a women's convent does nothing more than a service he owes to the brides of Christ.[64]

Only a century later, Gertrud the Great of Helfta, in her *Legatus divinae pietatis* gave testimonies of her empowerment for pastoral work by Christ himself. The praying Gertrud mentioned gratefully that she had received from Christ the commission to hear confessions and to judge the seriousness of the sins confessed to her. A fellow sister reported that, in a vision, Christ breathed upon Gertrud and spoke to her the words of Jn 20.22-23: 'Receive the Holy Spirit. Whose sins you remit, shall be remitted', and that she, not daring to believe, mentioned the restriction of this power to the priests, but received the following answer from Christ: 'Those whom you, discerning through my spirit, judge to be not guilty, will surely be accounted innocent before me, and those whose case you judge to be guilty, will appear such to me, for I will speak through your mouth.'[65] According to this and other texts in the same book, Christ regarded Gertrud as a minister of the church by his own gift, and she, in spite of feeling personally unworthy, was conscious of being in possession of the seven sacraments. Similar to Gertrud, her fellow sister Mechthild of Hackeborn was conscious of her ecclesiastical commission, both of them in a friendly cooperation with

---

63. Cf. E. Gössmann, *Mulier papa*, pp. 145-147.

64. Hildegard of Bingen, *Scivias* II.6, CC CM 43, 290. *Vita Ruperti*, PL 197, cols. 1086-87. Cf. Newman, *Sister of Wisdom*, p. 194. Gössmann, *Hildegard von Bingen*, p. 234.

65. Cf. Gössmann, 'History of Biblical Interpretation', pp. 32-34.

priests or monks. Thus it is evident that these women, feeling authorized by Christ himself, applied texts of the New Testament to themselves, with far reaching consequences.

In closing, I want to mention again Marie de Jars de Gournay who ridiculed men for mistaking their beard for the 'image de Dieu'. For her, the prophetesses of the Bible and the leadership functions of women in the history of the people of Israel were very important. As she could not distinguish between letters written by St Paul and those only ascribed to him, she excused 'St Paul' for excluding women from ministry in the church. Like other authors, she wrote that this was not because women were despised by him but because of the weakness of men who would have been distracted from liturgy by a woman priest. But she mentioned joyfully the female cooperators of St Paul and, according to the legends widely spread in her country, she praised Mary Magdalene as 'égale aux apôtres' ('equal to the apostles') who, exempt from the commandment to keep silence, preached for 30 years in the South of France.

Similar to all the ancient peoples who conveyed priesthood on women as well as on men, Marie argued that Christianity had acknowledged women's ability to baptize, but why, she asked angrily, were women not allowed to administer the other sacraments? The answer was easy for her: because men are not inclined to share power with women. For a seventeenth-century female writer this is a severe criticism of women's exclusion from priesthood.[66]

As can be learned from many prohibitions in ecclesiastical law during the time of the Counter-reformation, abbesses were blamed for reading the Gospel during the liturgy of the convent Mass, also for preaching, blessing their nuns and hearing their confessions. For such prohibitions to be in place, women must have taken such roles upon themselves.

Conclusion

Even if feminist theologians know enough about women's counter-tradition to give them support, there is still very much research work to be done in order to reconstruct women's theology throughout the centuries as far as possible. Of course, women and men are always children of their time, and feminists today are children of their time, sitting on

66. Cf. n. 27.

the shoulders of their foresisters even if they do not recognize it. Cooperation is needed to complete the work of reconstruction of women's theology in earlier centuries, and for this aim, it is necessary to study the languages our foresisters used, whether it is Latin, ancient French, Italian, Spanish, English or German.

From our foresisters in patriarchal and androcentric times we can also learn the methods of finding one's way in life and doing what is necessary to be done, whether by getting exceptional permissions or by ignoring limitations. I think it is a very important commission of women in the Catholic church of today to criticize the last Vatican documents, especially 'Mulieris dignitatem' (1988) for its biologistic concept of only male priests and 'Ordinatio sacerdotalis' (Pentecost 1994) for its imperfect and onesided concept of Christian tradition. Of course, according to the Vatican documents, 'Christian tradition' is only male, and different opinions, such as of the Franciscan school, are not included. The discriminations against woman, concerning her lower level of intellect and morality, originally legitimating the exclusion of women from ecclesiastical functions, are not mentioned any more. But as is well known, if the presupposition falls, the conclusion cannot stand. Is it so difficult for ecclesiastical authorities to understand this and to expand their concept of Christian tradition?

GENDER TROUBLE IN GALATIA?
PAUL AND THE RETHINKING OF DIFFERENCE

Brigitte Kahl

Nakedness, Reclothing, Disguise

There could be some reason to call Paul's letter to the Galatians the most 'phallocentric' document of the New Testament. Nowhere else have we so much naked maleness exposed as the centre of a deeply theological and highly emotional debate: foreskin, circumcision, sperm, castration, to name only some of the relevant terms.[1] Paul even links the Gospel to male anatomy, coining the unique terms 'Gospel of the foreskin' and 'Gospel of circumcision' (2.7). For most translations this seems to be too direct—they shamefully hide Paul's openness under more 'covered' phrases like 'Gospel to/for (the) Gentiles' and 'Gospel to/for (the) Jews' (Good News, NEB), or 'Gospel to/for the circumcised/ uncircumcised' (RSV/NRSV).

The well-known problem in Galatia is whether male non-Jews who convert to the Jewish Messiah Jesus should get the specific male Jewish identity marker of circumcision. Does it follow that Galatians is a letter addressing primarily male problems, suggesting more or less androcentric solutions to them, as some feminist critics have claimed?[2]

In contrast, it is Galatians where we find one of the most powerful prooftexts of emancipation and liberation throughout church history:

---

1. ἀκροβυστία 2.7; 5.6; 6.15; περιτομή/περιτέμνω 2.3, 7 , 8, 9, 12; 5.2, 3, 6, 11; 6.15; σπέρμα 3.16 (thrice); 3.19, 29; ἀποκόπτω 5.12. This makes more than 15% of the overall New Testament occurences of these terms.

2. L. Fatum, 'Women, Symbolic Universe and Structures of Silence: Challenges and Possibilities in Androcentric Texts', *Studia Theologica: Scandinavian Journal of Theology* 43 (1989), pp. 61-80 (66); S. Briggs, 'Galatians', in Elisabeth Schüssler Fiorenza (ed.), *Searching the Scriptures: A Feminist Commentary* (2 vols.; New York: Crossroad, 1994), II, pp. 218-36.

...for in Christ Jesus you all are children (sons) of God through faith. As many of you as were baptized into Christ have clothed yourself with Christ. There is no longer Jew or Greek, there is no longer slave or free, there is no longer male and female; for all of you are one in Christ Jesus (3.26-28 NRSV).[3]

The recent debate about the origin, meaning and literary embedding of Gal 3.26-28 is quite controversial.[4] Usually, the diachronic emphasis on the traditional, that is pre- and non-Pauline, character of the baptismal formula is rather strong.[5] A literary (synchronic) analysis, however, shows that every single part of 3.26-28 is closely tied to the overall context of Galatians; the key terms of sonship (implying descent, fatherhood, motherhood), oneness, slavery and freedom, male and female form the conceptual backbone of Paul's argument right through from the first to the last sentence.[6] Therefore, Paul's most fundamental

3.   All following translations are taken from the NRSV. Regarding the inclusive NRSV translation of 'sons' as 'children of God' cf. C. Osiek, 'Galatians', in Carole Newsom and Sharon H. Ringe (eds.), *The Women's Bible Commentary* (Westminster: John Knox Press, 1992), pp. 334-35.

4.   There is some consensus on the origin of 3.26-28 as a pre-Pauline baptismal formula (W. Meeks, 'The Image of the Androgyne: Some Uses of a Symbol in Earliest Christianity,' in *History of Religions* 13 [1974], pp. 165-208 [180-83]). Most other questions are fairly open: Does the statement mainly testify to egalitarian social practices in the congregations and missionary activities prior to Paul? (E. Schüssler Fiorenza, *In Memory of Her: A Feminist Theological Reconstruction of Christian Origins* [New York: Crossroad, 1985], pp. 208-211; Briggs, 'Galatians', pp. 218-19) Or, the other way round, is it rather Paul who disapproves of and changes a tradition that implies disdain of the body, misogyny and antisocial attitudes? In this case Gal. 3.26-28 would express Paul's own vision of sexual/social equality. Does the male and female of v. 28c echo Gen. 1.27 and the related myth of a primordial androgyne? (Meeks, 'The Image of the Androgyne', pp. 185-89; Fatum, 'Women, Symbolic Universe and Structures of Silence', pp. 67-68), or does it refer negatively to the order of procreation and marriage based on Gen. 1.27? (Schüssler Fiorenza, *In Memory of Her*, p. 211). Should Paul in 3.26-28 be primarily understood before a Hellenist philonic/platonistic background (D. Boyarin, *A Radical Jew: Paul and the Politics of Identity* [Berkeley: University of California Press, 1994]). Finally, how do the several occurences of similar unification statements in 1 Cor. 12.13; Col. 3.9-11 (both without the male-female opposites); 2 Clem. 12.2; *Gos. Thom.* 22; Gospel of the Egyptians 3.91 relate to each other?

5.   Schüssler Fiorenza, *In Memory of Her*, p. 208; Briggs, 'Galatians', p. 220.

6.   Sonship/genealogy/identity is the central topic of Paul's rereading of the Abraham-Sarah story in Gal. 3-4, slavery/freedom of the parenetic section chs. 5-6. Oneness (of God and in Christ) occurs as the focus of the whole letter: not only in

statement on border-transgressing unity of race, nation, class and sex is not just to be considered as a lighthearted aside to the gloomy rest of the letter (and of Paul), but as an integral part of the Pauline text—even if Paul quoted it from somewhere else.

If Gal. 3.26-28 is thus understood as the inner climax and focus of a coherent argument rather than a loosely connected prooftext from outside, then it should be asked how the baptismal reclothing and unification of male/female it proclaims relates to Paul's discourse on 'naked' maleness already described as central to Galatians.[7] According to Paul, how would it look 'to be clothed with Christ—all of you in oneness' (3.27-28)? A heavenly, invisible dress that leaves the earthly order of clothing untouched? Some kind of uniform, preferably male— just like the blue suits for men and women during the Chinese cultural revolution? Clerical robes that make femaleness completely disappear even if women are allowed to put them on? Something like a Christian counterpart to the 'universal' fashion standards of a worldwide Western consumerism (which cover differences of place and identity as perfectly as the poverty of the women in Asia and elsewhere who produce clothes for the warehouses of the West)?

The question at stake here is how Paul defines unity. Does 'oneness in Christ' primarily mean the elimination of hierarchies, inequalities and privileges which separate different nations, religions, cultures, classes and sexes—or is it difference and distinction as such that is erased?[8] The question can be put in a very simple way. If two are unified into one, what does that really mean? There are two possibilities. First, A

the key statements of 3.16, 20, 28; 5.13, but also in the most vital reflections on fellowship and mutuality in chs. 1–2 and 5–6 (cf. 2.1, 12; 6.2, 6). The pair of male and female is not mentioned again explicitly. But as male (ἄρσεν), contrary to female (θῆλυ), according to Gen. 17.14, 23 LXX is the object of circumcision, and as the whole section chs. 3–4 centres around the problem of biological/theological fatherhood and motherhood, one can hardly agree that 'the third pair of Gal. 3.28 has no connection with the immediate context nor with any of Paul's themes in Galatians', and that the baptismal formula as a whole 'stands out from its context' (Meeks, 'The Image of the Androgyne', p. 181).

7.   The unclothing /reclothing imagery is also central to Meeks's argument on baptism as rite of passage and the regaining of the original androgyne image of God (W. Meeks, *The First Urban Christians: The Social World of the Apostle Paul* [New Haven: Yale University Press, 1983], pp. 155-57).

8.   E. Castelli, *Imitating Paul: A Discourse of Power* (Louisville, KY: Westminster/John Knox Press, 1991), p. 22; Boyarin, *A Radical Jew*, p. 9.

plus B becoming C—that is finding a new way of co-existence, mutuality and community that both changes and preserves the old identities and distinctions; this would be a participatory, egalitarian and pluralistic model of unity. Secondly, a more hierarchical–unity model: A plus B united into A, that is the 'one' just swallows up the 'other one', making difference inferior or disappear. If this hierarchical–unity model of 'repressive sameness'[9] applies to Paul, then Galatians indeed would be one of the master narratives of the imperial cultural pattern of the West which puts identity markers like male, Christian, master, culture as superior to female, Jewish/Muslim/Gentile, slave, uncivilized/nature and all other kinds of otherness.[10]

There are, however, several observations which at first reading contradict the notion of a uniform male Christian superiority in Galatians. The most puzzling one is Gal. 4.19, where we come across Paul employing the imagery of a mother in labour who suffers heavily from birth pains and fears:

> My little children, for whom I am again in the pain of childbirth until Christ is formed in you... (4.19)

With only few exceptions,[11] commentators usually ignore or marginalize this most strange act of apostolic 'transvestism'. But perhaps Paul's symbolic self-feminization is less accidental than many believe. The whole of Galatians is about reversing and re-evaluating identities—on reclothing so to speak. Definitely, the primary concern of Paul is not gendered but religious, national and social identity: Jews and non-Jews. Nevertheless, I am going to argue that his rethinking of identity and difference, sameness and otherness, 'we' and 'them' inescapably has fundamental effects on the restructuring of male and female as well.

Who is Who in Galatians?

Galatians confronts us with a rather confusing picture if we try to look for clear cut identities. The oneness of Jew and Greek, slave and free,

---

9. Boyarin, *A Radical Jew*, p. 9.

10. Castelli, *Imitating Paul*, p.120.

11. B. Gaventa, 'The Maternity of Paul: An Exegetical Study of Galatians 4.19', in R. Fortna and B. Gaventa (eds.), *The Conversation Continues: Studies in Paul and John in Honour of J. Louis Martyn* (Nashville: Abingdon Press, 1990), pp. 189-210; Osiek, 'Galatians', p. 336.

and male and female proclaimed in 3.28 seems to produce something like a masquerade of identities.

(a) Male and female: Paul in 4.19 becomes a mother in labour, thus clearly showing non-male behaviour. Women in Galatians, on the other hand, are begetting their children without pregnancy or birth, without having a man, that is to say in a completely non-female (or even male?) way. New kinship bonds were created irrespective of blood ties.

> For it is written: Rejoice you childless one, who bear no children, burst into song and shout, you who endure no birth pangs; for the children of the desolate woman are more numerous than the children of the one who is married (4.27 = Isa. 54.1).

(b) Slave and free: freedom is one of the key words especially from Galatians 4 onwards.[12]

> ...we are children, not of the slave but of the free woman. For freedom Christ has set us free. Stand firm therefore, and do no submit again to a yoke of slavery (4.31–5.1).

But the freedom that Paul so vigorously defends throughout Galatians paradoxically is practised as mutual slave service: 'For you were called to freedom...but through love become slaves to one another' (5.13).

(c) Jew and Greek: even more astonishing is the handling of ethnic and religious identity. In ch. 3 we are confronted with non-Jews who before our eyes transmute into Jews of one hundred per cent Jewish descent—without having a Jewish mother or father and even without circumcision. They are merely implanted into the Jewish genealogy as sons, sperm, offspring of Abraham (3.7, 29) and children of Sarah together with born Jews (4.31).

Conversely, in Gal. 4.21-31 we see how pious Jews of probably perfect Jewish descent are presented with an 'Arabian' grandmother, Hagar. In a society where identity and status is very much based on genealogy this confusion of descent and kinship lines would be highly challenging and offensive.

---

12. Already in the narrative part of the epistle, chs. 1–2, it becomes clear that a focal point of the Galatian controversy is (violent) pressure exercised once by Paul himself (1. 13-14) and then by his opponents at Jerusalem, who want to destroy the freedom of the Pauline congregations by enslaving them (2.3-4). The pair freedom–slavery then becomes central to the passage about sonship of God (3.23–4.11), in the Sarah–Hagar allegory 4.21-31, and in the last two chapters.

To complicate matters further, Arabs (or Greeks or Galatians) become Jews and Jews become Arabs. 'Christians' in our sense of the word simply do not exist yet. The various terms Paul uses to denote Jews and non-Jews occur 22 and 14 times respectively, the term 'Christians' not once. This, of course, is well known. It has become one of the most subjective exegetical conventions explicitly or implicitly to insert the missing 'Christians' wherever it seems appropriate. Thus some of Paul's Jews and non-Jews get transfigured into Jewish Christians and Gentile Christians, and all of a sudden the controversy in Galatia separates 'Jews' (non-Christians) from 'Christians' (Jewish and Gentile Christians).[13] But is 'in Christ' (3.28) or 'of Christ' (3.29) really the same as 'Christian'? What changes if Paul speaks about Jews and Gentiles who ate together 'in Christ' at Antioch (2.12), instead of the common understanding of this as table fellowship of Jewish and Gentile Christians?[14]

Paul himself leaves us no doubt that he considers himself a Jew (he never says 'a Jewish Christian'). Rhetorically, large parts of Galatians are an inner-Jewish debate to which non-Jews are allowed access, most prominent is the famous dispute between the Jew Peter and the Jew Paul (2.14-15) about justification by faith and/or by works of law (2.11-29) at Antioch. But what then does it mean if the Jew Paul asks his non-Jewish Galatian addressees in 4.12: 'Become as I am, for I also have become as you are...'? Is this just the testimony of a slightly confused and even schizophrenic mind—or could it be that Paul is handling the question of identity in a much more dialectical and subversive way than our post-Pauline Christian identity patterns permit us to think?

Difference is not Different

To take one example, in his programmatic and very angry opening address in 1.6-9 Paul accuses the Galatians of turning to a different gospel (ἕτερον εὐαγγέλιον) ὅ οὐκ ἔστιν ἄλλο. Everyone who knows

---

13. H. Betz, *A Commentary on Paul's Letter to the Churches in Galatia* (Philadelphia: Fortress Press, 1979), pp. 28-29; Briggs, 'Galatians', p. 225.

14. These points have been made by Krister Stendahl already in 1976 in his programmatic book *Paul among Jews and Gentiles* (London: SCM Press, 1977), where he reintroduced the Jewish Paul and the original historical context of the cir-cumcision debate into the Protestant Pauline discussion, concentrating mainly on the doctrine of justification.

Greek will easily translate this as a very simple relative clause: 'A different Gospel which is not another one.' Nevertheless, with rare exceptions, such as, for example, the Latin Vulgate and the NEB, this literal meaning is usually not rendered; the majority of translations say something like 'a different gospel that does not exist'. Linguistically, this just means changing one single word, namely the relative pronoun 'that' into a 'there': 'a different gospel—there is not another one', rather than: 'that is not another one'. In semantic terms, however, there is a significant difference between these two translations.

I think that the common translation, which a priori denies the existence and the right of a 'different gospel', is quite symptomatic of the way in which Paul has been made to fit into our Western hegemonic discourse. Otherness, being different, is automatically thought of in terms of being wrong, marginal and inferior. Identity, on the other hand, is spelled out as sameness and, as such, opposed and superior to otherness/difference. The long and dreadful history of Christian occidental exclusion and expulsion, exploitation and extermination of 'others'—from the crusades to the Conquista and Reconquista, from witch hunting to the Holocaust, from 'Christian' wars to the destruction of nature—is rooted in this pattern.

To read Paul in this framework, or even to declare him (affirmatively or critically) as one of its early protagonists,[15] necessarily requires Paul to be given a clear cut Christian identity that is opposed to Jewish and all other 'Otherness'.[16] As in Gal. 1.6 'the different gospel', the proclamation of which is accused and even cursed (1.6-9), clearly is the 'gospel of circumcision' (2.7); these basic occidental opposites seem to be very well established: The 'Jewish' gospel of circumcision stands against the 'Christian' gospel of remaining uncircumcised, Christian being superior and 'correct' in opposition to Jewish as inferior, 'wrong', different, and excluded. This can be explained in the following diagram:

15. Castelli, *Imitating Paul*, pp. 124-28.

16. For example, Briggs, 'Galatians', p. 225: 'It is unquestionably clear that Paul replaced the distinction between Jew and Gentile in the Christian community with an in fact far more drastic one between Christian (Jew and Gentile) and non-Christian Jew.' This presupposition, however, which also underlies the commentary of Betz (*Commentary*) cf. pp. 28-33, and of course has the most far reaching hermeneutical consequences, does not seem so 'unquestionable'.

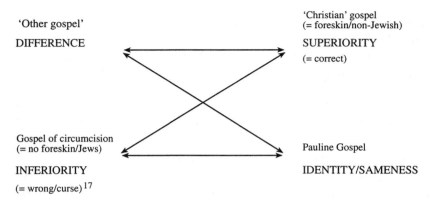

In the specifically Protestant version of this Christian occidental identity pattern the Jewish Law, understood as works of righteousness, (= inferior/excluded) is opposed to the gospel of Christ (= superior/ 'we'), spelled out as justification by faith alone. This explains how Luther, for example, in his commentary on Galatians of 1531, could easily transform the 'Jewish' opponents of Paul into Catholics and heretics of all kind, implying even the Turks/Muslims.

This pattern, which from the position of a dominant identity falsifies, excludes and suppresses otherness, easily applies to all other kinds of hierarchical dichotomies which, with Aristotle, have formed the basic structure of our occidental Christian thinking.[18]

identity	Christian	male	free/master	culture
otherness	Jew/Muslim	female	slave	nature

But what, then, if Paul has not said what we have consistently read and heard and taught about him? I believe that the literal translation of Gal. 1.6-7 is the correct one and very much in accordance with the the whole web of Paul's argument in Galatians: first, Paul does not speak of a 'Christian gospel' but of the 'gospel of Christ' (1.7). The gospel of

---

17. The sketch uses the structuralist pattern of the semiotic quadrangle which defines the relationships between A, non-A, B, non-B as opposites, contradictions and inclusions. Thus all positions in horizontal or diagonal order are mutually exclusive, i.e. either oppositional (A and non-A: difference and identity; B and non-B: superiority and inferiority) or contradictory (A and B: difference and superiority; non-B and non-A: inferiority and identity). The vertical positions are inclusive.

18. Cf. Elisabeth Gössmann, 'The Image of God and the Human Being in Women's Counter-Tradition', pp. 26-56.

Christ, however, exists only in a twofold way as 'gospel of circumcision' and 'gospel of foreskin' (2.7).

Secondly, he does not say that the 'different' gospel of circumcision is wrong; what he tries to make clear is that his own gospel of foreskin was for a long time regarded as 'different' and wrong. The whole narrative part of Galatians (1–2) deals with the tensions caused by this 'otherness' of Paul's preaching.[19] It fundamentally changed the conditions for male Gentiles to become full members of the people of God, without circumcision. But it could not claim any human authority or tradition to legitimize this 'heretical' move—just a revelation by God (1.10-24). No wonder that this caused serious quarrels, which Paul rather tries to play down when he tells the Galatians about it. There was not a forced circumcision for his Greek companion Titus at Jerusalem. There were *false brethren* acting as spies in the Pauline congregations (2.3-4). The whole story of these 14 years of the independent Pauline mission told in 1.11-23 must have been far more dramatic than usually believed. Nevertheless, in an historic act of community building an agreement could be reached at the famous Jerusalem conference. The leading Jerusalem authorities recognized the 'other' Gospel of Paul, the gospel of the foreskin, as an equally legitimate way of preaching Christ among non-Jews (2.6-10). They recognized difference.

The Galatians, however, are just about to betray this most fundamental agreement and the theological insight behind it. If they think they should get circumcised they act as if difference still mattered. But the 'different' gospel in fact is not another one (1.6-7). The two different gospels and the two different types of messianic ('in Christ') Jewish identity therefore must persist. This is at the heart of Paul's introductory attack on the circumcision plans of the Galatians. Paul allows identities and hierarchies to float and not to be fixed. It is difference as such that Paul is going to redefine.

This would change the whole semantic universe of Paul's theology in Galatians. Difference is not opposed to sameness/identity but to non-difference, implying pluriformity and oneness-in-difference.

---

19. That Paul's theology originally developed out of the struggles and experience of an 'outsider' would have had far reaching consequences for the interpretation of the 'canonical' Paul.

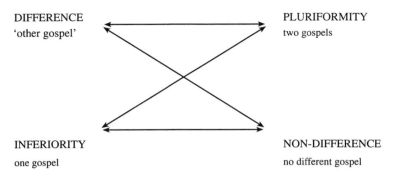

DIFFERENCE   PLURIFORMITY
'other gospel'   two gospels

INFERIORITY   NON-DIFFERENCE
one gospel   no different gospel

Oneness-in-Difference

Throughout the letter to the Galatians Paul is wrestling with the question of oneness/identity and difference/hierarchy. His basic concern is the messianic ('in Christ') transformation of Jewish identity toward an inclusiveness that can integrate difference without ceasing to be Jewish. His insistence that the Galatian non-Jews remain as they are, that is uncircumcized, refers to the symbolic field. Oneness (of God and of Israel) is no longer marked by sameness and superiority (i.e. all have to be circumcised as his opponents demand, as circumcision ranks above non-circumcision, at least from the perspective of his opponents). Oneness, therefore, is transformed from a vertical structure to a horizontal level, from an exclusive to an inclusive pattern.

This has fundamental practical consequences. The new pattern of behaviour became visible at Antioch, where Jews were eating together with non-Jews (2.11-21); or at the decisive meeting at Jerusalem (2.1-10) already mentioned, where after serious trouble it was agreed that the one gospel of Christ Jesus consists of two: not only the gospel of circumcision but also the gospel of foreskin to which the *right hand of community* (κοινωνία) is extended by the leading figures as a sign of acceptance (2.9). The representatives of the *foreskin*, namely Paul and Barnabas, on their side, promise to practise this community in terms of material solidarity with the poor (2.10). Likewise, in the section discussing parenthood in Galatians 5–6, Paul develops an ethics of mutuality that completely subverts the logic of dominance and subordination, identity and difference. Freedom is exercised as mutual slave service (5.13). Oneness and otherness are reconciled by *bearing one another's burdens* (6.2). The term *one another* (ἀλλήλος, from ἄλλος/ ἄλλος, literally, other-other), which in 5.13–6.10 occurs no less than seven times, seems to be pivotal here. The introductory claim of 1.6-7 that difference can turn out to be identity has to stand its test in the life practice of the messianic communities. If slaves who serve are free, implying even men serving women, then identity is no longer found on the level of a superior and exclusive oneness but on the level of the 'others'. The hierarchy between dominant and dominated is transformed into community.

If this is the description of a non-repressive, egalitarian and communitarian Christian identity and unity, it should also inform the interpretation of the key statement in Gal. 3.28. Paul's proclamation of the oneness of Jew and Greek, slave and free, male and female in Christ thus would not mean the erasure of difference; rather it would be directed against a dominant, exclusive identity concept of Judaism, freedom and masculinity, which prevents the messianic fellowship of Jews and non-Jews, slaves and free, men and women in Christ.[20]

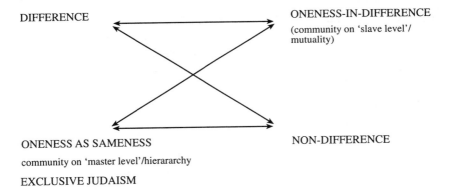

DIFFERENCE

ONENESS-IN-DIFFERENCE
(community on 'slave level'/ mutuality)

ONENESS AS SAMENESS
community on 'master level'/hierararchy
EXCLUSIVE JUDAISM

NON-DIFFERENCE

Paul's notion is deeply apocalyptic. In a divine revelation of the messianic event—the resurrection of Israel's crucified Messiah— Paul

20. In this point I differ from Elisabeth A. Castelli and Daniel Boyarin who claim that the Pauline concept is just sameness as 'Hellenistic desire for the One' (Boyarin, *A Radical Jew*, pp. 7, 16) and fear of diversity. I doubt that Paul sees difference as 'subversive of unity, harmony, and order' (Castelli, *Imitating Paul*, p. 86). He probably has to be understood much more from a Jewish apocalyptic than gnostic-Hellenist background, as, for example Louis Martyn, 'Apocalyptic Antinomies in Paul's Letter to the Galatians', *New Testament Studies* 31 (1985), pp. 410-24, and Neil Elliott, *Liberating Paul: The Justice of God and the Politics of the Apostle* (New York: Orbis Books, 1994) have pointed out—and from the biblical logic of the Genesis narratives.

'sees' that the binary oppositions and hierarchies (male-female, master-slave, Greek-Barbarian), which the Greeks thought to be the basic cosmic structures on which the world rested,[21] are no longer valid. This is the meaning of the new creation (6.15), the end of the old world, its order (1.4) and its powers.[22] The differences are not 're-unified' in the sense of making them disappear, but their hierarchical, polarizing order is abolished.

This, for example, happens in the Sarah-Hagar allegory (Gal. 4.21-31) where Paul completely confuses the traditional groups of binary polarities of Jewish and non-Jewish, slave and free, male and female. Identity markers of Jewish superiority (as Paul was experiencing it in his specific historical context of pre-70 CE) such as 'Sinai' and 'present Jerusalem' are 'wrongly' placed on the same side as 'Hagar/Ishmael' equating non-Jewish/Arab/Gentile and labelled with the inferior status of slavery and femaleness (4.23-25). On the opposite side of 'us' a similar mixture of Jewish ('Sarah/Jerusalem' above) and non-Jewish (Galatians) appears but receives the superior position of freedom and non-biological motherhood as children of 'promise' (4.26-28). Again difference is defined differently. Allegorical speech (in Greek, speaking 'differently'), which Paul explicitly claims in 4.24, can express this in unique ways,[23] even if being difficult to understand.

Nevertheless, the two 'mixed' columns of 'Hagar' and 'Sarah' in 4.21-31 are strongly antithetical and hostile (cf. persecute—drive out; 4.29-30). The new creation, already present but still waiting to become full reality, establishes new dichotomies (which, however, run queer to the old separation lines) and opponents.[24] But it is not yet a dominant church that triumphs over a victimized synagogue but the highly marginalized and persecuted Pauline vision of a universal and egalitarian messianic Jewishness which tries to defend itself against the superiority claims of a violently exclusive branch of pre-70 Judaism.[25]

21. Martyn, 'Apocalyptic Antinomies', pp. 413-16.

22. Elliott, *Liberating Paul*, p. 112.

23. E. Castelli, 'Allegories of Hagar: Reading Galatians 4.21-31 with Postmodern Feminist Eyes', in E. Struthers Malbon and E. McKnight (eds.), *The New Literary Criticism and the New Testament* (Journal for the Study of the New Testament, Supplement Series, 109: Sheffield: Sheffield Academic Press, 1994), p. 243.

24. Martyn, 'Apocalyptic Antinomies', p. 417.

25. The interpretation of 4.21-31 of course dramatically changes if Paul is

It could be shown that the Pauline technique of cross-changing identities and reversing superior and inferior statuses is deeply influenced by narrative patterns of the Genesis account where, from Cain and Abel onwards, the positions of firstborn and secondborn sons are continuously exchanged, as happens in Gal. 4.21-31 with Isaac and Ishmael.[26] The moving force behind this masquerade of identities does not aim at cementing the status quo of freedom-slavery, inferiority-superiority, but rather fundamentally subverts it.[27]

Likewise, the concept of oneness of God and of the people of God, which Paul so firmly links to his proclamation of oneness in Christ and to the Abraham story (3.16, 20, 28), could very well echo the exodus of Abraham out of Babylon, where the imperial unity of the Tower reigned and oneness was based on exploitation, submission and domination.[28]

defined as a 'Christian' who attacks 'the Jews' and deprives them of their identity, their father, their freedom (Briggs, 'Galatians', p. 230). If Hagar was 'the type of non-Christian Judaism' (Briggs, 'Galatians', p. 224) then Paul indeed would have created an early prototype of the anti-Judaistic 'Church and Synagogue' imagery, which throughout Christian mediaeval art represented the dichotomy between the two religions as two women, one (Hagar/synagogue) defeated and one (Sarah/ecclesia) in triumph. The hermeneutical shift making this (mis)use of Paul possible in my opinion happened only after Paul, in the processes of polarization and finally separation between Rabbinic Judaism and Christianity following the Jewish War (66–70) and later on the Bar Kochba rising (135).

26. B. Kahl, *Armenevangelium und Heidenevangelium: 'Sola scriptura' und die ökumenische Traditionsproblematik im Lichte von Väterkonflikt und Väterkonsens bei Lukas* (Berlin, 1987), pp. 93-96.

27. Contradictory to this interpretation Sheila Briggs thinks that Gal. 4.21-31 shows 'how deeply the metaphor of inequality was embedded in Paul's thought' ('Galatians', p. 230) and that he perpetuates the inferiority of the slave woman Hagar as hereditary and thus 'natural' (as it was already proclaimed by Aristotle; p. 224). This completely neglects the dialectic and subversive effect of the narrative technique of role exchange in Genesis and Galatians. Outsiders are made insiders and vice versa, strong opponents 'allegoricallly' (cf. 4.24) become weak, freedom means mutual slave service (chs. 5–6). Nothing is fixed. And the historical Paul, unlike the canonical, was not in a superior position.

28. Christoph Uehlinger has shown that the terminology of unity in Gen. 11.1-9 (one langugage, one people Gen. 11.6) has to be understood in the context of the Assyrian and Babylonian world empires; Uehlinger, *Weltreich und 'eine Rede': Eine neue Deutung der sogenannten Turmbauerzählung* [OBO, 101; Freiburg: Herder, 1990]). The unity destroyed by the One God then would be an imperial repressive oneness represented by the idols—cf. Paul's warning not to submit again to the non-gods in Gal. 4.8-10.

Contrary to this, Paul in Galatians tries to develop a theological pattern that makes it possible to think of the oneness of God and of Israel in a radically 'anti-Babylonian', that is non-hierarchical and inclusive, global and plural way. This, of course, would need further study.

Oneness as Split: Ethnic, Religious, Political Implications

Paul's inclusive concept of oneness integrates otherness at a horizontal, non-vertical level, rather than excluding and suppressing it. But if it is hierarchy that is excluded, not difference, who then are those 'others' attacked by Paul with such strong words: 'anathema', 'drive them out', 'castrate' (1.8-9; 4.30; 5.12)? Definitely not 'the Jews' in general but possibly radically observant and zealous (cf. 1.14) Jewish opponents of Paul, who insist on the circumcision of Gentile converts (i.e. 'same-ness') and obviously use force or violence against any dissidents (2.3, 14; 4.19; 5.11; 6.12)—exactly the same as Paul himself did prior to his call (1.13-14). This messianic call, which was not a 'conversion' [29], has not changed Paul's religious and ethnic identity as a Jew; rather it gave him a different perception of being Jewish. Paul continues to speak as a Jew (2.15), and it is a clearly Jewish identity that Paul creates for non-Jews 'in Christ'. The Galatians have to leave their former gods, family, nation, culture, tradition and social affiliation (4.8-9) to become children of the One God, of Abraham and Sarah, and sisters and brothers of Isaac. They receive the Jewish Scripture, the Jewish story and history are inscribed on them (chs. 3–4); and they are definitely not allowed to worship Caesar any longer. They possess all that builds up a Jewish national, religious, cultural identity.

But they remain uncircumcised. They become Jewish and they stay different. They have to preserve their foreskin—that tiny piece of otherness (which, however, is most significant in terms of religion, sociology, politics), in order to demonstrate, remember and practise that 'in Christ' difference has become different.

Within the framework of Jewish identity Paul thus develops a concept of descent, nation, religion and culture which fundamentally subverts any closed and separatistic group identity. By 'clothing' Paul with a Christian identity in the later sense and after driving the circumcized out of the church we have silenced and buried this highly challenging

---

29. K. Stendahl, *Paul among Jews and Gentiles* (Philadelphia: Fortress Press, 1976), p. 7-13.

discourse on identity and difference, which today could be one of the most precious contributions of Paul to the dialogue of religions and cultures, especially to the Jewish–Muslim–Christian encounter.

Within the context of the Hellenist cities of the Roman Empire where Jews and non-Jews co-existed, often in a mutually exclusive and rival/hostile way, being clothed with Christ could require quite a bit of courage. Probably this new clothing did not have anything to do with uniformity but rather with the tissue of the heavenly-messianic cloth (Acts 10.11) which made the eating table accessible for people who normally would never have eaten together (Gal. 2.11-21; Acts 11.3).

It should be added that this specific way of peacemaking in Christ the crucified was not only opposed to violent (zealot?) Jewish particularism but also subversive with regard to the Pax Romana, where Caesar was the exclusive medium of peace-making. Only 10 years later Paul was executed for his type of pacifism, which some Jews might have seen as a betrayal of Jewish identity, and the Romans as a new dangerous type of anarchy and lawlessness from the side of the ever-rebellious Jews.

Father God and Mother Paul

The trouble Paul is making implies gender problems as well. The inclusive new identity pattern automatically transforms the position and function of maleness and femaleness. Only two points should be mentioned here.

First, male (ἄρσην) does not bear one of the decisive physical distinction marks between Israel and non-Israel any more (cf. Gen. 17). The people of God no longer consist of circumcized male and uncircumcized female but of circumcized male and uncircumcized female and uncircumcized male. This pluriformity has a depolarizing effect, not only regarding the split between Jews and Greeks, but also between male and female. The symbolic superiority of male over and against female, which is marked by circumcision, loses theological foundation and dignity.[30] This could explain some of the difficulties that the male part of the Galatian congregations in particular were facing. Not only as (uncircumcized) Jews but also as men they must have been perceived as

---

30. The feminist debate about circumcision and women is quite controversial; see J. Lieu, 'Circumcision, Women and Salvation', *New Testament Studies* 40 (1994), pp. 358-70.

'different', irregular, even abnormal. Being a Jew and being uncircumcised—wasn't that a description exclusively for Jewish women? Were they not real Jews and not real men either? Maybe a 'third sex' in between? Especially in the light of the 'inferior' identity concept and a 'female' ethics of service already mentioned, one could imagine that the circumcision debates in Galatia were not only caused by socio-religious identity conflicts and ethical problems,[31] but by massive 'gender trouble' as well.

Secondly, the phallus is not only decentered theologically, but also biologically. In his rereading of the Genesis story in Galatians 3–4 Paul develops a concept of fatherhood and motherhood that could be a nightmare to anyone interested in 'orderly' patriarchal categories and cultural practices (as, for example, in the case of the Roman authorities). He introduces a specific christological spermatology where the whole web of kinship, descent and inheritance is built exclusively on the 'gene pi' = πίστις (3.7, 29 and the 'sperm chi' = Χριστός (3.16). Consequently, motherhood and fatherhood as well as sisterhood and brotherhood are completely de-biologized. As a result, the male line of descent is interrupted or horizontalized, which implies significant sociological and political consequences with regard to the father-centred Roman order. This, for example, becomes obvious in 'our' relationship to Isaac. 'We' are no longer children of Isaac (as it would correspond to the vertical genealogical pattern of father-followed-by son) but 'like' Isaac children of the promise, namely Isaac's sisters and brothers.

This rethinking of genealogy and descent, on the one hand activates kinship lines which so far have been dormant; non-Jews become Jews in Christ; and, on the other hand, de-activates branches of the genealogical tree. The Ishmaelites, alias Paul's Galatian opponents, who are full of zeal for Jewish identity, are not saved from being expelled by their claim to having Abraham as their biological father. In this case it is just the mother who counts (4.31). Following the logic of Paul's genealogical argument, there is no more significant role for human fathers (maybe with the one exception of Abraham). That is why the Galatians 'naturally' are children of father God and of mother Paul—together with mother Sarah.

---

31. J. Barclay, *Obeying the Truth: A Study of Paul's Ethics in Galatians* (Edinburgh: T. & T. Clark, 1988), p. 73.

Conclusion

The aim of these reflections on gender trouble in Galatia was not to once again criticize or canonize the androcentric Pauline thought patterns that undoubtedly exist. Rather, the intent was to study one weaving pattern in the fabric of the Pauline text which could very well change the whole cloth. How Paul, consciously or subconsciously, constructs gender and other identities by confusing them, implies a tremendously transforming potential, which mostly has been kept undercover throughout the centuries of Christian Pauline interpretation. By restricting the debate to isolated feminist proof or anti-proof texts we have cut ourselves off from what could be the most liberating and humanizing contribution of Paul's overall dialectic thought structure to the present gender discussion. The identity and place of male and female are fixed but have to be constantly re-negotiated towards a vision of oneness and difference not based on hierarchy but on κοινωνία. To discover this thread of the original Pauline fabric, however, requires getting Paul himself undressed from the thick layers of occidental cloth woven around him from Marcion, Constantine, Augustine and Luther onwards.

A FEMINIST CRITICAL READING OF THE ECCLESIOLOGY OF 'LUMEN GENTIUM'

Natalie Watson

It goes without saying that feminist critical involvement with the Christian tradition cannot avoid a study of the church as the main site of women's ambiguous experience within that tradition: the site of oppression and marginalization, of abuse and disembodiment, but at the same time the location of liberating discourse and identification and encounter with Christ. Surveying the work of feminist theologians we find that such a study of the church has in fact begun to take place. Yet we also find that the option for a liberation theological paradigm together with the primacy of experience by many feminist theologians has uncritically set the parameters of such a study. Rather than critically engaging with theological texts on the 'nature' of the church, on the kind of symbolism used in those texts that the churches have considered as relevant reflections on their own identity, some feminist theologians have 'reinvented' the church as 'women-church', as the discipleship of equals expressed in the form of feminist base communities. Such a neglect of ecclesiological texts and symbols seems almost universal and is best represented by the writings of Elisabeth Schüssler Fiorenza and Rosemary Radford Ruether, as well as the history of the women-church movement in the United States.

My intention is to question whether such a dismissal and neglect of traditional forms of theological discourse on the church may not have been too hasty. This means that feminist theology, and feminist ecclesiology as part of it, takes place at many levels, that of praxis being one, and that of critical theory being one of many other possibilities. Feminist theologians who consciously identify with the Christian tradition cannot afford to discard the study of theological and ecclesiological texts as the obsolete remainder of an androcentric theology. As well as reclaiming both biblical and other texts, feminist theologians may reclaim tradition for themselves by developing critical ways of re-reading those texts. Feminist theology can only fully take up its role as a critique of androcentric theology if it is also concerned with challenging patriarchy, where androcentric theologizing to a vast extent takes place: in the writing and critiquing of theological texts. Feminist theology not only has to be concerned with writing new texts and establishing new ways of practising the Christian faith. If it wants to establish its voice as an indispensable contributor to the praxis of theological discourse, it has to engage in a critical dialogue with those whose theological writings are considered influential.

Before I set out to give an example of such a feminist critical re-reading of an ecclesiological text, several methodological presuppositions have to be clarified.

First of all, it is necessary to construct the context in which such a re-reading can take place. We have to ask: Why discourse about the church at all? Why ecclesiology? If the church can be considered an institution, a context of life that is of importance and value for women, this points to the necessity of reflecting on what the church is. It furthermore points to the necessity of finding ways of expressing the importance and value of this institutional context of life in ways that are neither exclusive of women nor describe the church as an expression of religiously sanctioned male power over women. We must question the function of ecclesiology as a discourse that describes the church as a vital religious space, but does so in a way that supports a particular, predominantly patriarchal social symbolic order. For the purposes of this paper, 'church' signifies the Roman Catholic Church.

A feminist critical re-reading of 'Lumen Gentium' therefore has to proceed in two steps: first, certain ecclesiological discourses must be classified as to their essence: male self-reflections of a men's church. This identifies conventional ecclesiology as a male discipline. Second, the re-reading must start by establishing as its first presupposition that women are church and therefore must be involved in ecclesiological discourse. This involves searching for ways of re-reading ecclesiology that are in fact liberating and salvific for women. In so doing strategies of liberation and change may be developed in order to liberate the text itself from being a text that describes an institution that is oppressive and marginalizing for women.

Such a feminist reading is always a biased reading, but it seeks to overcome the myth of 'objectivity' that is claimed by conventional ecclesiologies as theology of the church that speaks for all of its members in all their diversity. It is not Scripture or a particular understanding of Scripture and the Christian tradition alone that is to be the measure of this reading of ecclesiological texts. Rather, this reading is one that seeks to advocate women's presence and representation in theological reflections on the church, in other words, to find ways in which particular ecclesiologies express or at least potentially express that women are church. A feminist critical reading of text from a male-defined genre is bound to be a subversive reading that does not aim at appreciating the timeless nature of the church or even the particular time and context-bound ecclesiology of particular authors. It aims to overcome the notion of 'legitimate' ways of doing ecclesiology by reclaiming the significance of women as authors of texts as well as agents of being church. As Marcella Althaus Reid argues,

> We are used to a universal reading of the scriptures (for example, 'for all humanity'), without suspecting that such an ample perspective excludes a lot of people from marginal groups. The universal reading is really European, male and white. To read from a different perspective does not sound 'legitimate'. But this is the point: it is not a legitimate reading that we want, since legitimization is the instrument of support of patriarchal ideologies, inside and outside the churches. Our interpretation wants to rescue elements of illegitimacy and subversion.[1]

Another reason for engaging in ecclesiological discourse is that the church as the community of men and women also becomes an important transfer point of power between men and women. A feminist analysis is therefore necessary in order to identify the gender-power interaction between men and women in an institution as important as the church. I identify issues of sexuality and gender as hitherto neglected dimensions of ecclesiology and argue that because of this neglect, dominating and oppressive power structures may, and do, develop. A feminist poststructuralist perspective, such as argued by Chris Weedon, can be extremely useful in such an analysis.

---

1.   Marcella Althaus-Reid, 'Walking with Women Serpents', *Ministerial Formation* 62 (1993), p. 32.

The assumption that sexuality is a historical construct which is the site of an especially dense transfer point for relations of power: between men an women, young people and old people, parents and offspring, teachers and students, priests and laity, an administration and a population makes sexuality an important site for the analysis of power without prescribing the precise importance of sexuality.[2]

My feminist critical reading of 'Lumen Gentium' takes three steps. First, I ask about women's participation in the authoring process of 'Lumen Gentium' as a conciliar text. With regard to the genre of conciliar texts, its process of development can be defined as one from which women were excluded. Second, one must look at women as readers and authors of new meaning. With regard to the genre of text with which I am dealing I can say that women as women have not been the intended readers of those texts and this point adds to the understanding of ecclesiology as a male dominated discourse. The essentially male genre of a conciliar text on ecclesiology may only be accessed by women if they agree to their temporary immasculation, their assumption of the role of the supposedly neutral male reader.

Often a woman reading an androcentric/patriarchal text is immasculated, that is, she reads and identifies as male. Yet as the reader identifies with the male as universal and dominant, she knows she is female. She constructs herself as Other... Hers is always a female difference and power that must be domesticated... Once a woman is aware of immasculation, she can read as a feminist. As she reads she recognizes the text immasculating her and the particular male reading strategies she uses. She also reads recognizing what the text forbids or tensions within it. She also reads recognizing that she and other feminists can resist or affirm the text, read it against the grain or transform it for feminist use.[3]

2.   Chris Weedon, *Feminist Practice and Poststructuralist Theory* (Oxford: Basil Blackwell, 1987), p. 7.

3.   Elizabeth Struthers Malbon and Janice Capel Anderson, 'Literary Critical Methods', in Elisabeth Schüssler Fiorenza (ed.), *Searching the Scriptures. I. A Feminist Introduction* (2 vols.; New York: Crossroad, 1993–94), pp. 241-54 (251). See also Judith Feterley's discussion of literature as male: 'In such fictions the female reader is co-opted into participation in an experience from which she is explicitly excluded; she is asked to identify with a selfhood that defines itself in opposition to her; she is required to identify against herself.' Judith Feterley, *The Resisting Reader: A Feminist Approach to American Fiction* (Bloomington: Indiana University Press, 1978), p. xii.

As readers of ecclesiological texts women, by the very fact of them being women, challenge conventional and intended forms of reading theological texts. Women as readers challenge the acceptance of their absence as authors and agents of ecclesiology by consciously embracing their identity as women readers in their particular socio-cultural situation. Ecclesiological texts cannot be seen as describing the empirical historical reality of the church but as texts that construct this reality and women as being part of it. Reflecting on the third aspect in this interactive process of reading one must ask what role women may play in the process of creating a text itself and/or the meaning of the text, and in what way meaning beyond an immediate context has been created for women.

After outlining some presuppositions of my study, I would like to turn to the particular application of this method in respect of the 'Dogmatic Constitution on the Church: Lumen Gentium'. The reason for choosing this particular text is that the Second Vatican Council can be understood as the most significant and revolutionary event in the history of the Roman Catholic Church in this present century.[4] In 'Lumen Gentium' the church reflects on its own identity in a changing world. In one of its other documents the Council in fact does acknowledge the changing role of women as part of that changing world. But its praise of the advancement of women remains restricted to the situation of women in society while the situation and role of women in the church remains unmentioned. The Council's concern for women does not reflect its willingness to correct a past theological error, but is driven by changes in the 'secular' world. This reflects a certain kind of belated disregard for women's concerns.

The council excluded women from its decision-making process and only reluctantly admitted women as observers at conciliar sessions.[5]

---

4.   See for example John Mahoney, *The Making of Moral Theology: A Study of the Roman Catholic Tradition* (Oxford: Clarendon Press, 1987), p. 302: 'The council itself was the major event of this century in the Church's life and the most momentous exercise to date of the Church's hierarchical *magisterium* in all its history, not only for the extent and depth with which it dealt, but also for the overall orientation which it gave to the Church's life and activity.'

5.   On the issue of the presence of women at the Council see Helen Marie Ciernick, 'Cracking the Door: Women at the Second Vatican Council', in Mary Ann Hinsdale and Phyllis H. Kaminiski (eds.), *Women and Theology* (Maryknoll, NY: Orbis Books, 1995), pp. 62-80; Carmel McEnroy, *Guests in their own House: The Women of Vatican II* (New York: Crossroad, 1996); and Carmel McEnroy,

Women have indeed not participated in 'Lumen Gentium' either as authors nor as readers, yet they have been affected by it as participants in a church that was thought to be changing and open to the concerns of a modern world. Since this is a discussion of feminist approaches to ecclesiology, I propose a reading of the 'Dogmatic Constitution on the Church' which, though perhaps not intended by the original authors, assumes women as readers of this document which, indeed, is part of the ongoing and changing tradition of the Roman Catholic church.

The church in the modern world sees it as one of its main characteristics that it provides room for diversity while simultaneously existing in unity under the supremacy of the Roman Pontificate. The emergence of local liturgies as well as the collegiality of the episcopate is encouraged, though the former still need the approval of the church and the bishops remain bound by the authority of the Roman Pontiff. Though the historical significance of the church for the first time presenting itself as a church that is aware of its world-wide dimensions should not be disregarded, we have to ask whether this emphasis on the diversity of local perspectives does not still suggest a rather limited understanding of diversity of ways of doing theology or liturgy. From a feminist point of view we might ask whether a diversity of locations and cultures can be enough or whether there also ought to be the celebration of a diversity of *bodies*.

The ambiguous body symbolism used by the authors of 'Lumen Gentium' is a profound source of alienation for women. The Church is defined as the body of Christ which is united by Christ as its head and under that condition celebrates the diversity of its members. For the church, traditionally often portrayed as female, to be defined as a body it has to be the body of Christ, a male body which, in addition to its denial of female bodiliness, is entirely dependent on its head, Christ. Such a concept of the church as the body of Christ does not take into account the reality of embodiment of human beings as men's bodies and women's bodies. It reduces the range of metaphorical meaning attached to the understanding of the body to the diversity of its members, while at the same time carefully limiting the range of such diversity. Diversity in such a limited understanding is only celebrated as diversity that is disconnected from an understanding of embodiment. It

'Women of Vatican II: Recovering a Dangerous Memory', in Pierre Hegy (ed.), *The Church in the Nineties: Its Legacy, its Future* (Collegeville: Liturgical Press, 1993), pp. 149-57.

is not the diversity of bodies, of particular embodied sexuate existence, which defines the body of Christ, but its submission to the male head of the body: Christ. Only such a literal deconstruction of what can be seen as one of the root metaphors of Christian ecclesiology can help to identify its potentially harmful character for the reality of women's lives both in the church and in society, but at the same time can leave room for a liberating re-reading of ecclesiology. Even though the dis-embodied androgyny that is created by identifying the essentially feminine church as the body of the male Christ appears absurd to a feminist understanding of embodied reality, it points to the significance of considering the relationship between ecclesiology and bodies, essentially between ecclesiology and women's bodies. What this feminist re-reading of 'Lumen Gentium' can point to here is the way in which ecclesiology has become a means of constructing women's bodies and their significance in a particular way. What we can retrieve for our reconsideration of ecclesiology is the importance of bodies, in fact of embodiment, for our understanding of the church, but this is only possible if we continue to struggle with the ambiguity of reclaiming ecclesiology by arguing for the importance of a different reading of 'Lumen Gentium' as a male conciliar text, and engaging in a critique of what is actually said in the text itself.

Gender does not appear as a category of difference and multiplicity that shapes the church in the modern world. Such a supposed gender neutrality helps to retain male dominance and essentially functions to exclude women as agents of ecclesial life. A feminist reading introduces the category of gender into the supposedly universal and gender-neutral concept of the 'people of God'. The concept of the people of God imposes a static concept of (gendered) hierarchies, which leaves no room for multiple forms as both personal and social identity reflected in the being of the church. The concept of the 'people of God' must be deconstructed in order to find out how it and other ecclesiological concepts become sites of the production of gender identities that are oppressive for women. The very identity of the people of God is built on the transmission of male power, whose disruption on the part of women is understandably resisted. The power of the college of bishops is dependent on the power of the pope as the supreme bishop and the college of bishops exercises power over the lower ranks of the hierarchy. What is presented here is essentially a male society governed by authoritarian power structures. Diversity within the church is expressed through diversity in the college of bishops. This concept of diversity is then used to assert the universality of the claims made by this hierarchical and exclusively male understanding of the church.

> This college, in so far as it is composed of many members, is the expression of the multifariousness and universality of the People of God; and of the unity of the flock of Christ, in so far as it is assembled under one head.[6]

It is a diversity of males exercising power that is essentially subsumed under the power of one male: the supreme pontiff.

The college or body of bishops has, for all that, no authority unless united with the Roman Pontiff, Peter's successor, as its head, whose primal authority, let it be added, over all, whether pastors or faithful, remains in its integrity. For the Roman Pontiff, by reason of his office as Vicar of Christ, namely, and as pastor of the entire church, has full, supreme and universal power over the whole church, a power that he can always exercise unhindered.[7]

Such an understanding of the 'people of God' identifies itself as essentially male and, though women's presence in it is presumed, the identity of the people of God hinges on the 'hierarchy' as the highest and essentially defining rank of the 'people of God'. Such an understanding of the 'people of God' constructs women as the 'Other', as those who might be included in 'the people' as those who participate in a mission that is not their own but that of a church in which they only participate through dependence on the male hierarchy. The present concept of relation as dependence must be replaced with one of being in relation as interdependence and connectedness, which enables us to develop models of church that are networks of human beings in particular sexuate identities interacting with each other.

The church of the Second Vatican Council understands itself as the sacrament of salvation for the world. By means of sacramental acts the church mediates salvation to individuals and therefore appears as an institution of salvation. As for the life of the church itself, the sacramental celebration of the Eucharist is its focal point and its dynamic centre. Such a focus on the Eucharist as the priestly celebration of the sacrifice of the mass confirms the church's self-understanding as an essentially male church that fosters the relationship of dependence

6. *Dogmatic Constitution on the Church*, III, p. 22.
7. *Dogmatic Constitution on the Church*, III, p. 22.

between hierarchy and laity as a basic characteristic. This structure cannot be disrupted as it would deprive the church of its dynamic centre, the celebration of the Eucharist. Sentences such as

> The ministerial priest, by the sacred power that he has, forms and rules the priestly people; in the person of Christ he effects the Eucharistic sacrifice and offers it to God in the name of all the people[8]

identify the church of 'Lumen Gentium' as an essentially male church that is centred around a male priesthood which alone can represent the people of God. This makes the sacramental priesthood essentially a structure of power over the people, and in particular as male power over women. To receive the sacraments, to participate in the sacramental life of the church, for a woman therefore means to give up her identity as a woman in order to be incorporated into a church which merely identifies her as Other, as 'second in line'. Sacraments are in theory understood as celebrations of the whole church, as means of establishing right relation with God and with the church. Yet, as with the core metaphor of priesthood, the sacraments are an area where women have experienced exclusion and denial of their bodily existence rather than affirmation of their being church. As long as we have not achieved a concept of the sacraments as celebrations of girls' and women's bodies embodied in the body of Christ, the sacramental nature of the church, expressed in the existence of the church as a whole as well as in individual sacramental celebration, will be a symbol of the exclusion of women from the body of Christ, from the people of God, rather than as expressions of women being church. The church of the Second Vatican Council understands itself as 'the church of the people' or 'the people of God', but a feminist analysis of the sacramental life of the church and the concept of sacramental celebration in 'Lumen Gentium' shows that the sacraments rather occur as celebrations of the priest, who is by definition male, on behalf of the people or for the people. Under such a definition of sacraments women are excluded from what it means to be the sacramental body of Christ.

The council had decided not to issue a separate statement on the subject of Mariology, but to include its Mariological pronouncements within its teaching on the church, since Mary is believed to be the mother and supreme personification of the church. While I do not want to elaborate on the details of Mariological ecclesiology, I want to point

---

8.   *Dogmatic Constitution on the Church*, X, p. 361.

out the fact that the addition of a Mariological chapter to a document which in its first part hardly mentions women at all can be seen as symbolic for the significance of the presence of women in the ecclesiology of the council. The chapter could perhaps be seen as the *acme* of 'Lumen Gentium', but on the whole appears as rather supplementary to the self-reflection of the church in the modern world. By constructing Mary as an idealized disembodied feminine figure that bears no resemblance to the reality of women's lives, but rather emphasizes their inevitable absence, 'Lumen Gentium' does not fill the space of the absence of women, but increases the exclusive maleness of the church by reducing women to the status of a supplement and denying the significance of their bodily being by substituting women who are church with a woman whose main strength is that she is *not* like women.

We can say that 'Lumen Gentium' can in fact be read in a way that makes it the starting point for possible feminist reconstructions of ecclesiology. Yet these readings can only happen after a process of feminist deconstruction that identifies the text as ignoring the reality of women's lives and at the same time is ridden with strong gender constructions that construct the reality of women's lives in a way that is suitable to patriarchy.

REDRESSING THE BALANCE, TRANSFORMING THE ART: NEW THEORETICAL APPROACHES IN RELIGION AND GENDER HISTORY

Sue Morgan

The growth of feminist consciousness and the corresponding emergence of gender as a primary analytical category in the study of religion has constituted a radical methodological re-orientation in research agendas, challenging the sufficiency of claims to intellectual objectivity and transforming existing interpretative models. While gender analysis has made far-reaching incursions into religious language, symbolism, biblical hermeneutics, ethics and theology, historical perspectives upon religion and gender have struggled to gain a purposeful foothold. As Gail Malmgreen has noted, 'some contemporary feminists have spoken and written as if the tradition of women's sacred wisdom is a direct legacy from ancient (even prehistoric) times to the present—with little of consequence happening in between'.[1] Eleanor McLaughlin has explained the 'deeply antihistorical bias' of many religious feminists as an understandable indictment of the 'depressing litany of theological justifications'[2] for ecclesiastical misogyny throughout the centuries. By way of a solution, and in order to explore the resistance of women to such negative traditions, McLaughlin proffered a revisionist approach to the Christian past that was simultaneously *responsible*, 'grounded in the historicist rubric of dealing with the past on its own terms',[3] and *usable*, interpreted through the prism of present concerns.

The retrieval of a 'usable past' has since become a truism among feminist scholars using history largely as a resource for contemporary

---

1. Gail Malmgreen (ed.), *Religion in the Lives of English Women 1760–1930* (London: Croom Helm, 1986), p. 1.
2. E. McLaughlin, 'The Christian Past: Does it Hold a Future for Women?', in C.P. Christ and J. Plaskow (eds.), *Womanspirit Rising: A Feminist Reader in Religion* (New York: Harper & Row, 1979), pp. 93-106 (94).
3. McLaughlin, 'The Christian Past', p. 94.

women's spirituality. The work of Elisabeth Schüssler Fiorenza springs to mind here, as does the scholarship of African-American feminists who have drawn upon the unacknowledged historical repository of black women's spiritual activism as a major element in their construction of a meaningful and transformative womanist theology. There is a profound connection between our foremothers' spiritual struggles and the enlargement of contemporary female self-consciousness. As Ursula King has argued in her seminal discussion of nineteenth-century women scholars of religion, historical investigation 'is not simply a matter of setting the record straight... it is also an issue of... personal and corporate identity'.[4]

Although the recovery of women as makers of their own spiritual history rather than as passive recipients of an imposed patriarchal order can be vital in the affirmation of contemporary feminist intellectual and political strategies, reading history solely as an inspirational resource is fraught with methodological difficulties. A primary focus of my research has been to explore the creative tension between the twin poles of the historical dialectic of responsibility and usability, in the belief that 'an over-simplistic translation of the language of the past into the interests of the present is a disservice to both'.[5] In women's appropriation of the historical religion/culture nexus, both resistance and collusion, status-defying and status-preserving responses to patriarchy have emerged. Conservative traditionalism and radical feminism alike form part of the religion and gender heritage. Rather than ascribing inspirational status to all women of the past therefore, challenging questions need to be asked concerning the historical dynamics of religion, gender and power.

---

4.   U. King (ed.), *Religion and Gender* (Oxford: Basil Blackwell, 1995), p. 222. See Elisabeth Schüssler Fiorenza, *In Memory of Her: A Feminist Theological Reconstruction of Christian Origins* (London: SCM Press, 1983); *idem*, *Bread Not Stone: The Challenge of Feminist Biblical Interpretation* (Boston: Beacon Press, 1984). For the use of history in womanist theology, see Delores Williams, 'Womanist Theology: Black Women's Voices', in J. Plaskow and C. Christ (eds.), *Weaving the Visions: New Patterns in Feminist Spirituality* (New York: Harper Collins, 1989), pp. 179-86; Katie Cannon, *Black Womanist Ethics* (Atlanta, GA: Scholars Press, 1988); and S. Morgan, 'Race and the Appeal to Experience in Feminist Theology: The Challenge of the Womanist Perspective', *Modern Believing* 34 (1995), pp. 18-26.

5.   Jane Williams, 'Recent Writings in Feminist Theology', *Epworth Review* (1989), p. 84.

The late nineteenth century provides a useful context from which to appraise the perplexing array of contradictory allegiances by devout women. Largely concerned with issues of doctrinal purity or denominational maturation, traditional accounts of Victorian church history have incorporated little, if any, gender analysis in their examination of the politics and policies of ecclesiastical government. Despite the shift away from bishops and synods, and a promising methodological rationale to address the various manifestations of popular piety, the new social history of religion has similarly failed to address the relations between the sexes in any meaningful fashion, focusing mainly upon economic stratification and the process of class formation.[6] Yet a study of gender, or what Patricia Crawford has described as the 'sexual politics of religion',[7] is crucial to a fuller understanding of Victorian religious culture. An obvious and pressing reason for the historical restoration of female piety is that women comprised the vast majority of church and chapel congregations throughout the period. The numerical 'feminization of religion' remains an uncontested feature of nineteenth-century devotion. We cannot speak confidently yet about the precise extent to which this occurred, but it owed much to the propagation of a pervasive feminine stereotype whose cardinal virtues—domesticity, purity, piety and submissiveness—were sanctioned by Christian values.[8] Shrouded in the flattering rhetoric of moral superiority, the conflation of the female sphere with the privatized, affective and religious aspects of Victorian society has been assessed by gender historians in highly negative terms, reflective of the increasing powerlessness of both women and the church as marginalized casualties of industrial modernization and the new species of Economic Man.[9]

The interpretation of nineteenth-century female religious experience

6. The classic text in traditional church history is still Owen Chadwick, *The Victorian Church* (2 vols.; London: A. & C. Black, 1971, 1972). See James Obelkovich's helpful discussion of the task of the social history of religion in *Religion and the People 800–1700* (Chapel Hill: University of North Carolina Press, 1979).

7. Patricia Crawford, *Women and Religion in England 1500–1720* (London: Routledge, 1993), p. 3.

8. See Barbara Welter, 'The Cult of True Womanhood: 1820–60', *American Quarterly* 18 (1966), pp. 151-74.

9. See Barbara Welter, 'The Feminization of American Religion, 1800–1860', in M. Hartmann and L. Banner (eds.), *Clio's Consciousness Raised: New Perspectives on the History of Women* (New York: Harper & Row, 1974), pp. 137-57 for a discussion of these issues.

as an elision of spiritual power and social impotence cannot be sustained, however, in a reading of history that takes seriously women's influential role in the shaping of denominational beliefs and practices. Research in modern British religion and gender history to date has convincingly illustrated the richness of women's involvement in their own discrete communities of faith. The work of Brian Heeney and Sean Gill on Anglican churchwomen, Susan O'Brien's accounts of women in Catholic conventual life and Deborah Valenze's study of female preaching in popular sectarian Methodism, for example, attest to the ideological and institutional import of religion as a vehicle for the emergence of an autonomous female spiritual matrix.[10] Women's role as domestic moral custodians, which extended through the local prayer-meeting, charity organization or district visiting society into a visibly public female world, espoused a keen awareness of gender solidarity displayed most emphatically perhaps in the mid-century religious sisterhoods and deaconess communities. Clerical dependence upon female labours in philanthropy, moral reform, education and missionary work, juxtaposed with women's continued exclusion from access to institutional leadership prompted contestations of authority between female laity and clergy that may be profitably analysed through a framework of gender.[11]

A related area of enquiry has been the impact of the numerical feminization of religion upon the doctrinal and theological progress of Victorian religious thought. In a century when, as Barbara Pope has observed, God became more merciful and less judgmental, heaven became progressively more domesticated and incarnational theology depicted a kenotic Christ in solidarity with suffering humanity, to what extent was the alteration of liturgy, doctrine and symbolism throughout the period an accommodation of the feminine tastes of the majority of

10. See Brian Heeney, *The Women's Movement in the Church of England 1850–1930* (Oxford: Clarendon Press, 1988); Sean Gill, *Women and the Church of England from the Eighteenth Century to the Present* (London: SPCK, 1994); Susan O'Brien, 'Lay-Sisters and Good Mothers: Working-Class Women in English Convents 1840–1910', in W.J. Sheils and D. Wood (eds.), *Women in the Church: Studies in Church History* (27 vols.; Oxford: Basil Blackwell, 1990), XXVII, pp. 453-65 and Deborah Valenze, *Prophetic Sons and Daughters: Female Preaching and Popular Religion in Industrial England* (New Jersey: Princeton University Press, 1985).

11. See Frank Prochaska, *Women and Philanthropy in Nineteenth-Century England* (Oxford: Clarendon Press, 1980).

spiritual consumers?[12] The courtship of Christian women may well have been a strategic response by a clerical elite concerned to withstand the fierce onslaught of secularization and quick to realize that their future lay at 'mother's knee'.[13] Certainly the Anglo-Catholic re-instatement of sisterhoods, the practice of auricular confession and the elaborate ceremonials of the ritualist churches are regarded by John Reed as directly related to the predominance of women within High Church congregations and devotion to the Virgin Mary continued to exert a powerful, albeit contradictory influence upon nineteenth-century constructions of femininity and motherhood.[14]

Was there in Britain therefore, as scholars have argued of Europe and America, a gradual 'softening' of harsh dogma in terms of an elevation of 'feminine' principles of meekness, humility and self-sacrifice in theological reflection, and to what extent could this be understood as an act of lay-based initiative rather than an ecclesiastical imposition?[15] The numerous instances of female Christologies proffered by religious reformers such as Ellice Hopkins, Josephine Butler or Florence Nightingale, in addition to the female messianic doctrines that proliferated on the edges of mainstream religion, (of which the most well-known was the millenarian sect leader Joanna Southcott), suggest that we have hitherto underestimated the theological creativity of pious Victorian women and the existence of a distinctive form of nineteenth-century female spirituality.[16]

Scholars have rightly cautioned against applying the formula of

---

12. See Barbara Corrado Pope, 'A Heroine without Heroics: The Little Flower of Jesus and her Times', *Church History* 57 (1988), pp. 46-60; and A. Douglas, *The Feminization of American Culture* (New York: Avon Books, 1977), the most celebrated statement on the feminization of nineteenth-century religion.

13. Barbara Corrado Pope's 'Immaculate and Powerful: The Marian Revival in the Nineteenth Century', in C. Atkinson, C. Buchanan and M. Miles (eds.) *Immaculate and Powerful: The Female in Sacred Image and Social Reality* (Boston: Beacon Press, 1985), pp. 173-200 (175).

14. See J.S. Reed, ' "A Female Movement": The Feminization of Anglo-Catholicism', *Anglican and Episcopal History* 57 (1988), pp. 199-238.

15. See Welter, 'The Feminization of American Religion'.

16. See especially Florence Nightingale's *Cassandra* with an introduction by Myra Stark (repr; New Haven, CT: The Feminist Press, 1979 [1860]). For Joanna Southcott and the issue of female messianism, see Barbara Taylor, *Eve and the New Jerusalem: Socialism and Feminism in the Nineteenth Century* (London: Virago Press, 1983).

feminization in such a way as to oversimplify and misrepresent complex theological negotiations of gender which must, of course, address men and masculinity as well as women and femininity. Through the dissemination of sermons, educational tracts, hymns, devotional poetry and prescriptive literature, Victorian religious discourse exercised unparalleled influence in defining the ideological parameters of both sexes. Many writers sought to countermand the feminization of religion in their concern to propound a robust, muscular Christianity that might entice men back into devotional worship. The contemporary exploration of masculinity is in itself the continuation of a dominant nineteenth-century genre in which commentators such as Thomas Carlyle, Thomas Arnold and Thomas Hughes looked variously at manly codes of chivalry, morality and athleticism. The seminal scholarship of David Newsome and Norman Vance, followed more recently by the work of Michael Roper and John Tosh has already begun to establish a lively, critical exposition of Victorian masculinity and its relation to the all-male hierarchy of churchmanship.[17] As Roper and Tosh have argued, gender studies facilitates an advantageous connection with the conventional focus of history, that of male elites, male institutions and the exercise of public power, by demonstrating that 'men's power in history has resided in their masculinity as well as their material privilege and their manipulation of law and custom'.[18] Thus, a gendered approach might illuminate ecclesiastical history by seeking to comprehend how clergymen viewed their actions in terms of contributing to their self-understanding and status *as men*, and how this defined them as separate from women.

As the two most formative ideological influences upon nineteenth-century women, the historical configuration between religious affiliation and first-wave feminism is of central importance to religion and gender history. Women historians have been among some of the most productive and creative commentators on the juxtaposition of Victorian faith and feminism, outlining the proto-feminist elements of religiously

17. See David Newsome, *Godliness and Good Learning: Four Studies on a Victorian Ideal* (London: John Murray, 1961); Norman Vance, *The Sinews of the Spirit: The Ideal of Christian Manliness in Victorian Literature and Religious Thought* (Cambridge: Cambridge University Press, 1985); and Michael Roper and John Tosh (eds.), *Manful Assertions: Masculinities in Britain Since 1800* (London: Routledge, 1991).

18. Roper and Tosh (eds.), *Manful Assertions*, p. 8.

inspired projects such as temperance, abolitionism or rescue work. This type of philanthropic endeavour was an important, if ambivalent, location for the development of organizational and public speaking skills, fuelling demands for equal access to ministry across a range of denominations. Unitarian and Quaker women figure prominently in these accounts. The relative autonomy afforded to women preachers within these communities and their active support of various reform causes has led historians to recognize these denominations as the major religious wellspring for the broader women's movement.[19] Initial examinations suggest that despite mounting cultural indifference to formal religious worship, 'religion remained a significant if diminishing aspect of the British feminist tradition, even after it had been taken over by socialism'.[20] The defining features of a nineteenth-century religious feminism have yet to be delineated, but there is strong indication that both orthodox and heterodox forms of spirituality were of fundamental emotional and intellectual import to Victorian and Edwardian feminists.

The wide-ranging agenda of research possibilities indicated above must be offset against considerations of the practical difficulties confronting the historian of religion and gender. These are invariably source-related, both in terms of the scarcity of certain types of evidence and the limitations of available material. The documentation of working-class women's religious experience is particularly problematic and requires a highly creative use of extant data. Letters, diaries, autobiographies, memoirs, hymns, devotional writings, sermons, educational tracts and prescriptive literature constitute the bulk of potential primary sources. These documents are also subject to the exigencies of class, however, for they represent the history of a predominantly articulate and literate group of women. Given the range of themes and approaches encompassed by religion and gender history, the need for methodological clarification is vital. The key phrases 'religion and gender' and 'women and religion' are often used interchangeably, yet there are hugely complex debates around these terms with serious ramifications for the type of historical project undertaken, subjects studied and con-

19. See, for example O. Banks, *Faces of Feminism: A Study of Feminism as a Social Movement* (Oxford: Basil Blackwell, 1993); and J. Rendall, *The Origins of Modern Feminism: Women in Britain, France and the United States 1780–1860* (London: Macmillan, 1985).

20. O. Banks, *Becoming a Feminist: The Social Origins of 'First Wave' Feminism* (Sussex: Wheatsheaf Books, 1986), p. 60.

clusions drawn. The following discussion will explore briefly the central theoretical models of 'women's history', 'feminist history' and 'gender history', along with their possibilities and limitations for the study of religion.

Women's history, defined quite simply as historical work on women, seeks to retrieve and interpret the lives and experiences of those multitudes of women hitherto hidden from history.[21] From the depiction of 'women worthies' with their personification of emulatory Christian qualities found in the earliest hagiographies of female saints and notable churchwomen, this model has continued to provide a foundational approach for the exploration of women's religious beliefs and practices. Its emphasis upon the tools of straightforward historical retrieval—excavation of new data, empirical analysis and descriptive narrative—has proved essential in reconstructing the role of religion in women's lives, including their status within and contributions to various communities of faith. And there is still much groundwork to be done. Studies of women in nineteenth-century Baptism, Catholicism, Unitarianism, Congregationalism and a myriad of smaller, nonconformist sects have yet to be undertaken. As a methodology, women's history has been prone to accusations of producing a supplementary, compensatory narrative and of merely fitting fresh subjects into received historical categories, thereby falling short of the full radical theoretical potential of feminist and gender analysis. Women's history, Joan Scott has contended, ' has contributed new information, but not a distinctive methodology'.[22]

Criticisms like this are misplaced when applied to such uncharted territory as British women's religious history. New findings must be related to established themes of enquiry so as to refine dominant historical consensus, and the women's history paradigm contains considerable transformative scope for a revised perspective upon nineteenth-century religion. In focusing upon the female sphere, the dominance of male-defined histories that privilege public events and achievements is undercut and new horizons concerning the study of domestic spirituality, daily devotions or structures of family religion are opened up as

21. See June Purvis, 'Women's History in Britain: An Overview', *The European Journal of Women's Studies* 2 (1995), pp. 7-20.

22. Joan Scott, 'The Problem of Invisibility', in S.J. Kleinberg (ed.), *Retrieving Women's History: Changing Perceptions of the Role of Women in Politics and Society* (Oxford: Berg, 1988), pp. 5-29 (12).

equally legitimate areas of historical research. Similarly, charting the contributions of women to public religious activity may require serious re-evaluation as to the relevance of traditional periodizations of Victorian structures of faith.[23] Gauging the expansion and contraction of female responsibility and access to power throughout various churches may well provide a quite different chronology of denominational development than that determined by male interests. Periods regarded as watersheds in ecclesiastical historical change are not necessarily the same for women as for men.

Despite areas of overlap, the terms 'women's history' and 'feminist history' are by no means identical. Whereas women's history is defined by its subject matter, feminist history—'historical work infused by a concern about the past and present oppression of women'[24]—is designated by its mode of analysis. Women's history contributes partially to the feminist project in terms of its revelation of previously neglected aspects of female activity, but need not evince an explicitly feminist perspective and often avoids the more difficult questions relating to the sexual dynamics of historical access to power.[25] Rather than viewing historical retrieval as a sufficient end in itself, feminist historians politicize female invisibility by asking who, or what structures and policies benefit from such invisibility. In seeking to discern trends of female oppression and their mode of accomplishment, feminist history is committed to the study of patriarchy, defined by Judith Bennett as 'a familial-social, ideological, political system in which men...through ritual, tradition, law and language, customs, education, and the division

---

23. See Joan Kelly-Gadol's essay, 'Did Women have a Renaissance?' in R. Bridenthal and C. Koonz (eds.), *Becoming Visible: Women in European History* (Boston: Houghton Mifflin, 1977), pp. 137-64 for a seminal discussion of periodization.

24. Judith Bennett, 'Feminism and History', *Gender and History* 1 (1989), pp. 251-72 (253).

25. Many practitioners of women's history have disavowed connections with political labels. Others exhibit an overt anti-feminist tendency. Judith Bennett has commented on an increasing trend towards less explicit feminist perspectives in women's history scholarship, and bemoans the corresponding loss of political nerve and 'feminist indignation'. One may also wonder to what extent the increasing severance of feminist perspectives from women's history impinges upon its contemporary relevance? Bennett has argued that the feminist perspective may well be the cutting edge that continues to inform contemporary theory and define issues for research. Bennett, 'Feminism and History', pp. 251-72.

of labour, determine what part women shall or shall not play, and in which the female is everywhere subsumed under the male'.[26] Use of the term 'patriarchy' remains controversial, with many scholars concerned at the projection of women solely as victims and the concomitant denial of female historical agency. The unequivocal assertion of the guilt of all men and the virtue of all women is a practice which, according to Bridget Hill, serves only to alienate our male allies.[27] Appropriated as an all-purpose, convenient shorthand for the diverse dynamics of the reality of female subordination, patriarchy has emerged as something of a transhistorical, monolithic spectre for women. Nevertheless, because church hierarchies have formed such key sites of male-exclusive, anti-female sensibilities, patriarchy remains a highly pertinent category in the study of religious history, although not without pressing need for more careful application of the term.[28] Ecclesiastical patriarchy has been responsible for the creation of a thriving network of male-serving customs and rituals of which women's denied access to religious leadership has proved most symbolic, historically speaking. Judith Bennett has argued that what is required is sustained, precise examination of the multiple, changing expressions of patriarchy in order for feminist scholarship to avoid accusations of propagandism or anachronism.[29] Reconstructing the ways in which historical forms of religious patriarchy have survived by isolating the differing mechanisms of clerical adaptation to specific gender-political crises is of real significance in the development of religion and gender history. Recent feminist research has concentrated on women's simultaneous resistance *and* mediation of patriarchy at a given historical moment, illustrating that while faced with considerable ideological and institutional barriers to equality of representation with men, women were never merely passive victims of patriarchy, but often crucial to its perpetuation. As Bennett has observed, Victorian women 'colluded in, undermined and survived patriarchy'.[30] Only by fully historicizing patriarchy can the complexity

26. Cited in Bennett, 'Feminism and History', p. 260.
27. See Bridget Hill, 'Women's History: A Study in Change, Continuity or Standing Still?', *Women's History Review* 2 (1993), pp. 5-22 (19). See also Brian Harrison and James MacMillan, 'Some Feminist Betrayals of Women's History', *The Historical Journal* 26 (1983), pp. 375-89.
28. See Bennett, 'Feminism and History', p. 261.
29. Bennett, 'Feminism and History', p. 261.
30. Bennett, 'Feminism and History', p. 260.

of how women both benefitted from, and suffered under its regime, be appreciated.

The shift to a paradigm of gender with its incorporation of male as well as female experience is a methodological insight of huge import to religious history. Many scholars have proffered gender as a welcome departure from the separatist rhetoric of women's studies.[31] Segregating the study of women as a discrete socio-historical grouping has not only reinforced a static model of polarized relations between female and male, they argue, it has confirmed rather than challenged female stereotypes, preventing any appreciation of how men and women both participate in and reinforce the institutional structures that oppress, liberate, join or divide them.[32] In elucidating the interdependence of male and female sexual identity, a more authentic placing of men and women in history is proposed that goes beyond the inflexibility of the female oppression/liberation dualism typical of feminist methodology. Masculinity and femininity are relational constructs, 'incomprehensible apart from the totality of gender relations'.[33]

Critics of this model have argued that in giving equal space to men and women, gender history deradicalizes and depoliticizes previous theoretical frameworks. Attention to men and masculinity 'decentres the study of women *as* women'.[34] It also undermines the original challenge of feminist history by playing down male privilege and diminishing the impact of patriarchy. In a helpful discussion of this theoretical tension, Roper and Tosh have demonstrated that historical emphasis on the changing and varied forms of masculinity need not necessarily be 'uncongenial to feminism'. A clear connection exists between feminist history's focus on patriarchy and gender history's call for more informed perspectives on masculinity that is particularly promising for scholars of religion. Without a fuller understanding of 'why men sought

---

31. See, for example Ursula King's comment that 'the strength of a critical, but more inclusive gender studies lies in its greater comprehensiveness through seeing femaleness and maleness, and the attendant constructions of masculinity and femininity, as closely interrelated' (Introduction to *Religion and Gender*, p. 8).

32. See Scott 'The Problem of Invisibility', pp. 5-29.

33. Roper and Tosh (eds.), *Manful Assertions*, p. 2.

34. Purvis, 'Women's History in Britain', p. 15. See also Mary Evans, 'The Problem of Gender for Women's Studies', in J. Aaron and S. Walby (eds.), *Out of the Margins: Women's Studies in the Nineties* (London: Falmer Press, 1991), pp. 67-74 (73).

to control and exploit women' we run the risk of 'returning to themes of an inherent male tendency towards domination',[35] and the obfuscation of the complex connections between masculinity and ecclesiastical power. Interpreting the position of religious women in the past 'requires not only an engagement with the experience of the oppressed, but an insight into the structures of domination'.[36] Thus, understanding men's power over women as a central organizing of principle of masculinity can provide common ground between advocates of gender, and feminist historians.

Recent interpretations of gender in history have shifted away from the causes and effects of the social organization of sexual difference to the poststructuralist emphasis upon textual analyses of the varied, conflicting *meanings* attached to gender. Here, as Joan Scott has explained in her seminal book *Gender and the Politics of History*, 'the story is no longer about the things that have happened to women and men and how they have reacted to them; instead it is about how the subjective and collective meanings of women and men as categories of identity have been constructed'.[37] In this theoretical model, gender is studied not through material experience, but through language and discourse, in the attempt to discern how knowledge of sexual difference is articulated and given meaning at specific historical moments. The thoroughgoing relativization of knowledge, truth and subjectivity that underpins the postmodern project refutes the existence of any unitary, essentialist, transhistorical category of 'woman' or 'man'. Instead, sexual difference is ascribed meaning though discourse and the constant renegotiation of competing cultural representations of masculinity and femininity.[38] Throughout the nineteenth century, dominant discourses such as that of the church, the law, politics or science and their organizational technologies operated upon available cultural symbols of femininity and masculinity, classifying and circulating competing representations of gender knowledge. According to discourse theory therefore,

35. Roper and Tosh (eds.), *Manful Assertions*, pp. 7, 10.

36. Roper and Tosh (eds.), *Manful Assertions*, p. 7.

37. Joan Scott, (*Gender and the Politics of History* (New York: Columbia University Press, 1988), p. 6.

38. As Scott argues, 'The point of new historical investigation is to disrupt the notion of fixity' (*Gender and the Politics of History*, p. 43). See also Denise Riley, *'Am I that Name?' Feminism and the Category of 'Women' in History* (London: Macmillan, 1988).

the role of the religious historian would be to trace the process through which gender was articulated by popular or hierarchical religious discourses, and why certain constructions of Christian womanhood and manhood emerged in particular socio-historical settings.

Postmodern readings of gender deal primarily with the issue of reality and representation, and the reciprocal shaping force between them. They provide a useful framework for approaching the abundance of Victorian didactic texts such as sermons, domestic handbooks or moral literature. Educated churchwomen and pious clergymen alike made substantial contributions to defining normative identities of femininity and masculinity, espousing meanings of gender that resonated very differently in various historical contexts. It is impossible to equate behavioural models proposed in prescriptive literature with the way in which people actually thought or conducted themselves. Discourse theory deals with the tenuous relationship between ideology and social practice by acknowledging literary narratives outright as products of human agency, as ideological and social constructions that are less descriptions of material reality than reflections of a shifting system of cultural values. In the historical search for authorial intent, postmodern readings of gender can elicit careful examination of covert messages, deconstructing the seeming transparency of language in order to reveal the historical and political positioning of the writer. Consequently, postmodern readings of gender as discourse enable the history of religion and gender to extend beyond its valid, compensatory function as corrective to the incomplete record of the past, and embrace a related critical project, revealing the way in which religion has operated historically as a significant location of the production of gender knowledge and under what circumstances.

As an aid to understanding gender, the 'linguistic turn' in history has not passed unchallenged.[39] Some scholars regard the focus on cultural representation as opposed to material reality as undermining the very foundations of the historical enterprise. As Lawrence Stone has com-

---

39. There is a vast amount of material on this subject, but see especially Lawrence Stone and Gabrielle Spiegel, 'History and Postmodernism', *Past and Present* 135 (1992), pp. 189-208; J. Hoff, 'The Pernicious Effects of Poststructuralism on Women's History', *The Chronicle of Higher Education*, 20 October 1993, B1-B2; S. Jackson, 'The Amazing Deconstructing Woman', *Trouble and Strife* 25 (1992), pp. 25-31; and Susan Kingsley Kent, 'Mistrials and Diatribulations: A Reply to Joan Hoff', *Women's History Review* 5 (1996), pp. 9-18.

mented, if we can only access the 'real' of history through its representational forms, then 'history as we have known it collapses altogether, and fact and fiction become indistinguishable from one another'.[40] Women historians such as Joan Hoff and Stevi Jackson have expressed particular disquietude at postmodernism's anti-experientialist predilection in which representations of the female self as infinitely diffuse or as a mere juxtaposition of culturally isolated scripts appears to abstract and intellectualize tangible sexual inequalities out of existence. As little more than a series of disembodied literary constructs, women become disconnected from their own historical experiences, and disempowered from real instrumentality.[41] Reconstructing the history of religion and gender, where the 'contributions' paradigm is still very much the dominant one, requires methods of research that are grounded in concrete historical realities. Discourse analysis remains an extremely useful methodological tool in the historicization of religion and gender as long as the excesses of anti-experientialism and extreme cultural relativism are avoided. Ultimately, material conditions produce texts and subjects. Yet a meaningful account of human experience cannot be achieved without reference to the way in which those subjects are interpreted culturally. The interdependence of historical reality and symbolic representation, and how shifts in the discursive meanings of gender related to changes in people's actual lived experiences of faith, is postmodernism's methodological challenge for religion and gender history.

A fully integrated model of gender can either deepen our understanding of existing accounts of religious history, introduce new concerns, or, in some cases, compel serious re-examination of assumed categories and explanations. Restoring women to the past means reshaping the landscape of Victorian religious history, and the distorted, male-specific nature of research so far. Indeed, through its methodology and rationale, history—providing substance, texture and depth to our knowledge of the past and of ourselves in relation to that past—offers a primary impetus for the recovery of female visibility and a new, more adequate version of the Christian narrative. In this sense history contributes significantly to the central epistemological challenge posed by contemporary religion and gender scholarship and its critique of androcentric

40. Stone, 'History and Postmodernism', p. 190.

41. See Jackson, 'The Amazing Deconstructing Woman', pp. 25-31 and Joan Hoff, 'Gender as a Postmodern Category of Paralysis', *Women's History Review* 3 (1994), pp. 149-68.

conflations of the norms of masculinity and humanity. Whether simply redressing the balance, or more radically, transforming the art of history-writing, a critically sensitive exploration of our spiritual predecessors that does not compromise historical context in the interests of current concerns can reveal a rich, complex heritage of women and men of faith who negotiated an exuberance of self-identities and activism through the multiple alliances of spirituality, politics and gender.

Part II

NEW DIRECTIONS FOR THE NEW MILLENNIUM

FEMINIST THEOLOGIES IN CONTEMPORARY CONTEXTS:
A PROVISIONAL ASSESSMENT

Ursula King

My title does not imply that I intend to provide some kind of definite assessment of feminist theology in general, or of specific feminist theologies in different cultural, intellectual and ecclesiastical contexts in particular. It is in any case much too early for such an analysis of what is still a somewhat fluid, fast changing and expanding field of enquiries. I can only offer some provisional fragments of reflection, intended as a very preliminary interrogative reading of the contexts, texts and subtexts of the bewildering variety of feminist theologies now in existence, and trace some of their visions of hope and empowerment. These three major perspectives will inform the lines of thought that follow. In other words, I am trying to take stock, however provisionally, and provide an assessment from where to where feminist theologies have journeyed.

Different Contexts

It is impossible to suggest an unequivocal, encompassing definition of what feminist theology is, apart from the fact that it is born out of women's experience and commitment, and involves advocacy and engagement. Feminist theology is a new, critical way of doing theology which is not imprisoned by traditional disciplinary boundaries, but characterized by multidisciplinarity. It is a new way of women doing theology rooted in praxis. For historical and structural reasons it occurs to a great extent outside traditional academic institutions, but pursues a multiplicity of methods and tasks.

Born out of the struggle to overcome the oppression and subordination of women, feminist theologies are linked to a powerful vision of equality, justice, liberation and hope, rooted in a faith that knows of redemptive transformation and wholeness of being. Doing such theology out of the perspective of praxis, the concrete socio-economic and personal histories of particular women in particular communities and churches, means that it can only occur in contexts of radical plurality. There is no one single, universal feminist theology; there are only feminist theologies in the plural. Their plurality represents a celebration of diversity and differences, but this does not simply mean utter fragmentation and rampant individualism. The doing of such theologies occurs along certain trajectories and possesses some commonalities and shared patterns, although by now enough feminist theology has been produced to begin to take stock, to reflect on the achievements and some of the shortcomings too.

The term 'feminist theology' is to some extent a programmatic self-description, accompanied by the claim that it is a new, critical theology that calls into question the false universalisms, dualisms and idealized abstractions of traditional theology. However, feminist theology's own critical claims must themselves come under critical examination, and there is now sufficient material of enough substance and variety to do this in a spirit of openness and critical reflexivity. Depending on the position of the speaker, there is no doubt that feminist theology can elicit both strong negative and positive associations. On the negative side criticisms have been raised that feminist theology is unbiblical and heretical, pseudo-theological and confused, that it is uncontrollable because it is being developed outside the sphere of influence of official church institutions, and that it is not much more than a narcissistic search for self-realization. At worst it is accused of a complete rejection of the Judaeo-Christian heritage and of representing a new kind of syncretism. Some western feminist theology appears so strident as to lead to a complete separatism and a separate women-church, and how can such separateness ever claim to work towards the wholeness of humanity and the coming of the kingdom of God?

Some of the strongest objections have come from evangelical critics, but also from very conservative, right-wing churchmen. But when, by contrast, drawing on strongly positive associations, feminist theology can be seen as a new synthesis rather than as syncretism, it gives expression to the voices and experiences of contemporary women; it celebrates and gives witness to the Christian faith in today's world; it expresses a new religiosity and spirituality; it represents a more inclusive ecumenism; it respects other religious and spiritual traditions and seeks connections with some of their insights; it provides an effective critique of the sexism, androcentrism and patriarchy of the traditional churches and their hierarchical structures. To unravel any of these associations—whether positive or negative—in full and evaluate whether they are really justified, would require a rather longer discussion than can be pursued here.

Feminist theologies are so thoroughly pluralistic and open-ended because women's struggles, their experiences, actions and reflections, their ways of doing theology with each other and within communities, are so diverse, resulting in ways of thinking, discourses, strategies, hopes, dreams, visions and transformative actions, all of which are in the plural. The contexts which gave and give birth to feminist theologies are diverse and plural too. They relate to individual, local, national, international and global situations without which it would have been impossible for feminist theologies to emerge. The dynamic interaction of both the local and global contexts must be especially underlined, for it would be quite wrong to see feminist theology as only a white, western, urban, middle-class phenomenon. On the contrary, the consciencization of women across different churches, religions, cultures, peoples and races is now globally observable. The process of globalization, which the sociologist Roland Robertson has among others described as 'the consciousness of the world as one', has acted as a strongly enabling factor in the recent history of women and their theological education, in the emergence of women's studies and in the growth of feminist theologies.[1]

The rich plurality of contexts is not only created by the diverse experiential, cultural and geographical settings, but also by the different histories of women's struggle and women's education, their different methods of articulation and self-reflective critical analysis, and their different energies in formulating and enacting an emancipatory, liberating and transformative praxis.

I hope these remarks make clear how feminist theology, even when referred to in the singular, is not so much a discipline than a field, an activity that involves the breaking open of theology into plural visions and voices, the counter-voices of women which have existed in the past, but were muted or suppressed, whereas now they have come out to affirm alternative theological insights by deconstructing traditional

---

1.   I have discussed some of the cross-cultural and global connections that have shaped the development of feminist theologies in the so-called Third World in the U. King (ed.), *Feminist Theology from the Third World: A Reader* (Maryknoll, NY: Orbis Books; London: SPCK, 1994). See especially my Introduction, pp. 7-16.

readings of texts and histories, by recovering the lost experiences of women and by constructing a more inclusive theology.

Women's hermeneutic of suspicion concerns the universal truth claims of traditional theology and its dualistic, androcentric foundations where male experience has been presented as universal human norm. In feminist theology the long-established understanding of God, the human being, and the world—the central core of traditional theological treatises—have all been rendered problematic. This leads to a critical reassessment of all theological work, whether in exegesis, doctrine, ethics, ecclesiology, church history or other fields. For feminist theologians the Christian past is an important source, not least for its evidence of women's counter-cultural traditions, but it acts no longer as a norm.

In reflecting on the development of feminist theology since 1981, Pamela Dickey Young has argued that we have now arrived at a stage where there are already, in North America at least, two generations of feminist theological scholars.[2] Whereas the first generation was self-trained and had to create feminist theology as it went along, the second generation of women has had feminist teachers itself. One of the differences she notes is the more specialized and focused sense in which the term 'feminist theology' is now primarily applied to studies of the Christian tradition, whereas earlier on it was used more generally in connection with all feminist critical studies of religion.

This has happened for some time, and I only understand feminist theology in this sense—as referring to Christianity rather than the study or practice of any other religion—in this essay. My discussion will therefore also not take into account the development of 'thealogy' where non-traditional, alternative patterns prevail, many of which are concerned with women's spirituality and the worship of the Goddess.[3] It is

2.   Pamela Dickey Young, 'Feminist Theology from Past to Future', in Morny Joy and Eva K. Neumaier-Dargyay (eds.), *Gender, Genre and Religion* (Waterloo, ON: Wilfrid Laurier University Press and The Calgary Institute of Humanities, 1995), pp. 71-82. See also her interesting earlier reflections on the feminist challenge to theology: Pamela Dickey Young, *Feminist Theology/Christian Theology: In Search of Method* (Minneapolis: Fortress Press, 1990).

3.   I have discussed these themes elsewhere; see my book *Women and Spirituality: Voices of Protest and Promise* (London: Macmillan, 2nd edn, 1993) and some of the contributions in my edited volume on *Religion and Gender* (Oxford: Basil Blackwell, 1995). See also Cynthia Eller, *Living in the Lap of the Goddess: The Feminist Spirituality Movement in America* (Boston: Beacon Press, 1995).

important, though, to realize the growth and extent of the field of feminist theology in terms of its stronger focus and its new generation of women theologians. This will make all the difference, for what was once a novelty, a breakthrough and a breakaway, will eventually become established in its own right, as a new praxis wedded to new intellectual and academic traditions.

Very summarily, the field feminist theology is also concerned with questions of feminist biblical scholarship, with Christian scriptural texts and tradition which raise questions about authority—the authority of the past, the authority of the church, the authority of women's experience—and the very difficult question about what of the past remains usable in the present and whether patriarchy is inevitable or reformable. The emphasis on women's experience connects up with the development of narrative theology, a narrative related to and rooted in women's lives, but it also suggests new theological topics not treated before.[4] The greatest existential challenge is that of being a feminist whilst still remaining a Christian, how to resolve the tension between the two and hold in balance two mutually enriching experiences and perspectives.

Pamela Dickey Young speaks of the challenge of diversity as also 'the challenge of fragmentation' and voices the legitimate question of 'How can feminists privilege diversity without fragmenting into "communities" of one?' I agree with her assessessment that

> The gains of feminism are great but fragile; in church, in university, in society. Too much fragmentation could easily allow a return to the previous status quo...
>
> The fragmentation of the once all-encompassing term 'feminist theology' into a variety of feminist studies of religion is also a strength and challenge for feminist theology today. Again, the abundance of available material presents the problem that one can no longer be conversant with all of it... The danger this presents to feminist theology is the danger of being marginalized... Feminists, including feminist theologians, need to find creative ways to value and discuss difference without marginalizing those whose conclusions differ from one's own.[5]

Enough has been said about the factual existence of diversity, its importance and challenges that are part of the multiple contexts of feminist

---

4. For a more detailed discussion of these questions see Young, 'Feminist Theology from Past to Future'.
5. Young, 'Feminist Theology from Past to Future', pp. 76, 77.

theologies. To make my discussion more concrete, some texts will now be looked at in more detail in the hope that some of their subtexts will thereby be rendered more transparent.

Texts and Subtexts

From what I have said so far it is clear that I cannot speak any more of feminist theology in the singular, although I have done so in the past. The inherent, extraordinary plurality of feminist theologies is one of their strengths which must be given explicit recognition. It is acknowledged in the titles of some publications, though not in all. Thus it is interesting to look at some examples of recently published texts which illustrate what has been achieved in the field of feminist theology. The development of this field has gained enough volume and critical mass for summaries, dictionaries and critical appraisals to appear ever more frequently.

Enough new knowledge has been generated to make possible the publication of comprehensive dictionaries. I mention three that have recently come into existence. First in the field was the German *Wörterbuch der feministischen Theologie*, published in 1991.[6] It contains substantial essays (each with extensive bibliographical references, supplemented by a subject and name index) on key concepts and developments, written with few exceptions by women theologians from Germany, Switzerland and Austria. It provides a somewhat different and much needed complementary perspective to the publications in English that dominate the feminist theological debate. Published quite a few years ago, it is interesting to note that this work does not directly address questions of gender studies and methodological issues raised by feminist theory, although it contains an entry on *Feministische Forschung* which includes a discussion of *Feministische Wissenschaftskritik*.[7]

During 1996 two dictionaries were published in English, one in England—*An A to Z of Feminist Theology*,[8] the other in the United

6.   See Elisabeth Gössmann *et al.* (eds.), *Wörterbuch der feministischen Theologie* (Gütersloh: Gütersloher Verlagshaus Gerd Mohn, 1991).

7.   Gössmann *et al.*, *Wörterbuch der feministischen Theologie*, pp. 98-102.

8.   See Lisa Isherwood and Dorothea McEwan (eds.), *An A to Z of Feminist Theology* (Sheffield: Sheffield Academic Press, 1996).

States—*Dictionary of Feminist Theologies*.[9] The first was planned before the second, but they were both published at the same time. The majority of articles in *An A to Z of Feminist Theology* are written by British women, though some contributions from abroad are also included, with a helpful cumulative bibliography at the end of the book. This reference work is very accessible for a first orientation and contains material not found in the German dictionary, such as entries on 'Asian Women's Hermeneutical Principle', 'Empowerment', 'Interfaith Dialogue', as well as articles on 'Gender', on 'Methodology', and many others.

The North American publication *Dictionary of Feminist Theologies* is the largest, the most international in its list of contributors, and the most wide-ranging in its approach and entries (again with a cumulative bibliography at the end, but no index and unfortunately also no alphabetical list of the entries which would help cursory reading). It explicitly acknowledges the existing diversity of feminist theologies in its title and maintains its thoroughly pluralistic perspective also in its entries on 'Methodologies' and 'Feminist Theories'. There is much to be found here not captured by the other two dictionaries, such as 'Gender Construction', 'Gendered Institutions', 'Gender Representation', and 'Thealogy', besides many other topics. 'Theologies, Contemporary' are in the plural, and so are 'Theologies of Liberation' and 'Theologies, Evangelical', but it seems odd that this plurality is not acknowledged for 'Spirituality', even though several articles deal with different historical and contemporary forms of spirituality, including 'Spirituality, Women's'. This difference in treatment between 'theologies' in the plural and 'spirituality' in the singular raises the question of how far spirituality is still approached in an essentialist perspective rather than in a thoroughly historicized and contextualized framework.

Overviews of the development of feminist theologies are not only available in dictionaries, but through specialized articles, journals and anthologies which document in increasing numbers the fast growing extent of this field, still largely unknown before the 1980s. The earliest regular journal, still in existence, is the Asian publication *In God's Image*, published since 1982. Internationally, the academic debate about feminist theologies is well reflected in the North American *Journal of*

9. Letty M. Russell and J. Shannon Clarkson (eds.), *Dictionary of Feminist Theologies* (Louisville, KY: Westminster/John Knox Press; London: Mowbray, 1996).

Feminist Studies in Religion, published since 1985, which is concerned with feminist theologies in the wider, more comprehensive sense mentioned earlier in the assessment given by Pamela Dickey Young. Then there is also the younger British journal of *Feminist Theology*, which has appeared since September 1992.

These journals are complemented by several anthologies of which I shall only mention the three largest. Ann Loades edited *Feminist Theology: A Reader* in 1990, but this deals only with western developments.[10] To supplement this perspective through non-western writings Ursula King edited *Feminist Theology from the Third World: A Reader* in 1994,[11] and most recently, in 1996, Elisabeth Schüssler Fiorenza edited *The Power of Naming*, a selection of articles on feminist liberation theologies published over the years in the international theology journal *Concilium* which has devoted specific issues to feminist theological themes since 1985.[12] The first number of this journal for 1996 carries the title *Feminist Theology in Different Contexts* and provides on overview of recent international developments thematized in terms of 'struggle'.[13] At the planning stage this number was to be entitled more pluralistically as *Feminist Theologies in a Global Context*, but for reasons unknown to me the editors changed the plural into the singular 'feminist theology' and pluralized the 'contexts'. The overall organizing foci for the themes from around the world are the 'sites of struggle', perceived as different geographical, religious and theoretical sites of struggle. The preparatory working paper described the planned issue as aiming

> to create a rhetorical space where different sites of struggle, theological conflicts and tensions can be discussed and assessed rather than become reified as fixed positions. Such a discussion is especially appropriate in a context of global right-wing back-lash against women. At the same time this issue of *Concilium* also seeks to communicate to a wider public the rich theological argument and religious vision articulated by feminist theologies in different global contexts.[14]

10. Ann Loades (ed.), *Feminist Theology: A Reader* (London: SPCK; Louisville, KY: Westminster/John Knox Press, 1994).
11. King (ed.), *Feminist Theology from the Third World*.
12. Elisabeth Schüssler Fiorenza (ed.), *The Power of Naming* (A Concilium Reader in Feminist Liberation Theology; Maryknoll, NY: Orbis Books; London: SCM Press, 1996).
13. See *Concilium* 1 (1996).
14. Unpublished working paper. For comparison see the brief 'Introduction' to

At a certain level it may not be all that important whether one speaks of feminist theology and its wider context in the singular or plural. The fluidity of usage may point to the dynamic growth and youthfulness of the field; it may also hide an uncertainty or lack of agreement among its various practitioners and thus show that a definite, commonly agreed terminology has not been established yet. Nor may that be desirable either.

More important than the terminology and use of words is the question of who are the women creators who delineate the boundaries of the field and choose the words to speak its content. Here a healthy hermeneutic of suspicion is needed too, for I do not think that feminist theologies should only be conceptualized in terms of 'struggle' and 'liberation'. Suspicion is in order as to the implicit claims and subtexts of much writing on feminist theology, whether by women or men. Whereas I can agree with the description of feminist theology as a non-traditional way of doing theology which is not imprisoned by traditional disciplinary boundaries, and in which liberation is of central concern, feminist theologies are not only liberation theologies, but include complex patterns of transformation in all areas of praxis and theory.

The language of struggle and resistance is too antagonistic at times; it disempowers and makes dependent rather than energizes and affirms, constructs and creates. I refuse to see myself working as a victim rather than a creative agent, and protest against some of the inauthentic consciousness and arrogant rhetoric present in some feminist theological writing. The field is also far too dominated by North American women authors who exploit their powerful positions to the full, so that it is difficult for European and non-western women's voices to get a hearing, or for their work to find acknowledgment in North American publications. This problematic situation is not unique to feminist theology, of course, but I would like to argue that to situate feminist theologies only in terms of struggle, in terms of oppression and liberation, is a diminished rather than the full picture. It is not the only possible definition and view point but a particular interpretative stance whose specific value, but also inherent limitation, must be recognized. It is a matter of choice, as well as critical strategy, whether one wishes to emphasize hope, empowerment and transformative potential, or underline instead

Concilium 1996/1 by Elisabeth Schüssler Fiorenza, bearing again a title in the plural: 'Feminist Theologies in Different Contexts', pp. vi-ix.

oppression, struggle and liberation as key concepts and features of feminist theology. Perhaps Elisabeth Schüssler Fiorenza wants to point to such a more balanced possibility of assessment when she writes in her introduction to the edited papers of *The Power of Naming* on 'Feminist Liberation Theology as Critical Sophialogy'.[15] She says there that feminist theology (here again in the singular)

> seeks to rectify our gendered knowledge and spiritual perception of the world which is still one-eyed to the extent that it continues to be articulated in the interest of elite white western men. How then does feminist theology seek to restore the world's full spiritual vision? How can it correct the fragmentary circle of Christian vision and change its narrow and biased perception of the world and G*d?[16]

In other words, it is important to get away from a perception exclusively focused on struggle. I agree with those who emphasize the richness, the depth, the commitment, the power of vision and spiritual energy that form the heart and blood of feminist theologizing. At the same time we need to acknowledge the deeply haunting presence of *ambivalence* and *ambiguity* which runs though all attempts of interpretation and existential transformations. These afflict human endeavours everywhere with deep resonances of contingency, incompleteness and ultimate unsatisfactoriness, and feminist theological efforts are no exception to this. This experience is currently enhanced by the interrogative mode of the postmodern approach which, to some, appears deeply disempowering. Yet it can also be perceived as utterly challenging by inviting and encouraging a profoundly transformative new creativity in living, being and thinking. It seems almost like the 'wilderness experience' of which some womanist theologians speak and, as wilderness often does, this can lead to a transformative new spiritual vision.[17]

What I want to express here, however imperfectly, is the recognition that the legitimate feminist critique of the false and narrow universalisms of past theologies must not in turn lead to arrogant new claims of a different universality. Similarly, in spite of all the genuine critique, but sometimes also barely disguised rhetoric, regarding traditional dualisms, it must be said that certain feminist thinking works to such an

15. Fiorenza (ed.), *The Power of Naming*, pp. xiii-xxxix.

16. Fiorenza (ed.), *The Power of Naming*, pp. xxxv-vi. G*d is her spelling of the Divine, explained on p. xxxv-vi, and dependent on Jewish usage.

17. See Dolores S. Williams, *Sisters in the Wilderness: The Challenge of Womanist God-Talk* (Maryknoll, NY: Orbis Books, 1993).

extent with binary oppositions that new dualistic patterns emerge again. In addition, the isolation of feminists from other people can in practice lead to insularity and separatism, when in theory relationality is so much stressed as a desideratum.

Thus, on closer examination, many contradictory patterns can be revealed as hidden substructures present within the developing field of feminist theology. Nowhere is this perhaps more true than in the claims of a post-Christian feminist theology. It has of course been said many times that contemporary feminism is a form of postmodernism, that feminist diversities have developed within the context of global modernities and are now taking part in the rejection of much, if not all, of that modernity. Yet it has also been pointed out that much of the debate about modernity and postmodernity[18] is locked into an entirely western vision that cannot sufficiently account for the genuine gains of modern social, political and economic developments from which many people in the world, and especially women, have gained a great deal.

What is the word 'post' in any case meant to refer to in such compounds as postmodernism, post-patriarchal and post-Christianity? Is it primarily pointing to a sequence in time or to a substantive change, a qualitative difference that expresses greater inclusiveness, perfection or fullness? Or is it rather an expression of disintegration and decline, more a loss than a gain? These questions are too large to be debated here, but I want to mention that the notion of 'post-Christianity' is now associated with multiple meanings and allows both positively and negatively charged interpretations. Many Christians, when they speak of 'post-Christianity', often really mean 'post-Church' as a critical rejection of an institution rather than the outright denial of Christianity itself. Even such a passionately argued book as Daphne Hampson's *After Christianity*[19] does not really answer the question of what might come after Christianity and only makes sense from a particular, concrete perspective which is perhaps more rooted in a historical, conceptual and ethnic ghetto mentality than in a genuine Christian universalism and catholicity that are the hallmarks of certain forms of Christian denominational and global interfaith ecumenism.

18. I have looked in more detail at this debate in my introduction to U. King (ed.), *Faith and Praxis in a Postmodern Age* (London: Cassells, 1998), pp. 1-14.

19. See Daphne Hampson, *After Christianity* (London: SCM Press, 1996). A more extensive discussion of the unsatisfactoriness of her views is found in my review of this book in *Journal of Beliefs and Values* 18 (1997), pp. 243-45.

In spite of all that has been achieved there is still a need for feminist theologians to get out of their own isolation—whether institutionally imposed or intellectually adopted—and develop a more fully dialogical approach, not only among themselves in different parts of the world or with women of many different faith traditions, but also through reflecting from their experience of solidarity and sisterhood on some of the burning questions of our time. In the areas of ethics and ecology, of justice and peace, and of spirituality, this is already happening. But feminist theologians are at present still little explicitly engaged in or critically challenged by interfaith dialogue[20] nor are they concerned with the great debates between theology and science, nor are they particularly noted for efforts to rethink what kind of religious education is needed in the secular educational institutions of contemporary society.

Some of the liveliest debates, some of the most challenging encounters and dialogues are occurring today among the women theologians of the so-called Third World. It is by listening to their voices that we can discern much hope and vision, for it is amid their struggles and pain that we see the greatest transformation, a new world being born.

Visions of Hope and Empowerment

If doing feminist theology is about sharing experiences, then it is important to share with each other not only those of oppression, resistance and struggle, but also those of hope and empowerment, mutually enriching new awareness and affirmation. Nowhere is this more apparent than in the empowering effect that Christian feminist theology has on women in different parts of Asia, Africa and Latin America.

The concept of empowerment has been widely used in the development debate and refers to the powerless or disempowered gaining a greater share in the control over resources and decision-making. Women are often the most disempowered in society, and their empowerment is associated with the struggle for social equality and greater justice, for a

---

20. Feminist theological reflections on interfaith dialogue are still rare; see on this theme Kate McCarthy, 'Women's Experience as Hermeneutical Key to a Christian Theology of Religions', *Studies in Interreligious Dialogue* 6 (1996), pp. 163-73; also my article 'Feminism: The Missing Dimension in the Dialogue of Religions' in John May (ed.), *Pluralism and the Religions: The Theological and Political Dimensions* (London: Cassell, 1998), pp. 40-55.

more just and peaceful world. But more than that, the word empowerment in feminist writing has come to mean the recognition of one's own
inner capacities, one's strength and ability in going out and changing
situations and social relations, in influencing and shaping not only
one's own life, but also the world around us. It is also linked to a
deeper spiritual experience in feeling more hopeful and strong, in being
affirmed and encouraged by a greater spiritual power that enables us to
grow, be healed and transformed.

Strong voices of empowerment that can give hope to others are found
in many writings from women around the world. A wide selection of
theological reflections are gathered in my edited volume on *Feminist
Theology from the Third World* (1994) or in the more recently edited
collection of papers *The Power of Naming* (1996) edited by Elisabeth
Schüssler Fiorenza, both of which I mentioned earlier. As the Korean
woman theologian Chung Hyun Kyung has pointed out, women's
theology from the Third World is woman-affirming, life-affirming and
cosmos-affirming. The affirmation of and struggle for life is also a very
central theme of the newly emerging spiritualities coming out of the
religiously, culturally and ethnically pluralistic situations of the Third
World. How inspiring and truly empowering and hopeful these
spiritualities for life are, can be gauged from the publication *Women
Resisting Violence: Spirituality for Life*[21] which resulted from the international women's meeting of the Ecumenical Association of Third
World Theologians, held in Costa Rica in December 1994, and bringing
together for the first time women theologians from the Third World
with those from the First World.

Dialogue is getting more diverse and complex among women around
the world and, increasingly, more discerning and critical voices are
being heard. To give two examples: the Finnish woman theologian
Elina Vuola has brought feminist theology and liberation theology in
South America into dialogue, pointing out that the methodological
principle of praxis has very definite limits in not tackling burning issues
of sexual ethics as part of liberation in Latin America.[22] In her general
assessment of 'Feminist theologies in the plural' she writes:

21. See Mary John Mananzan *et al.* (eds.), *Women Resisting Violence:
Spirituality for Life* (Maryknoll, NY: Orbis Books, 1996).
22. See E. Vuola, *Limits of Liberation: Praxis as Method in Latin American
Liberation Theology and Feminist Theology* (Helsinki: Suomalainen Tiedeakatemia,
1997)

In the 1990s, feminist theology has grown into a worldwide, global ecumenical movement. There are feminist theologians in all major religious traditions, including non-Christian. This globalization of feminist theology has been a process similar to that of liberation theology. It is a process of simultaneous globalization and particularization. A false abstract universalism is replaced by particularism and concrete universalism.[23]

Another assessment of the diversity and obstacles of doing feminist theology as 'multicultural theology' comes from Linda Moody who sees women's theology today as being a 'theology across boundaries of difference' where women's theological reflections and the dialogue about their experiences move in terms of both commonalities and differences which counteract a falsely constructed unity and an imposed singular worldview that obliterates real differences.[24]

Where will feminist theologies be in the next ten to fifteen years? How will they develop during the first decade of the new millenium? This is hard to predict—a large agenda has been set; much has been accomplished; much can now be critically assessed, sifted through and transformed under the challenge of further diversity and greater refinement of concepts and models, of further networking and restructuring. The task is both a practical and intellectual one; it represents a tremendous challenge and even greater opportunity for women to bear witness to the transformative power of faith. It seems to me inappropriate and misleading to consider feminism the deathknell of Christianity, for although the institutional structures may be changed beyond recognition, there is no doubt that Christianity still possesses great reservoirs of hope and large scriptural, historical and spiritual resources for empowering women to seek liberation and justice.[25]

In the next decade or so there will be another generation of women singing a new song, and no doubt also another generation of women

23. Vuola, *Limits of Liberation*, p. 110.

24. See Linda A. Moody, *Women Encounter God: Theology across Boundaries of Difference* (Maryknoll, NY: Orbis Books, 1996).

25. A detailed study of the scriptural resources available to Christian and Muslim women in Bangladesh can be found in Mukti Barton, *Scripture as Empowerment for Liberation and Justice: The Experience of Christian and Muslim Women in Bangladesh* (CCSRG Monograph Series; Bristol: University of Bristol, 1999). I have argued, contrary to Daphne Hampson, that Christianity and feminism are not incompatible; see my chapter on 'Women and Christianity: A Horizon of Hope', in Teresa Elwes (ed.), *Women's Voices: Essays in Contemporary Feminist Theology* (London: Marshall Pickering, 1992), pp. 147-58.

theological scholars who, we may hope and expect, will further strengthen the new and exciting field of feminist theologies through creative, critical and lively debates that will not only affect and transform women's experience and reflections, but also make a lasting mark on the future shape of theology itself. One of the most remarkable affirmations about this comes from the Brazilian theologian María Clara Bingemer who has reflected on 'Women in the Future of the Theology of Liberation'.[26] For her the Christian teaching that God is love can only mean that 'God can only be... the object of desire; not of necessity, not of rationality' and therefore she sees the challenge and promise of women doing theology as the challenge 'to restore the primacy of desire within theological discourse'. With a theological message uttered in favour of life and light, denouncing the forces of darkness and death, woman, in Bingemer's words,

> is called to inaugurate new ways of listening to revelation, of expressing the experience of faith, of reading and interpreting the word of God, of thinking about and unfolding the great themes and chapters of theology. And all the while she allows herself to be possessed by the desire that inflames and summons, that keeps alight, not consumed, the flame of love in the face of everything that threatens to extinguish it.[27]

There could be no stronger expression of the hope, power and promise of feminist theologies existing now and in the future to come.

---

26. In Marc H. Ellis and Otto Maduro (eds.), *The Future of Liberation Theology: Essays in Honor of Gustavo Gutiérrez* (Maryknoll, NY: Orbis Books, 1990), pp. 473-90.

27. Ellis and Maduro (eds.), *The Future of Liberation Theology*, pp. 478, 479.

GLOBAL SISTERHOOD OR WICKED STEPSISTERS: WHY DON'T GIRLS WITH GOD-MOTHERS GET INVITED TO THE BALL?

Tina Beattie

One morning recently, I went into my local Catholic church to pray. A small group, mainly women, was saying morning prayers in one of the side aisles. In this particular parish, morning prayers are always led by women although the priests usually participate. This is not a gesture in the direction of gender politics—indeed, I suspect most of the women who lead the prayers would be outraged if I suggested such a thing. It is just the way things happen. At the back of the church, a young mother with her toddler was lighting a candle. In front of the altar there was a coffin, awaiting a funeral Mass. For a moment, I had a sense of women's lives held cupped in the palm of God's hand, a murmuring collective of prayer and hope, anxiety and grief, motherhood and death, warmly encompassed in a candlelit space. Yet this space is invisible to the majority of people in our society, and particularly to those women who believe that to be feminist means to define yourself in opposition to religion, or, to be more particular, Christianity. I enjoyed Sara Maitland's robust review of Daphne Hampson's book, *After Christianity*, in *The Tablet*. Maitland begins her review by saying, 'This book is fundamentally wrong. Hampson's central argument is that a person cannot be a feminist and a Christian. Well, I am.'[1]

I want to begin by saying a little about my use of language. In the ongoing tension between particularism and universalism, I am wary of expressions such as 'religion', 'feminism' and even 'Christianity', because these are imprecise terms that so easily eliminate difference and diversity. However, in a short paper such as this, it is not possible to develop the linguistic elaborations that would define these words more precisely. So when I refer to religion it is in the context of the

---

1. Sara Maitland, 'Feminist Dead End', review of *After Christianity* (London: SCM Press, 1996) by Daphne Hampson in *The Tablet*, 1 February 1997, p. 146.

western religious tradition, and I therefore tend to mean beliefs and practices associated with Christianity. In a longer paper, I would make more of the differences between Catholic and Protestant Christianity, and I would pay greater heed to the diversity of feminist theories.

I locate this paper at a complex intersection of academic questions, where feminist theory, scientific scholarship and Christianity cross paths, without necessarily acknowledging one another in the process. I argue that secular feminism, claiming to have removed the blindfold of historical conditioning and positioning itself where it can expose the nakedness of all the patriarchal emperors who parade past, still has a patriarchal blind spot with regard to the significance of Christianity in many women's lives and the role of theology in the shaping of western thought. In the work of feminist theologians it is difficult to find any acknowledgment of just how effectively the secular sisterhood silences women's theological voices. It is as if Cinderella is pretending that of course she has been invited to the ball, and steadfastly refuses to acknowledge that she has been confined to the entrance hall while the ugly sisters are having a ball without her in the banqueting rooms of the ivory tower.

A glance at the contents page of any feminist reader would demonstrate my point. For example, Rosemarie Tong's *Feminist Thought: A Comprehensive Introduction* includes Mary Daly in the section on radical feminism,[2] but this is the book's only engagement with any form of theological discourse, and it focuses on a philosopher who defines herself diametrically in opposition to the Christian tradition. Tong allows no space to feminists whose engagement with religion is less oppositional than Daly's. *Ethics: A Feminist Reader*, edited by Elizabeth Frazer, Jennifer Hornsby and Sabina Lovibond, is entirely devoted to the secular sphere. The implicit assumption is that there is no point of encounter between Christian and feminist ethics, and those feminists who are working in the area of Christian ethics are—what?—not really feminists, not really ethical, or simply not worth listening to?[3] It is

2. Cf. Rosemarie Tong, *Feminist Thought: A Comprehensive Introduction* (London: Routledge, 1992), pp. 102-109.

3. Cf. Elizabeth Frazer, Jennifer Hornsby and Sabina Lovibond, *Ethics: A Feminist Reader* (Oxford: Basil Blackwell 1992). Susan F. Parsons has written on Christian ethics elsewhere, but her interesting essay in this collection, entitled 'Feminism and the Logic of Morality: A Consideration of Alternatives', pp. 380-412, makes no specific reference to a Christian perspective. Cf. Susan F. Parsons,

intellectually blinkered to compile a reader about ethics in western culture that ignores Christianity's fundamental and ongoing role in the shaping of ethics. This leads me to wonder what feminist magisterium dictates the conditions for inclusion in the canon.

Gerda Lerner writes in the preface to the second volume of her two-volume study on *Women and History*,

> The insight that religion was the primary arena on which women fought for hundreds of years for feminist consciousness was not one I had previously had. It was won in work on Volume One; I listened to the voices of forgotten women and accepted what they told me.[4]

This is a rare insight for feminist scholars in the secular field, with few being quite so open to what 'the voices of forgotten women' are telling them. When religion does get mentioned in feminist studies, it is rarely any form of traditional Christianity. For instance, in a reader edited by Gill Kirkup and Laurie Smith Keller entitled *Inventing Women: Science, Technology and Gender*, there are a number of academically rigorous and thought-provoking essays, but when spirituality is discussed in the essay on 'Eco-feminism', the focus is entirely on spiritualities that have arisen since the 1970s.[5] There is only a passing reference to 'traditional religion as a vehicle of patriarchy'[6] and no mention is made of feminist theologians who write on eco-feminism. Mary Daly's *Gyn/Ecology* is discussed—apparently being a radical post-Christian feminist makes one something of an authority on these things.[7]

Annabel Miller, reporting in *The Tablet* on the United Nations Fourth World Conference on Women in Beijing, writes that the event had 'Janus faces' in which 'everyone wore their prejudices on their sleeves'.[8] She was particularly interested in the intolerance aimed at the

Feminism and Christian Ethics (Cambridge: Cambridge University Press, 1996).

4. Gerda Lerner, *The Creation of Feminist Consciousness: From the Middle Ages to Eighteen-Seventy* (New York: Oxford University Press, 1993), pp. vii-viii. The first volume is entitled *The Creation of Patriarchy* (New York: Oxford University Press, 1986).

5. Cat Cox, 'Article 4.5: Eco-Feminism', in Gill Kirkup and Laurie Smith Keller (eds.), *Inventing Women: Science, Technology and Gender* (Cambridge: Polity Press, 1992), pp. 282-93.

6. Cox, 'Eco-Feminism', pp. 292-93.

7. Cf. Cox, 'Eco-Feminism', pp. 283-84.

8. Annabel Miller, 'The Holy See in the Public Square', in *The Tablet*, 23 September 1995, pp. 1192-94 (1192).

Vatican delegation, which was made up mostly of women. The delegation was led by Professor Mary Ann Glendon, twice-married Harvard law professor who once worked for the black civil-rights movement in Mississippi, and the team included Kathryn Hawa Hoomkwap, a former Nigerian health minister and mother of four who was imprisoned for nine months during a military takeover. Miller writes that these women 'had clearly been chosen not only for their loyalty to the Church, but for their intellectual—and street—credibility', but she goes on to say, 'this was not enough to break through the wall of prejudice, even hatred, among some secular feminists'.[9] A partial explanation for this prejudice obviously might relate to the Catholic Church's stand on issues of fertility and sexuality, but this is not sufficient to justify the apartheid that prevails among secular feminists with regard to their Christian counterparts. It must be added that secular feminisms are hardly problem-free with regard to issues surrounding women's bodies and fertility. Moreover, when one looks at the Vatican's arguments, they are at least as concerned about questions of development, education and poverty as abortion, which is more than can be said for many advocates of population control.

Penelope Margaret Magee argues that the sacred–profane opposition is an ideology based on repressive dualisms and perpetuated in the exclusion of feminist theological and religious discourses from academic feminism. This results in a situation in which, 'Feminist theologians and scripture scholars have been marginalized or made invisible as humanist-liberal "reformers" within religions which, it is assumed, should either be condemned or ignored.'[10] Magee goes on to say that, 'The declaration of total war on one polarity of an opposition is always repressively anti-intellectual and exclusivist.'[11]

Magee's essay makes frequent reference to Luce Irigaray's work, and it is to Irigaray that I now turn to give a focus to the above general observations. My concern here is not with Irigaray's writings per se, but with their reception among English-speaking scholars within what might be broadly termed the Anglo-Saxon academic tradition.

Serene Jones, in her article on Barth and Irigaray entitled 'This God

9. Miller, 'The Holy See', p. 1192.
10. Penelope Margaret Magee, 'Disputing the Sacred: Some Theoretical Approaches to Gender and Religion' in Ursula King (ed.), *Religion and Gender* (Oxford: Basil Blackwell, 1995), pp. 101-20 (103).
11. Magee, 'Disputing the Sacred', p. 105.

Which is Not One', says of Irigaray,

> Throughout her writings, she returns again and again to the question of 'God'; and she does so with such rigor and persistence that one cannot help but sense that this particular question stands at the very heart of her project.[12]

This creates problems for many feminist theorists who engage with Irigaray.

By way of illustrating my argument, I am going to look at the work of two scholars, Elizabeth Grosz and Margaret Whitford, both of whom show a nuanced understanding of Irigaray but appear determined to rescue her from her own mystical and religious inclinations, particularly when these focus on Christianity rather than Greek mythology. Whitford deals at some length with Irigaray's treatment of the divine in her study entitled *Luce Irigaray: Philosophy in the Feminine*, but her exposition is hedged in with a self-consciously apologetic tone that seems to assume her readers will find this dabbling in religion quite bizarre. She calls the divine 'one of the most controversial aspects of Irigaray's latest work',[13] and goes on to suggest that '"God", like other terms in Irigaray's discourse, is a symbolic category... although it is perhaps rather more difficult to handle, because of the enormous weight of symbolic meaning it already bears'.[14] Whitford argues that Irigaray attempts to avoid the 'dangers in the attempt to reclaim the divine for women' by 'conceptualizing the divine as (1) corporeal; (2) sexuate, either male or female; (3) subject to becoming; (4) multiple; (5) incarnated in us here and now'.[15] But having offered this analysis, she adds, 'The point to be stressed here is that the realization of the divine is *in language and ethics*, i.e. it is firmly within the symbolic order, in its possibilities for becoming'.[16] Given her description of Irigaray's divine as being incarnated, corporeal, and so on, I am not sure how to interpret her repeated assertions that Irigaray's God is firmly a product of the

---

12. Serene Jones, 'This God Which is Not One: Irigaray and Barth on the Divine', in C.W. Maggie Kim, Susan M. St. Ville and Susan M. Simonaitis (eds.), *Transfigurations: Theology and the French Feminists* (Minneapolis: Fortress Press, 1993), pp. 109-41 (121-22).

13. Margaret Whitford, *Luce Irigaray: Philosophy in the Feminine* (London: Routledge, 1991), p. 140.

14. Whitford, *Luce Irigaray*, p. 140.

15. Whitford, *Luce Irigaray*, p. 144.

16. Whitford, *Luce Irigaray*, p. 144.

symbolic order. Certainly, Irigaray sees the signifier 'God' in the context of western philosophy and traditional Christianity as an oppressive function of the symbolic order, but she also suggests that 'God' is a means for challenging the symbolic order, that Christianity has a self-subverting potential in which the symbolic, the corporeal and the transcendent might become integral to one another and not be in conflict. William Large, reviewing *Marine Lover of Friedrich Nietzsche* in *Radical Philosophy*, refers to Irigaray's,

> ...incredible inversion of Nietzsche's attack upon Christianity. It is the Greek myths of Dionysus and Apollo which are found to be lacking, and the Christian story—with its vision of the word becoming flesh—which supplies the resources for a possible displacement of the masculine hegemony.[17]

These are immensely subtle and difficult areas of Irigaray's work, but the nature of the questions she raises demands that we do not explain them away or wrap God up once again in a manageable symbolic package that disempowers the word. This I would suggest is exactly what Whitford is trying to do.

Elizabeth Grosz offers an illuminating study of Irigaray's work in her book, *Sexual Subversions*, and has also contributed an essay to *Transfigurations: Theology and the French Feminists*. It is to these two texts that I refer. Grosz's exposition of the divine in Irigaray's work is well worth reading, but again she manifests a desire to rescue Irigaray from the ambivalent relation she has to religious discourse by locating her firmly on the outside. While Irigaray refuses to define herself in opposition, regarding such strategies as a mirror image of the patriarchal order, Grosz sometimes seems overly anxious to do just that. Magee writes of Grosz that,

> ...her fear of interpretative lapses into religious essentialism causes her to reassure her readers that Irigaray is not 'a 'born-again' Christo-feminist', an unnecessary warning which carries with it an implied horror of 'Christo'-feminism, rather than any helpful information about Irigaray... Within Grosz' 'spiritual'/'academic' dichotomy, Irigaray is placed within the 'academic', almost in spite of possible contamination by theological concerns.[18]

---

17. William Large, review of *Marine Lover of Friedrich Nietzsche* (trans. Gillian C. Gill; New York: Columbia University Press, 1991) by Luce Irigaray, in *Radical Philosophy* 71 (1995), pp. 50-51 (51).

18. Magee, 'Disputing the Sacred', pp. 103-104, quoting Elizabeth Grosz,

Irigaray herself strives to avoid categorizations such as these which uphold rather than disrupt the patriarchal boundaries of thought and discourse.

Referring to Irigaray's treatment of religion, Grosz writes,

> Irigaray is not advocating a return to the kinds of pious devotion that have hitherto marked women's submission to religious orthodoxy. She disdains the kinds of religiosity attributed to such female saints as Lacan's favourite, St Teresa, and the large list of devout women who, in protest at their social subordination, and in a manner similar to that of the modern-day hysteric, use patriarchal religion as a kind of expression of and compensation for their social powerlessness.[19]

This criticism is hard to square with Irigaray's recognition that,

> The love of God has often been a haven for women. They are the guardians of the religious tradition. Certain women mystics have been among those rare women to achieve real social influence, notably in politics.[20]

Irigaray certainly disdains Jacques Lacan's interpretation of Teresa, but I am not convinced that she disdains Teresa's religiosity as such. The following passage is written in conversation with Lacan and gives a sense of Irigaray's teasing and ironic engagement with her male counterparts. She quotes Lacan, "Just go look at Bernini's statue in Rome, you'll see right away that St Teresa is coming, there's no doubt about it','' and she goes on:

> In Rome? So far away? To look? At a statue? Of a saint? Sculpted by a man? What pleasure are we talking about? Whose pleasure? For where the pleasure of the Theresa in question is concerned, her own writings are perhaps more telling.[21]

Sexual Subversions: Three French Feminists (St Leonards, NSW: Allen & Unwin, 1989), p. 155.

19. Elizabeth Grosz, *Sexual Subversions: Three French Feminists* (St Leonards, NSW: Allen & Unwin, 1989), p. 151.

20. Luce Irigaray, *Sexes and Genealogies* (trans. Gillian C. Gill; New York: Columbia University Press, 1993), p. 63.

21. Luce Irigaray, *This Sex Which is Not One* (trans. Catherine Porter with Carolyn Burke; Ithaca, NY: Cornell University Press, 1985), pp. 90-91. Irigaray is referring to Jacques Lacan's seminar entitled 'God and the *Jouissance* of The Woman' which is published in Juliet Mitchell and Jacqueline Rose (eds.), *Feminine*

I think Irigaray is considerably more respectful of women's religious experience than Grosz suggests. Grosz's comments tell us more about her own anti-religious prejudice than about Irigaray's work.

Grosz's essay 'Irigaray and the Divine' begins with the words, 'Irigaray's recent writings on the divine have evoked shock, outrage, disappointment, and mystification in her readers',[22] which suggests the extent to which feminism has embraced an ideological commitment to secularism. After her careful analysis, Grosz concludes the essay with the words,

> This is not a religious conversion, a leap of faith; it is a political and textual strategy for the positive reinscription of women's bodies, identities, and futures in relation to and in exchange with the other sex.[23]

Apparently it is permissible to engage in political and textual strategies, but religious conversions and leaps of faith are out. Who is making up these rules, and what women, indeed what political ends, are they intended to serve? What is a leap of faith, if not a willingness to fling oneself against the far horizons of meaning and existence in order to ask the unaskable, to know the unknowable, to encounter that which is always other, mystical, wondrous—and to make this leap knowing that there may be nothing there, only meaninglessness, the void and absence? It is a risk that Irigaray willingly takes. This has far more to do with religion and faith, even if we have to use those words in a sense that immediately breaks under the weight that the words carry, than it has to do with the more manageable, containable and safe categories of politics and textual analysis.

I would suggest that this feminist disempowering of religion is perpetuating certain conceptual changes that took place in the seventeenth century and that stand in urgent need of deconstruction with regard to the religious/secular divide. I want to gesture in the direction of those changes without in any way being able to do justice to the complexity of historical developments that they represent, so what follows is very broad and necessarily over-simplified.

Much feminist thought is built on an unquestioned acceptance of the

---

Sexuality: Jacques Lacan and the école freudienne (trans. Jacqueline Rose; Basingstoke: Macmillan, 1982), pp. 137-48.

22. E. Grosz, 'Irigaray and the Divine', in C.W. Maggie Kim *et al.* (eds.), *Transfigurations*, pp. 199-214 (199).

23. Grosz, 'Irigaray and the Divine', p. 214.

Enlightenment principle that religion works in opposition to human freedom and self-attainment, and even those forms of feminism that call into question the rational man of Enlightenment thought rarely do so by appealing to pre-Enlightenment Christian anthropology. The widening gulf between scientific and theological models of knowledge can be traced back to a shift in western attitudes to religion, nature and women during the sixteenth and seventeenth centuries. Carolyn Merchant's book, *The Death of Nature*, argues that with the scientific revolution, the earth stopped being metaphorically described as a bountiful and nurturing mother and began to be regarded instead as a sexual female body to be penetrated and brought under control by the rational masculine intellect.[24] In this respect, it is interesting to read Freud's work, *The Future of an Illusion*, in which he says of nature, 'She destroys us— coldly, cruelly, relentlessly', and goes on to argue that 'the principal task of civilization, its actual *raison d'être*, is to defend us against nature'.[25] The main argument of Freud's essay is the need to mature beyond a religious world view (that is, an illusion), in order to attain to the realism offered by scientific rationalism. Scientific man clearly feels he must pit himself against the unholy trinity of woman, nature and religion if he is to gain control of his world. John Donne's poem, 'To His Mistress Going to Bed' (c. 1593–98), expresses a rather different way of describing the relationship between the conquest of women and the conquest of land:

> Licence my roaving hands, and let them go,
> Before, behind, between, above, below.
> O my America! my new-found-land,
> My kingdome, safeliest when with one man man'd,
> My Myne of precious stones, My Emperie,
> How blest am I in this discovering thee![26]

Rowan Williams observes that by the seventeenth century, western Europe had, on the whole, 'succumbed to a collective amnesia about

---

24. Cf. Carolyn Merchant, *The Death of Nature: Women, Ecology and the Scientific Revolution* (San Francisco: Harper & Row, 1983).

25. Sigmund Freud, '*The Future of an Illusion*', in Albert Dickson (ed.), *Civilization, Society and Religion: Group Psychology, Civilization and its Discontents and Other Works* (The Penguin Freud Library, 12; trans. James Strachey; Harmondsworth: Penguin Books, 1991), pp. 179-241 (194).

26. John Donne, *Complete English Poems* (ed. A.J. Smith; Harmondsworth: Penguin Books, 1971), pp. 124-26 (125).

the meaning of the word "God"'.[27] This collective amnesia was willed by those who had the power to shape and dictate the intellectual tradition, which does not include all men but all of whom were men, (although I am not denying that women colluded in the process). The desire of the man of reason to distance himself from the man of faith has had a powerful influence upon the ordering of academic disciplines, and the tendency to marginalize theology gains in momentum with the increasing ideological commitment of western learning to the dictates of science and technology. One of the preconditions for the hegemony of science has been the discrediting of theology as a legitimate area of academic enquiry. To the extent that feminists in the human sciences perpetuate this model, they leave unquestioned one of the premises upon which the modern structures of power are constructed. Unless feminist scholarship attempts to reweave the fabric of spirit and body, nature and culture that was violently torn apart in the making of the modern mind, it will never be able to create a conceptual tapestry that is intricate enough to depict the realities of human life in all its rich diversity, joy and pain; but such reweaving surely entails some engagement with Christianity, as the foundational religious and spiritual resource available to western scholars. The task is one of tremendous complexity and subtlety, since it risks either regression born of a futile nostalgia for a golden age, or a Mary Daly type rebellion that ends up defining itself in opposition to and therefore dependent upon existing categories. This is why I think Irigaray's project is such a compelling challenge to both secular and theological ideas. The radical daring of her thought is manifest in the fact that she dares to breach the last scholarly taboo, the one that separates the sacred from the profane, a taboo that continues to distort and restrict secular feminist scholarship.

Yet who can offer a critique of the inherent blind spot in secular feminism if not feminist theologians, even if it means bursting into the banqueting halls like latter day Jeremiahs and spoiling the party? This raises vital questions regarding the relationship between Christianity and culture and the role of Christianity in society and in the academic world. If Christianity uncritically conforms itself to secular discourses, including feminism, does it lose its identity and become the poor relation of secular theory, always struggling to catch up and show its credentials and never able to face up to the fact that nobody is interested in

---

27. Rowan Williams, 'A Ray of Darkness', in *idem*, *Open to Judgement: Sermons and Addresses* (London: Darton, Longman & Todd, 1994), pp. 118-24 (119).

what it has to say? In a longer essay, I would ask this question in the context of John Milbank's *Theology and Social Theory: Beyond Secular Reason*,[28] which despite its astonishing neglect of feminist issues, nevertheless poses an important challenge along these lines.

Christianity cannot understand itself as just another voice in the 'babel' of postmodernity. An incarnational theology calls Christian scholars to regard nothing as profane but everything as touched by grace, potentially sacred and capable of revelation. Nevertheless, an incarnational theology also demands a recognition of the crucifying power of this world, the treachery of the social order, and the ultimately fickle allegiances of populist movements, even those that are politically correct. Initially, perhaps the development of feminist theology necessitated an uncritical engagement with the resources of secular feminism, but the time has come to develop a more critical spirit of discernment. In the materialist and consumerist ideologies that dominate modern life, there is a profound difference between secularism and faith, and women of faith are often belittled and marginalized, socially as well as academically, by their secular sisters. I began by referring to the women at prayer in my parish church. They might not be card-carrying feminists, but that does not make their lives any less significant, any less womanly, than the lives of the theorists who so arrogantly ignore their existence. For those working in the academic world, there is a loss of intellectual and ethical integrity if these issues are overlooked in the interests of conforming to a broad and uncritical feminist ecumenism.

With Sara Maitland, I believe that it is possible to be a feminist and a Christian. However, I also believe that honest debate and scholarly rigour are only possible if there is an acknowledgment of difference and sometimes painful conflict between Christian and secular feminisms. Then, Christian voices might be heard as saying something distinctive, challenging, and possibly even worth listening to, rather than as a ghostly and anachronistic echo of feminist theory which attempts to reconcile what might ultimately prove to be the irreconcilable—the wisdom of women, and the foolishness of God.

28. John Milbank, *Theology and Social Theory: Beyond Secular Reason* (Oxford: Basil Blackwell, 1990).

WOMEN'S NATURE AND THE FEMINIZATION OF THEOLOGY

Sally Alsford

Rosalind Shaw suggests that a universal female reality is now assumed by few feminist scholars *except in religious studies* and that this is because of the universalizing and essentializing tendencies of its mainstream discipline.[1] This paper is in some senses a mapping exercise, as I hope to see whether Christian feminist theology does make such assumptions and whether these do lead it into such universalizing tendencies.

With regards to definitions of female nature the beginnings of feminist theology are clear. First, there has been an identification of the negative ways in which female nature has been defined over the centuries through a process of opposition to male nature, and secondly, there has been an examination of the concomitant systematic oppression of women. These patriarchal identifications of female nature not only purported to be descriptive but also, of course, were prescriptive. One of the starting points of feminist theology was the insistence that these definitions were not true to the reality of women's nature, and that their use both as a prescriptive ideal and as a means of devaluing women was not only inappropriate but oppressive. Patriarchal definitions of women's nature were rejected as neither true nor useful. It was the proclamation of founding mothers such as Ruether and Russell that the task of feminist theology was to liberate itself from such patriarchal definitions and to recover the inclusive, egalitarian and liberating message of Christianity.

The first stage of this process has been a deconstruction with which we are all familiar: a re-examination of the ways in which female nature has been defined and the uses of these definitions, and of the ways in

---

1. Rosalind Shaw, 'Feminist Anthropology and the Gendering of Religious Studies', in Ursula King (ed.), *Religion and Gender* (Oxford: Basil Blackwell, 1995), pp. 65-76 (73).

which women of the past have, or have not, conformed to these characterizations; and a hermeneutics of suspicion and the search for a usable past. In its constructive or reconstructive phases, Christian feminist theologians have also sought to reinterpret their traditions and claim them as potentially liberative. These concerns have led to various areas of study that seem to break down and subvert the patriarchal male-female distinctions. The discovery in the tradition of female characterizations of God (through God-language, Spirit-Christologies and the female Logos) and the discovery of 'significant women' who, far from conforming to patriarchal prescriptions of female nature, are women of leadership and spirituality are potent subversive examples.

So Christian feminist theology begins within the early concerns of feminism for equality in sharp reaction to the difference that had been used to oppress. Drawing on the essentialism and universalism of the Christian tradition, feminist theologians have argued for the liberation of human nature per se as created 'male and female' in the image of God, their concern being with humanity rather than solely, or in the long term, with specifically female nature. So we have: Ruether's criterion of the full humanity of women,[2] Russell's concern with human worth and dignity,[3] Fiorenza's identification of the vision of the kingdom as the wholeness of everyone, the restoration of humanity,[4] McFague's 'life of freedom and fulfilment for all',[5] Moltmann-Wendel's aim to recover 'true humanity', and 'recovery of the status of being a child of God'.[6]

However, Christian feminist theology has come to mean, or to include, something rather more or rather different from what this might suggest, as it has gone on to reinterpret and explore its tradition from the perspective of women,[7] specifically in relation to the experience and

2.   Rosemary Radford Ruether, *Sexism and God-Talk: Toward a Feminist Theology* (London: SCM Press, 1983), pp. 18-19.

3.   Letty Russell, *Human Liberation in a Feminist Perspective* (Philadelphia: Westminster Press, 1974), p. 63.

4.   Elizabeth Schussler Fiorenza, *In Memory of Her: A Feminist Theological Reconstruction of Christian Origins* (London: SCM Press, 1983), pp. 120-22.

5.   Sally McFague, *Models of God* (London: SCM Press, 1987), p. 48.

6.   Elizabeth Moltmann-Wendel, *A Land Flowing with Milk and Honey* (London: SCM Press, 1985), p. 71.

7.   Cf. Fiorenza, who notes that while feminists generally agree on the deconstructive moves in sociocultural gender analysis, it is at this point of articulation of a positive position from which to struggle that they often part company. See

concerns of women. Sallie McFague talks of the way the Christian paradigm, 'can name women's experience as it has named men's' and Letty Russell of the necessity that, 'the discernment of what oppression and liberation mean for women has to be rooted in the experience of women'.[8] There is clearly a sense in which much Christian feminist theology, as it has developed, is not simply a theology for all, a theology of human-ness, but rather is theology *for women* in a specific way.

This, of course, presupposes and raises again the question of defining women's nature. It seems to me that while Christian feminist theology has up to now rested on rejection of patriarchal definitions of female nature and on the articulation of a theology for women, it has not tended to formulate *explicit* alternative essentialist views of female nature. There are likely to be a number of reasons for this, including the intractability of nature/nurture debates, where statements about the essential nature of women often function more as statements of aims/ideals, as prescriptions, than as conclusions or descriptions we could ever be sure about; a desire to get away from such oppositional thinking; growing awareness of diversity; a concern for praxis rather than theory; and the impact of postmodern questions about the very notion of human nature. However, the developing theologies for women that are emerging do seem to me suggestive *in practice* of some growing acceptance of difference and of a view of women's nature as having at least some broadly describable shape, and this raises some interesting questions about the nature and tasks of feminist theology.

Feminist theology as a theology for women begins necessarily from women's points of view and is informed by the questions, concerns and values of women. As innumerable feminist writers have agreed, it is both necessary and valid to acknowledge one's stance and starting point and the ways in which this will shape one's interactions with any traditions. Furthermore, few would deny the ways in which women's experience has been shaped by patriarchal culture and social constructions of women's nature—even if these were seen as entirely extrinsic. Thus the fact of some levels of difference seems unlikely to be contested, though its explanation remains contentious and we are

Elisabeth Schüssler Fiorenza, *Discipleship of Equals* (London: SCM Press, 1993), p. 340.

8.   Sally McFague, *Metaphorical Theology* (London: SCM Press, 1983), p. 153 and Letty Russell, *Church in the Round* (Philadephia: Westminster Press, 1993), p. 40.

increasingly aware of the dangers of universalizing such differences.

Much recent feminist theology has been influenced by such work as Chodorow's and Gilligan's analyses of differences characterizing masculine and feminine personality and roles, and of the ways in which these differences are reproduced and evaluated.[9] This has contributed to a range of feminist theologies which focus on mutuality and interconnectedness as a primary theme, theologies concerned with the full humanity specifically of women as a matter of interrelatedness, growth, nurture and integration and as a notion of female nature as differentiated from men's nature.[10] Ruether has also drawn on the work of palaeo-anthropologists, identifying a matricentric process (which persists under male hierarchy) where male identity is a matter for anxiety and social construction unlike female identity which is rooted in basic life processes and relationships.[11] She also draws on analyses of left and right brain processes, which suggest the tendency towards greater integration in women than in men.[12]

While it is, of course, unwise to make universal claims about feminist theology as if it were a single or unified approach or method, this theme of interconnectedness seems to be widely accepted as a common, dominant characteristic. Interconnectedness here indicates an approach that is concerned not only with understanding women's nature in terms of human relationality and embodiedness, but also in terms of context; the context of history and of social and cultural setting. It is seen to be part of women's nature to be constituted by, and realized through, such interconnections, and this is seen as a strength. To cite some examples, Ursula King talks of the holistic nature of feminism, in its quest for integration and wholeness. She states that, 'Being more conscious of a web of interrelationships and connections, women are perhaps less

---

9. Nancy Chodorow, *The Reproduction of Mothering* (Berkeley: University of California Press, 1978). Carol Gilligan, *In a Different Voice* (Cambridge, MA: Harvard University Press, 1982).

10. Cf. Anne Carr, *Transforming Grace* (San Francisco: Harper & Row, 1988), p. 204 on a range of such theories of difference.

11. Ruether, *Sexism and God-Talk*, pp. 73-75 and especially, Rosemary Radford Ruether, *Gaia and God: An Eco-Feminist Theology of Healing* (London: SCM Press, 1993), pp. 157-72 (esp. pp. 169-70).

12. Ruether, *Sexism and God-Talk*, pp. 89-90. Ruether insists that this analysis does not offer a biological basis for differentiation between male and female as different psychic profiles—but that it does suggest a possible biological basis for male dichotomizing. See pp. 111-12.

tempted than men to see spirituality as something apart from life.'[13] Rebecca Chopp notes embodiment and connectedness/mutuality as leading values in feminist theologies[14] and Naomi Goldenberg talks of the way in which any serious reflection on women, 'turns... into reflection on interconnectedness'.[15]

There are numerous specific examples of this characteristic and concern from across the spectrum of Christian feminist theological study. Caroline Walker Bynum argues that there is some degree of consensus in mediaeval studies on differences between women and men in the use of symbols. Here, women's mode is claimed to be characterized by synthesis, reconciliation and continuity, whereas men's mode appears to be characterized by an emphasis on opposition, contradiction and conversion.[16] Linda Woodhead analyses Christian ethics as fundamentally relational. She argues that this conception is particularly acceptable to women for whom relationship is a more fundamental and important category than for men.[17] Mary Grey's work on sin and redemption is another clear example, in a study that re-envisions redemption and power in terms of mutuality. Although Grey notes the danger of dualism and separatism, she is concerned with the 'different voice' of women and states that whether or not historically all women have experienced the capacity for relationality and healing, 'they have often been holding alive all humanity's yearning for deeper and more satisfying patterns of relating'.[18] Letty Russell describes feminist ecclesiology as to do with connection and relationship, and feminist spirituality 'as the practice of bodily, social, political, and personal

---

13. Ursula King, *Women and Spirituality* (London: Macmillan, 1993), p. 30, 36 and throughout, and p. 107.

14. Rebecca Chopp, 'Feminist and Womanist Theologies', in David Ford (ed.), *The Modern Theologians* (Oxford: Basil Blackwell, 1997), pp. 395-96 along with openness to transformation, or anticipatory freedom.

15. Naomi Goldenberg, 'The Return of the Goddess: Psychoanalytic Reflections on the Shift from Theology to Thealogy', in King (ed.), *Religion and Gender*, pp. 145-64 (154).

16. Caroline Walker Bynum (ed.), *Gender and Religion: On the Complexity of Symbols* (Boston: Beacon Press, 1986), p. 13.

17. Linda Woodhead, 'Feminism and Christian Ethics', in Theresa Elwes (ed.), *Women's Voices* (London: Marshall Pickering, 1992). Woodhead uses Weil and Oppenheimer as examples.

18. Mary Grey, *Redeeming the Dream: Feminism, Redemption and Christian Tradition* (London: SPCK, 1989), p. 126.

connectedness so that life comes together...'[19] Other examples include Ruether in much of her work, McFague's concern for models of connectedness and embodiment, Primavesi's ecological paradigm of connectedness and Fiorenza's call for a discipleship of equals, which she expresses as a community of mutuality and plurality. We can also consider the work of a range of writers on images and language for God which arise out of a focus on the relational qualities of the divine.

Qualities of relatedness are of course very much part of Western cultural stereotyping of women's nature, but this is one element of traditional definitions of women's nature that is claimed within much feminist theology as being both true and useful. There is a good deal of consensus in practice about women's nature, that it is fundamentally interconnected, shaped by and expressed in terms of such interconnectedness in a way that is not equally true for men's nature, not necessarily because of some theory of innate or essential differences, but for historical, psychoanalytical and/or sociological reasons. While this trend cannot be simply identified with the Jungian type of dual-nature anthropology that Fiorenza is particularly concerned to oppose,[20] it probably should be included in what she terms the 'revalorization of the feminine'.[21]

It seems to me that there are critical questions to be asked about the direction and aims of this feminist theology of interconnectedness. One possible aim for a theology of interconnectedness might be simply the aim of providing a theology for women. Its rationale and purpose might be related explicitly to a developing theology of difference and Christian feminist theology thus might follow the path of other separatist

19. Russell, *Church in the Round*, p. 187.

20. Because it is based not on an essentialist account of two eternal or innate natures or sets of qualities/categories, but grows from the emphasis of feminist theology on the significance and value of women's experience and perspectives, which can be explained in terms of socialization etc, rather than ontology. Its aims, equally, are not to perpetuate this description as a way of differentiating between women and men or between feminine and masculine. It does not lead to an idea of complementarity, but advocates connectedness for all.

21. Fiorenza, *Discipleship of Equals*, pp. 340-41. Fiorenza finds this revalorization disturbing because of recent deconstructions of unitary, essentialist notions of women from around the globe, and because of the recent emergence of the work of Third World feminists which theorizes on the basis of difference. See also King, *Women and Spirituality*, pp. 76-78, who is also concerned about the idealizing and narrowing down of women's experience particularly in terms of bodily experience.

feminisms. This seems to me unlikely however, given the particular desire of Christian theologians for unity and inclusiveness. As Anne Carr says, 'In the light of gospel values, then, a "separatist" position cannot be a final one for Christians: the ultimate goal is an inclusive mutuality.'[22]

A second possibility is that this theology of interconnection is seen as an interim stage, as playing a part in 'the ongoing development of a more complete theology', as becoming pro-woman in order to become pro-human,[23] as women occupy for themselves for a time the space that has been occupied by men for so long.[24] A third possibility, and this is the area that particularly interests me here, is that this feminist theology of interconnectedness might be either presented or read as an inclusive theology of liberation *for all*.

Consider the specific example of Valerie Saiving's classic study, which identifies the ways in which sin has been defined from a specifically male perspective and which offers alternative definitions of sin which have roots in, and significance for, women's nature (as it is shaped by 'biocultural' processes of socialization).[25] This analysis clearly has relevance for women as women. However, Saiving wants to guard against the suggestion that her study is significant solely for women or that the 'feminine' sins she lists are confined to women. Her analysis is presented as having universal significance, particularly by being located in the context of a 'growing trend... toward the feminizing of society itself...in which the character traits inherent in femininity are being increasingly emphasized, encouraged, and absolutized.' [26]

It is interesting to overlay onto this suggestion recent feminist theologies that seem to offer not only a descriptive account of women's nature as basically interconnected, but also a potentially (at least)

22. Carr, *Transforming Grace*, p. 129.

23. Russell, *Human Liberation*, pp. 62, 68.

24. Morny Joy, 'God and Gender: Some Reflections on Women's Invocations of the Divine', in King (ed.) *Religion and Gender*, pp. 121-44 (140). Cf. Carr, *Transforming Grace*, 'Strictly feminist spirituality... is, one hopes, a temporary stage on the way to a fully human and Christian spirituality', p. 210.

25. Valerie Saiving, 'The Human Situation: A Feminine View', *The Journal of Religion* 40 (1960), pp. 100-12. Saiving uses the work particularly of Margaret Mead on processes of differentiation between females and males.

26. Saiving, *Human Situation*, pp. 110-11, referring to Arendt and Reisman. Saiving closes with the suggestion that in this context theology may have to reconsider and redefine its categories.

prescriptive account of true, liberated humanity per se as fundamentally interconnected, of interconnectedness as 'a' or even 'the' basic model of humanity and of salvation. Rebecca Chopp talks of the way, 'connectedness becomes the centre and central value of Christian spirituality'[27] and this is arguably seen in Ruether's claim, on behalf of women-church, to 'the authentic mission of Christ, the real agenda of our Mother-Father God'.[28] The escape of humanity from inhumanity and into wholeness is clearly an inclusive quest, which women are in the process of revealing and so Ruether talks of, 'the humanist promise of feminism'.[29]

Felicity Edwards, in her exposition of Bruteau, presents the category of neo-feminine consciousness as being 'much wider and fuller than masculinist focussed selectivity'. It is real knowledge of the self and the other, unlike the pseudo-knowledge of superficial, masculinist modes. She relates this form of consciousness to a broader paradigm shift, including for example contemporary physics, which understands reality in terms of networks of interrelationships.[30] Mary Grey claims the vision of redemption based on mutuality-in-relating as having the widest possible embrace, so as to be the vision of Shalom of the kingdom of God. The power of relatedness is 'a power, finally, which can unite the opposing polarities of affectivity and reason, of being and action'.[31]

A reading of such theologies as universalizing and potentially prescriptive could be supported by their appeal to Trinitarian and incarnational foci. For example, Felicity Edwards presents Bruteau's 'participatory feminine consciousness' as linked to the role and achievement of Jesus, and to the Trinity. It is presented as 'spiritual experience' and as a 'definite advance in the evolution of consciousness'.[32] The model and story of Jesus and the concept of Trinity are widely presented within

27. Chopp in Ford, *Modern Theologians*, p. 395.

28. Rosemary Radford Ruether, *Women-Church* (San Francisco: Harper & Row, 1988), pp. 69, 72-73.

29. Ruether, *Gaia and God*, p. 171.

30. Felicity Edwards, 'Spirituality, Consciousness and Gender Identification: A Neo-Feminist Perspective' in King (ed.), *Religion and Gender*, pp. 177-91 (188).

31. Grey, *Redeeming the Dream*, pp. 155-76 (157). Cf Fiorenza, *Discipleship of Equals*, p. 67 who argues—from a rather different perspective—that feminist theology can integrate the traditionally separate areas of male/female, public/personal, intellectual/emotional.

32. Edwards 'Spirituality, Consciousness and Gender Identification', pp. 189-90.

Christian feminist theology as prototypical or paradigmatic for the ideal of inclusive human relationality.[33]

It seems to me that the present course of such feminist theology could be characterized as a feminization of theology per se, where the notion of interconnectedness which is seen as basic to women's nature is 'increasingly emphasized, encouraged and absolutized' in relation to Christian theology in general and in every area of theology. Feminism, of course, is not the only source of such concerns and values and McFague notes how the organic model with which she is concerned, stressing radical interrelationship and interdependence, is another version of a story derived not only from feminism, but also from the sciences.[34] However, in feminism these concerns have a particular significance because they are linked specifically with 'women's nature'. Here, women's experience is providing the basis not only of the critical, deconstructive mode of feminist theology, but also of its creative and transformative role. A focus on women's experience as a response to oppressive essentializing and dichotomizing, and as an engagement with diversity, can thus end up as another mode of essentialism.

Such theology might also be read as offering salvation in some sense through women. At the very least there seems to be a logical implication that salvation as interconnectedness may be easier in some sense for women than for men. Ruether, talking about the need for relationality and integration, says that, 'It is the male rather than the female lifestyle that needs, however, the deeper transformation'.[35] Grey, in relation specifically to connection with nature, says that, 'women have been engaging in the work of redemption on behalf of all humanity'.[36] Fiorenza, despite her concerns about the ascription of special qualities or gifts for women, argues for the need for women-church, for women

---

33. For example, McFague presents Jesus as paradigmatic for interconnectedness and embodiment (*Models of God*, p. 53 and *Metaphorical Theology*, pp. 109, 111). Also Grey discusses the redemptive power of Jesus in terms of divine relational energy (*Redeeming the Dream*, p. 97). Anne Carr also discusses a range of Christian feminist interpretations of Christology and of Trinity as final community of mutuality, in *Transforming Grace*, pp. 149-61.

34. Sally McFague, *The Body of God* (London: SCM Press, 1993), p. x. Cf. Grey who relates her concept of interrelatedness to systems theory, *Redeeming the Dream*, pp. 28-35 (32).

35. Ruether, *Gaia and God*, p. 266.

36. Grey, *Redeeming the Dream*, p. 42.

to develop their own institutions for theological education and spirituality, 'as the central embodiment and incarnation of a "renewed church"',
'the "birthing" of a new vision of community and church'.[37]

A 'salvation through women' approach could be a very clear example
of feminist theology occupying the space men have for centuries occupied, but it would seem an unlikely assertion for Christian feminist
theologians whose presuppositions are likely to include an insistence on
inclusiveness and on equal involvement in both sin and salvation. This
could also be a form of reverse sexism, if not totalism. It could indeed
reflect the observation of Caroline Walker Bynum (in relation to mediaeval spirituality) that women seem to have more sense of their own
gender as a positive route to union with God.[38] We should also, however, note the danger that this kind of model of salvation as being
through women or through interconnectedness, which is in some sense
female, could have the effect of re-enforcing or reinstating a model of
female service. As Ursula King notes, amid all her emphasis on interconnectedness, women also may need to find their true selves and that
the experience of separateness may be a necessary part of this process.[39]
Much will depend, of course, on what kinds of claims are actually being
made for this theology. McFague, for example, argues always for a
polysemic, multivalent vision, which itself can be seen as an example
of interconnectedness[40] and this sort of claim may help to guard against
totalism.

We also need to examine the ways in which the designations 'feminine', 'female' and 'neo-feminist' are being used. Clearly for Ruether
and for Edwards, for example, the intention is to reach towards a truly
inclusive vision of humanity for men and women who may experience

37. Fiorenza, *Discipleship of Equals*, p. 193, 197-205. Cf. p. 330 where Fiorenza
argues that women-church is, 'not an end in itself, but has as its goal to make
experientially available here and now the well-being and inclusivity of the basileia,
of God's intended world'.

38. Walker Bynum, *Gender and Religion*, p. 260. Bynum contrasts this with
men's stories and spirituality where there seems to be more sense of the need for
reversal and renunciation.

39. King, *Women and Spirituality*, pp. 108-109.

40. McFague, *Models of God*, pp. 38-40. As well as talking about the pluralistic
nature of metaphorical theology, McFague also talks about the impermanence of all
paradigms. Cf. Fiorenza (*Discipleship of Equals*, p. 77), who stresses that in the
search for new images and myths, no one single image or myth should be singled
out and absolutized, rather, a variety should be put forward.

both 'masculine' and 'feminine' modes of being. Edwards states (like Saiving) that she does not want to identify the categories of masculine and feminine with men and women in an oppositional way and she talks of re-imaging sexual polarity.[41] It may be that salvation is being offered not through women, but through 'female nature' as dissociated from women, or at least as not necessarily associated with women. So if Christian theology is being 'feminized', it may be that gender language is being used in a new way. Bynum notes with reference to Confucianism, where wholeness is a feminine image and the ultimate is feminine, 'it is so only with an expanded meaning of feminine that leaves its referent in social experience far behind'.[42] This seems to present something of a dilemma; would it be better to avoid any such use of gender language, given the possibilities of misunderstanding or of perpetuating oppositional dichotomies? Is it possible or desirable to use such gender terminology in a way that is detached from social reference? Many women rightly want to claim the strengths of their perspective and experience, and are unlikely to want to detach their visions of wholeness from its roots in their social and historical experience.

In conclusion, however, it must also be important to remember these roots of feminist theology that lie not only in women's experience of

41. Edwards, 'Spirituality, Consciousness and Gender Identification', pp. 180-81. 'For while the polarity between masculine and feminine is an energizing reality of a kind, we do not have to go along with the popular (and false) polarization between female and male, black and white. We can choose to re-image sexual polarity, to experience it differently.'

42. Bynum, *Gender and Religion*, p. 3. This is consonant with her characterization of female mediaeval spirituality as more likely to see humanity as genderless. Cf. Eleanor McLaughlin, who talks of the 'feminized' human nature represented by male and female mediaeval saints, and how this feminized human nature was seen not as feminine, but 'as Christian, typical, the image of God'; cited in King, *Women and Spirituality*, p. 105. Cf. Mercy Oduyoye, *Hearing and Knowing: Theological Reflections on Christianity in Africa* (Maryknoll, NY: Orbis Books, 1986), p. 121. Here Oduyoye talks of feminism as one contribution towards inclusive anthropology, one '-ism' among many—and goes on to say that, 'feminism is not the word of the female; it is the word of all who are conscious of the true nature of the human community as a mixture of those things, values, roles and temperaments that we divide into feminine and masculine. It is the word of all who seek a community in which all will be enabled to attain the fulness of their being... Feminism stands for openness, creativity and dynamic human relationships.'

interconnectedness as offering salvation, hope and growth, but also in women's experience of the *breakdown* of interconnectedness. Feminist theology cannot be defined and will not be shaped only by its understandings of women's nature, but also by its experience of oppression and exclusion, and it is this too that will shape its aims and future hopes and any claims which it makes for itself. It may also be the experience of oppression which shapes notions of interconnectedness; as Ruether says, the relative powerlessness of women within history has led to the cultivation of, 'values and modes of relationship that are less de-humanized than male culture'.[43] Mary Grey also roots women's intuition of the relational core of the world in women's exclusion from the competitive/aggressive/dominance ethic controlling the public arena.[44]

However, I must also note in passing a fact of more than fleeting significance, which is that interconnectedness itself can be a means or tool or form of oppression. Feminist theology has grown out of women's experience of oppression and exclusion and out of the identification of systematic sexism and patriarchy as sinful, and for Christian theology, understandings of sin and salvation tend to shape and define each other. This is consonant with Fiorenza's alternative to Jungian and other forms of valorization of the feminine

> Rather than remaining within the psychoanalytic story of gender system … women-church needs to look for an interpretive frame that neither reinscribes nor denies, but that undercuts the totalizing binary sex-gender system.

This interpretive frame she envisions as the struggle, or the various struggles, against oppression, so that 'not gender and biology but historical experiences and struggles against patriarchy are constitutive for a feminist identity formation'.[45]

Women and men are *equally* caught up in the processes of this breakdown and this struggle, which is *not* necessarily to say *in the same ways*. Both women and men are seen within Christian theology as in need of salvation, and any vision of wholeness that is offered may be perceived differently not only by women and by men (if some account of difference *is* accepted) but also by each individual human being. Difference, however, is surely a prerequisite for interconnectedness as

---

43. Ruether, *Sexism and God-Talk*, p. 231.
44. Grey, *Redeeming the Dream*, p. 31.
45. Fiorenza, *Discipleship of Equals*, pp. 347-48.

true mutuality. Feminist theologies centred around such a notion of interconnectedness must acknowledge the need for a range of male and female responses and contributions to their critique and de-constructions and to their emerging visions of wholeness; they should also confront the implications of this form of essentialism, and the possibility of alternative accounts of women's, and of human, nature.

MONOTHEISM IN CONTEMPORARY FEMINIST GODDESS RELIGION: A BETRAYAL OF EARLY THEALOGICAL NON-REALISM?

Melissa Raphael

From the late 1970s to the present, the study and practice of thealogy in the academy has largely focused on its non-realism. Among the relatively small number of thealogians and scholars of thealogy holding academic posts, Goddess discourse is primarily instrumental in character; as an archetype, image or metaphor the Goddess heals the psycho-spiritual/political wounds of patriarchy and 'open(s) up new avenues for self-exploration'.[1] This Goddess is not a real divinity who fits the description 'female'. She is, instead, an image for the sacred power of the self.

But perhaps the academy is paying insufficient attention to the growing phenomenon of realism in contemporary popular thealogy, while continuing to generalize about thealogy as a broadly non-realist discourse. As recently as 1995, Beverley Clack stated quite categorically, and presumably on behalf of all Goddess feminists that:

> The Goddess is not understood ontologically; she is not understood as an entity distinct from human individuals whose existence could be proved... When a thealogian approaches the concept of divinity, she is using the language of the Goddess as a way of exploring what it means to be a woman.[2]

Clack claims that, 'At the heart of talk of the Goddess is the denial for the necessity for establishing the objective existence of such a being.'[3] Graham Harvey (writing in 1996) also regards Goddess talk as

1. E. Culpepper, 'The Spiritual, Political Journey of a Feminist Freethinker', in P.M. Cooey et al. (eds.), After Patriarchy: Feminist Transformations of the World Religions (Maryknoll, NY: Orbis Books, 1991), pp. 146-65 (153).

2. B. Clack, 'The Denial of Dualism: Thealogical Reflections on the Sexual and the Spiritual', Feminist Theology 10 (1995), pp. 102-15 (104).

3. Clack, 'Denial of Dualism', p. 106. Cf. S. Heine, Christianity and the God-

being primarily 'about the embodied living of life by women. "The Goddess" is not exactly equivalent to "Woman" but is more like "the innermost being of women"'[4]

Understanding the Goddess as an existential symbol for the trans-formed, realized female self is characteristic of Naomi Goldenberg, Emily Culpepper, Nelle Morton, Mary Daly and the early work of Carol Christ.[5] This was the first feminist theory of the Goddess and it remains an important one. But Clack's claim, that 'in thealogy, the task of the Goddess is to provide a framework for the process of conscious-ness raising',[6] is based on quotations from Starhawk and Christ that are nearly 20 years old and seems an unwarranted totalization of thealogical discourse.[7]

The reduction of Goddess feminism to an offshoot of the Con-sciousness Raising movement might have been appropriate in the mid-1970s when the needs of individual feminists took precedence over the coherence or truth of thealogy[8] and when, according to Asphodel

dess: Systematic Criticism of a Feminist Theology (London: SCM Press, 1988), p. 149, where Heine offers a generalization which, if ever true, is now out of date: 'the women who revive their goddesses do not believe in them'.

4.   Graham Harvey, 'The Authority of Intimacy in Paganism and Contem-porary Goddess Spirituality', *DISKUS* 4 (1996), p. 42.

5.   See for example N. Goldenberg, *The Changing of the Gods: Feminism and the End of Traditional Religions* (Boston: Beacon Press, 1979), pp. 42-43; N. Morton, 'The Goddess as Metaphoric Image', in J. Plaskow and C.P. Christ (eds.), *Weaving the Visions: New Patterns in Feminist Spirituality* (New York: HarperSanFrancisco, 1989), pp. 111-18 esp. pp. 111, 115; M. Daly, 'Original Rein-troduction' [1985] to *Beyond God the Father: Towards a Philosophy of Women's Liberation* (London: The Women's Press, 1985), p. xix; C.P. Christ, 'Why Woman Need the Goddess: Phenomenological, Psychological and Political Reflections', in C.P. Christ and J. Plaskow (eds.), *Womanspirit Rising: A Feminist Reader in Religion* (New York: HarperSanFrancisco, 1992), pp. 273-86.

6.   Clack, 'Denial of Dualism', p. 106.

7.   Since the Gender Issues and Contemporary Religion colloquium at which a version of the present paper was first presented, Beverley Clack and I have agreed that our difference is essentially one of emphasis. Clack is correct in noting that non-realism is a feature of thealogical discourse, but in my view, a strong non-real-ist emphasis is increasingly that of a minority in the Goddess movement. See fur-ther, B. Clack, 'The Many-Named Queen of All: Thealogy and the Concept of God/ess', pp. 151-59 in the present volume.

8.   This kind of pragmatism is still in evidence. See for example C. Matthews, *The Goddess* (Shaftesbury: Element Books, 1989), pp. 18-19, where she claims that

Long, the Goddess functioned as 'a synonym for a woman with newly regained self-worth'.[9] It is only to be expected, though, that like theology, thealogy will reflect its own time. For example, it is not surprising that Emily Culpepper, one of the principal prophets of thealogical non-realism, studied 'Death of God' theology with Thomas Altizer during the late 60s and describes her passage out of Christian realism as an existential liberation.[10] For Culpepper, monotheism is an 'inertia' which 'fails to leave behind patriarchal patterns of thought'.[11] That may or may not be the case. But I suspect her non-realism owes as much to the prominence of non-realism in the theological academy at that formative period of her intellectual and political development, as it does to thealogical thinking itself.

After all, during the late 1960s thealogy barely existed: Goddess feminism had yet to distinguish itself from secular radical feminism.[12] It has taken about twenty years for Goddess feminism to gain in numbers and develop a religious and institutional identity of its own. (State recognition of Goddess religion as a legal religion confers tax benefits and other practical advantages.) The ordination of women as priestesses of the Goddess by a number of legally recognized pagan institutions in the United States is already shaping what Goddess women do and believe. The heated debate among Goddess religionists of the early 1990s over whether priestesses are formally trained and ordained or are self-appointed and self-defined is a case in point.[13] And where thealogy is housed and produced within institutional frameworks such as The Women's Thealogical Institute, [14] the Goddess might well become less

the 'truth' of the Goddess is entirely experiential; the only criteria in 'finding a myth of the Goddess to live by' is *'does it work for you?'*

9. A. Long, 'Goddess Movement in Britain Today', *Feminist Theology* 5 (1994), pp. 11-39 (15).

10. Culpepper, 'Spiritual Political Journey', p. 149.

11. Culpepper, 'Spiritual Political Journey', p. 153.

12. Thealogy is still (principally through the work of Naomi Goldenberg) strongly associated with psychotherapeutic feminism.

13. W. Griffin, 'Diana's Daughters: Postmodern Priestessing in America', a paper delivered at the colloquium 'Ambivalent Goddesses: An Exploration of the Current State of the Study of Goddesses and Goddess Spirituality', held at King Alfred's College of Higher Education, Winchester, 26 March 1997.

14. See Jade (no surname given), 'The Six Paths of the Inner Mysteries: A Spiritual Leadership Program for Women', *Woman of Power* 24 (1995), pp. 81-82. This institute is run by the Wisconsin-based Re-formed Congregation of the

a symbol of individual self-realization than a publicly mediated and available collectivized religious commodity.

So while a commentator like Clack (who is herself sympathetic to Don Cupitt, Stuart Sutherland and D.Z. Phillips's non-realism) might like to think thealogy is definitively and excitingly non-realist, that does not mean that it *is* so. As I see it, a more realist picture is now emerging—among many grass-roots spiritual feminists at least. Thealogical language is no longer, it seems to me, predominantly self-referential.[15] There is evidence of a discursive shift, such that despite their considerable overlap, there may now be deeper differences between popular and academic thealogy than was previously the case.

However, thealogians, realist or otherwise, do not engage in technical philosophical arguments for the existence of the Goddess;[16] or not yet anyway. And as Clack rightly points out, 'the importance of the Goddess cannot be established by providing evidence for the existence of such a celestial entity'.[17] Even if the Goddess were not 'true' but a figment of women's spiritual-political imagination, she would still be politically, psychologically and historically significant. (If the Goddess did not exist, spiritual feminism would, no doubt, have to invent her.) Of course, not all Goddess feminists are realists, even today. Those who are disinclined towards religion per se remain convinced that the meaning of the Goddess is primarily political and also a matter of private choice. The British Goddess feminist Asphodel Long insists that 'it does not matter' whether the Goddess is one or many, real or symbolic. As might be expected of one who, in her seventies, very much represents the old guard of second wave feminism, Long claims that the point of thealogy is a political one: namely, to challenge the ideology of masculinity as normatively and exclusively divine. For her, an interest in promoting a thealogically unified picture of a real Goddess continuous with that worshipped by Neolithic peoples has only come to the fore as part of the defensive response of 'born-again Gimbutians' to

Goddess and offers the Cella Training Program completion of which gives legal ministerial credentials.

15. It is now customary for all types of Goddess feminists to capitalize the pronoun 'She', and the use of the definite article 'the' before the noun 'Goddess' invites a conception of her as a sacred object in her own right.

16. Clack, 'Denial of Dualism', p. 104; Long, 'The Goddess Movement in Britain Today', pp. 15, 16.

17. Clack, 'Denial of Dualism', p. 105.

academic criticism of Marija Gimbutas's theory of Goddess worship in matrifocal Old Europe.[18]

Nonetheless, the majority of contemporary feminists in the popular Goddess movement *do* postulate the kind of Goddess who would exist even if no one believed in her, and more precisely, they believe that she *continued to exist* during the Christian millennia in which no one *did* believe in her. In 1993, Cynthia Eller's sociological study of the American Goddess movement found that 'most spiritual feminists grant the goddess a much more substantial existence than one of concept, symbol, or linguistic device'.[19] So too, according to Eller, genuine polytheism is very rare among spiritual feminists as they tend to prefer belief in one Goddess with many names.[20]

To claim that Pagan feminism is becoming realist and monotheist is not to claim that its thealogy is moving closer towards traditional theological models. Despite some Pagans' conviction that one cannot be both a Pagan and a monotheist, as Pagans affirm 'that reality (divine or otherwise) is multiple and diverse',[21] where thealogians *do* appear to reverence a single, real divinity, they do not attribute qualities such as omniscience, omnipotence and immutability to divinity, as does classical theism. And in thealogy, the Goddess is not a spirit whose meaning or activity is detachable from the natural material, embodied process. Hence, for Wiccans, the almost credal status of the line from the Charge of the Goddess, 'Truly, that which is not found within you will never be found without.'

---

18. A. Long, 'Perceptions of the Goddess: The One and the Many', a paper delivered at the colloquium 'Ambivalent Goddesses: An Exploration of the Current State of the Study of Goddesses and Goddess Spirituality', held at King Alfred's College of Higher Education, Winchester, 26 March 1997. In her review of my book *Thealogy and Embodiment: The Post-Patriarchal Reconstruction of Female Sacrality* (Sheffield: Sheffield Academic Press, 1996) in *Wood and Water* 55 (1996), pp. 14-15, Long criticizes the book as exemplifying 'a current new phase of feminist spirituality where comprehensive doctrinal statements are being made on its behalf'. For Long, thealogy, as a project, is to be distrusted: there are only 'many many women working towards a revolutionary overthrow of their patriarchal conditioning and finding the divine female for themselves and in their own way'.

19. C. Eller, *Living in the Lap of the Goddess: The Feminist Spirituality Movement in America* (Boston: Beacon Press, 1995), p. 141.

20. C. Eller, *Living in the Lap of the Goddess*, p. 133.

21. M. Adler, *Drawing Down the Moon: Witches, Druids, Goddess-Worshippers and other Pagans in America Today* (Boston: Beacon Press, 1986), p. 25.

Those Pagans who speak of the Goddess as 'real' do not believe that the divine constitutes or belongs to a reality outside the natural realm, as most theologians do. For many, the Goddess is real and her existence is separable from the individual, but not from nature. In 1996, Zszusanna Budapest, giving an interview to Susan Bridle, was asked, 'When you speak of the Goddess in your religion, is there a transcendent aspect to it, or is it purely immanent?' Budapest replied, 'You mean is any part of the Goddess beyond nature? No there is nothing beyond it. There's just more nature beyond nature.' Even so, in the same interview, Budapest goes on to speak of the Goddess as a real hypostasis within the natural:

> All you need is to walk out in nature. If you have nothing, just a blade of grass, you pray with that one blade of grass and she will still come. It seem[s] like a loving, ever present deity who like[s] to take care of her own, appreciate[s] being prayed to.[22]

This kind of confession is easily found in the contemporary literature. For example, a flyer for the 1997 Goddess Conference in Glastonbury promises 'adorations' of the Goddess. Or again, Monica Sjöö described flying back from the International Goddess Festival in California. She writes,

> The night I was flying back to London was the full moon of June 23, and for a while I could see Her in the dark sky above the clouds, the radiant Queen of the Night.[23]

Although this real Goddess is within the immanent natural/political process, her presence generally requires some sort of mediation. In other words, for feminist witches at least, the Goddess is the kind of deity who needs to be invoked from *outside* the self by rituals such as the priestess's circle casting and 'drawing down the moon', both of which rituals are described as ways of 'opening our spirits to allow Her to come through us'.[24] Here among this influential group of Goddess feminists, the Goddess is not merely immanent as an archetype or

---

22. S. Bridle, 'Daughter of the Goddess: An Interview with Z. Budapest', *What is Enlightenment?* 5 (1996), pp. 67-68.

23. M. Sjöö, 'My Journeys in USA and Canada: '94 Int. (sic) Goddess Festival and British Columbia Travels', *Goddessing Regenerated* 5 (1996), p. 27.

24. Bonnie Wodin, 'New England Brigid Celebration', *Goddessing Regenerated* 5 (1996), p. 7.

symbol, but the sole or principal object of worship.[25] Of course, for some witches, the 'reality' of the Goddess is not at issue because what is real is what effects a willed change, and a fantasy about a divinity can do that kind of magic as well as a real divinity. Even so, the feminist Wiccan De-Anna Alba makes unselfconsciously monotheistic and realist claims for the Goddess:'Although I know the Goddess dwells in me and works through me, I do not and cannot contain the totality of what She is and what She knows.' Similarly, she writes, that the Goddess is 'differently located'; 'Not only is the Goddess within us, She is "out there" too—amongst the stars in deep space.'[26] D.J. Conway also refers to the Goddess as one who 'in all Her aspects resides on another plane of existence and will help those who learn how to reach and call upon Her'.[27]

And some of those who might, intellectually, prefer to speak of the Goddess as a symbol of female existential becoming, also, on occasion, speak of her as a self-existent deity who reveals herself to those who, in whatever way, confess her. Nelle Morton, for example, while describing the Goddess in non-realist terms as a 'metaphoric image', also recalls two occasions in which she experienced the unbidden self-revelation of the Goddess in her living room and on an aeroplane. During the latter experience, Morton was feeling extremely apprehensive about flying, but reports that the Goddess came to her as a comforting presence in an hour of need: 'it was as if someone had eased into the vacant seat next to me and placed her hand on my arm'.[28] Even if it were argued that such texts should not be read too literally and that Morton did not intend a thealogy of real intervention, 'to experience' is a transitive verb and it is difficult to stop experiences *of* the Goddess taking her as a real direct object, especially when, as in this case, the Goddess-self begins to act as an independent agent within the woman-self.

This gradual evolution of the Goddess from woman-self to Goddess-self to Goddess-in-herself is most importantly exemplified in the

25. See Adler, *Drawing Down the Moon*, p. 212. Here she notes that other Pagans have criticized feminist Wiccans for their monotheistic tendencies.

26. De-Anna Alba, *Cauldron of Change: Myths, Mysteries and Magick of the Goddess* (Delphi Press, 1994), pp. 19, 14.

27. D.J. Conway, *Maiden, Mother, Crone: The Myth and Reality of the Triple Goddess* (Llewellyn Publications, 1994), p. 25, see also, e.g., p. 5.

28. N. Morton, 'The Goddess as Metaphoric Image', p. 113.

spiritual biography of Carol Christ. In 1978, at one of the events that marked the rise of the feminist Goddess movement, the University of California at Santa Cruz Extension conference 'The Great Goddess Re-emerging', Carol Christ gave a keynote paper that later became something of a foundational document of Goddess feminism. In this paper, 'Why Women Need the Goddess: Phenomenological, Psychological and Political Reflections', Christ claims that the Goddess is, essentially, a symbolic 'affirmation of the legitimacy and beneficence of female power'; 'a symbol of the new-found beauty, strength and power of women'.[29] Yet by the time of the publication of her 1987 book *Laughter of Aphrodite*, Christ has begun to refer to the goddess Aphrodite as speaking to her 'clear as a bell', bestowing wisdom upon her, speaking through 'golden laughter'—a revelatory experience that confirmed and initiated her as a priestess of Aphrodite.[30] Nearly two decades after her presentation of a non-realist thealogy, Christ's moving autobiographical narrative thealogy, *Odyssey to the Goddess: A Spiritual Quest in Crete* has become quite evidently realist. Here, Aphrodite is a divinity with whom Christ has a complex, intimate relationship that she herself perceives as a relationship with a divinity outside and beyond herself. Christ is unequivocal that her auditory revelations of the Goddess are not self-generated:

> The words come into my mind, but they do not seem to me to be my words, or even to come from an unconscious, deeper, or split-off part of myself. Rather they feel like a gift from a source outside myself, and I choose to interpret them as such.[31]

Aphrodite claims, calls, leads and speaks to Christ. She answers Christ's prayers, though sometimes appears to abandon her.[32] Summarizing a particularly significant part of her life, Christ writes,

> What strikes me most about [] my odyssey is how little I chose it and how much I resisted it. But the Goddess was persistent. She wanted me back.[33]

29. Christ, 'Why Women Need the Goddess: Phenomenological, Psychological and Political Reflections', in *idem*, *Womanspirit Rising*, pp. 273-87 (276), 286. See also, p. 278.

30. Christ, *Laughter of Aphrodite* (New York: Harper & Row, 1978), p. 191.

31. Christ, *Odyssey with the Goddess: A Spiritual Quest in Crete* (New York: Continuum, 1995), p. 169.

32. Christ, *Odyssey with the Goddess*, e.g., pp. 9, 11, 13, 14, 15 and *passim*.

33. Christ, *Odyssey with the Goddess*, p. 31.

Christ's latest book, *Rebirth of the Goddess*[34] indicates no less realist a thealogy than the more confessional *Odyssey with the Goddess*. This latter text leaves the reader in no doubt that the Goddess is real and, although for Christ, the Goddess is named Aphrodite, she is one.

Christ feels that the feminist movement has not kept its promises to women. She writes that, 'the feminist movement had betrayed me because it told me that I could "have it all" [love, family, and a career]. I had ended up with nothing.'[35] While Christ remains a feminist, it may be that she now has less faith in women's power to transform their lives through feminism than in the power of the Goddess to transform the lives of women in and through the women who seek her. It is, after all, the Goddess who has kept her promises to her; not the political movement of which she was an emblem. In other words, where the link between Goddess religion and feminism is weakened or damaged, thealogical discourse and its divine object may achieve a discursive autonomy outside or at least to the side of the movement that gave it birth.

Although, as we have seen, not all Goddess feminists will be persuaded that thealogical/philosophical deliberations over the senses in which the Goddess is real are interesting or helpful, phenomenologists of religion will inevitably question whether a Goddess feminist's ontological assumptions about the Goddess make any difference to her religious experience. I suggest that they do. For example, in a 1996 issue of the American Goddess feminist journal, *Goddessing Regenerated*,[36] in which most of the space is devoted to Goddess feminists' accounts of their pilgrimages to ancient sites of Goddess worship throughout the Mediterranean countries and the British Isles, it is quite clear that what is being sought on these pilgrimages is an *encounter* with the Goddess and that such an encounter entails more than self-discovery. Self-discovery is more the effect than the purpose of the pilgrimage. Throughout this issue of the journal the contributors emphasize less the political/ existential consequences of regenerating the Goddess, than the satisfactions of *knowing about* her. The articles here are not about their authors but about the history of the Goddess's existence, her many names, her association with specific locations, and experiences of her in those

34. *Rebirth of the Goddess: Finding Meaning in Feminist Spirituality* (Reading, MA; Addison-Wesley, 1997).
35. Christ, *Odyssey with the Goddess*, p. 52.
36. *Goddessing Regenerated* 5 (1996).

locations at which she is believed to remain as a real and continuous presence.[37]

In conclusion, it is clear that feminist and non-feminist Goddess religionists mean a variety of things when they use the word 'Goddess'.[38] Also, what constitutes the reality of a real Goddess remains open to debate. Thealogy, whether realist, non-realist or something in between, is never dogmatic or exclusive.[39] Starhawk, for example, while *tending* towards identification of the Goddess with the liberated self and with nature, makes a bid to have her cake and eat it early in her career, writing: 'I have spoken of the Goddess as psychological symbol and also as manifest reality. She is both. She exists, *and* we create her.'[40] Although Starhawk stretches thealogical inclusivity to the point of meaninglessness, we have seen that others, like Culpepper, have feared feminist monotheism as a tyranny-in-the-making. Yet these fears might prove unfounded. Reading the work of a realist monotheist like the feminist witch De-Anna Alba, it becomes apparent that a spiritual feminist monotheism may be more subtle and open than earlier commentators might have supposed. Spiritual feminist monotheism may not *necessarily* betray the liberative principles of early thealogians. A feminist monotheism might not *inevitably* produce the type of deity who would arrogate the immanent divinity of human women to herself. Women and the Goddess could have some kind of ontological commonality that would not exclude the Goddess being more than the sum of empowered womankind as such.

Moreover, it would be a mistake to equate realist thealogical monotheism with a *literalist* thealogy. It is possible to affirm the basic reality of a divinity whose cyclic generativity would warrant the description 'female', and whose will for socio-ecological justice and harmony would warrant the loose description 'feminist', without saying that that

37. See also Christ, *Odyssey with the Goddess*, pp. 77-152 for a detailed account of a Goddess pilgrimage in Crete led by Christ herself.

38. See Harvey, 'The Authority of Intimacy in Paganism and Goddess Spirituality', p. 35-36.

39. In *Thealogy and Embodiment* I argue that thealogy is creatively ecological and organicist precisely because it is intrinsically chaotic or anti-systematic. Its process is one of flux, with an emergent discursive order constantly pushing in from its own margins.

40. Starhawk, *The Spiral Dance: A Rebirth of the Religion of the Great Goddess* (New York: Harper & Row, 1979), p. 81.

divinity is *actually* or *literally* a woman with three faces living under the earth or up in the moon. Moreover, to make a claim for the reality of the Goddess need not imply any certainty that one is right. Nor need thealogical realism *necessarily* make heretics of those who beg to differ. Realist monotheism may postulate one Goddess, but need not reduce thealogy to *one* account of her nature. After all, Goddess feminists unanimously agree that a defining characteristic of the Goddess is that of cyclicity and change symbolized by her many names.

In sum, I want to suggest three things. First, it may be that concepts of the Goddess are evolving more rapidly than many of those teaching thealogy in the academy suppose. Second, I suggest that conceptual precision in radical religious feminism is not an authoritarian contradiction in terms. Concepts are merely provisional frames or structures that exist to be subverted. Certainly thealogians insist that thealogy is experiential before it is conceptual. But experience is surely only experienced when it is conceptualized as such and playful negotiations with received thealogical concepts are signs that the discourse is alive and open to the future. And third, I am recommending that religious feminists critically revisit received views about realist language and discourse. Thealogical realism is not necessarily politically retrogressive or a 'fundamentalist' betrayal of religious feminist freedoms. Goddess feminists should not be indifferent to the possibility of a transcendent, wholly Other Goddess; the *tremendum* of whose real will for change would underwrite the religious feminist struggle more than as its emblem. Speaking for myself (a Jewish feminist), I am not hopeful that humanity and its political systems—spiritually depleted as both so often are—can be sufficient to their own transformation. Indeed, Enlightenment, and now postmodernist, assumptions that real transcendent divinities are incredible, oppressive and somehow intrinsically unfeminist is not self-evidently true and might put the future of any religious feminist community or tradition in jeopardy.

'THE MANY-NAMED QUEEN OF ALL':
THEALOGY AND THE CONCEPT OF THE GODDESS

Beverley Clack

Over the last twenty years or so, feminist approaches to the study of religion have interacted with the main expressions of human spirituality found in the world's religions. Notably, in western feminist theology this has involved a critique of the dominant religious tradition in the west, namely Christianity, often with a view to revising and reclaiming that tradition for women.[1] This attempt to reclaim the tradition has been challenged, not only by anti-feminist writers, but also by feminist scholars. The question asked by feminists critical of Christian feminists is this: To what extent is this continued interaction with Christianity appropriate to the aims and hopes of the women's movement?

For some feminists—notably the 'post-Christians' Mary Daly and Daphne Hampson—feminists would be well advised to reject this revisionist approach to a male-defined religious tradition.[2] As Hampson points out, it is not merely *aspects* of Christianity that are sexist and in need of reform; rather, the religion *as a whole* supports and sustains a sexist understanding of human relationships.[3] Rather than continue the attempt to make Christianity non-sexist, it would be more fruitful to turn our attention to alternative religious and spiritual ideas that are not hindered by the sexist history and forms of this historical faith.

---

1. Cf. for example Rosemary Radford Ruether, *Sexism and God-Talk: Toward a Feminist Theology* (London: SCM Press, 1983); Elisabeth Schüssler Fiorenza, *In Memory of Her: A Feminist Theological Reconstruction of Christian Origins* (London: SCM Press, 1983).

2. Mary Daly, *Beyond God the Father* (London: Women's Press 1986); Daphne Hampson, *Theology and Feminism* (Oxford: Basil Blackwell, 1990) and *After Christianity* (London: SCM Press, 1996).

3. For further details of Hampson's critique, see Chapters 1–4 of her most recent work, *After Christianity*.

Hampson's assessment of Christian feminism is, as usual, provocative:

> Why anyone who calls herself (or himself) a feminist, who believes in human equality, should wish to hold to a patriarchal myth such as Christianity must remain a matter for bafflement.[4]

As a woman brought up within the Christian tradition, I would until recently have considered myself feminist *and* Christian. It has taken me some time to arrive at the place at which Hampson stands. However, I am beginning to believe that the attempt to make Christianity more 'user-friendly' to women is a distraction from the exciting possibilities open to feminists engaged in theology. Reading Hampson's attempt to formulate her own understanding of the divine *outside* the parameters prescribed by Christian theology was a truly liberating experience. While I do not share her theology, I share Hampson's conviction that the time has come for feminists to explore the meaning of religion and the concept of God *without* the shackles imposed by male-defined and male-determined Christian theology.

In this article I want to consider the effect that such an approach might have upon the conceptualization of God (or, to use a more inclusive, if somewhat clumsy term, God/ess). As such, I am aware that I am engaging in an area that has traditionally been part of the subject matter of the philosophy of religion. This discipline, like Christian theology, has been dominated by male ideals of what constitutes the divine. However, in this paper I want to explore the way in which the subject provides a useful sounding board against which to explore notions of divinity, with a view to suggesting how a concept of God/ess which takes its lead from feminist thealogy presents a very different understanding of the relationship between God and humanity than that habitually offered. In offering a thealogical approach, it is not simply the idea of the patriarchal God that is being rejected; an alternative approach to human life and culture is also being offered. The first part of this paper offers a thealogical approach to the concept of God/ess, which focuses on the implications of such an approach for theological methodology. The second part of the paper illustrates the extent to which a thealogical understanding of God/ess affects the interpretation of a key issue for philosophical approaches to religion; in this case, immortality.

4. Hampson, *After Christianity*, p. 50.

Thealogy and the Concept of God

The kind of thealogical approach that I wish to explore takes its lead from the nineteenth-century philosopher Ludwig Feuerbach.[5] If Feuerbach's ideas are taken seriously, the notion of God/ess finds its rightful place in the context of human life and culture. As such, I am offering a non-realist account that suggests that spirituality is not a response to a different dimension or kind of reality, but is rather a response to this world which endows this world with significance. Thus, the concept of God/ess reflects human desires and values, and is a vital component of human self-expression. In offering a concept of God that reflects masculinist values, the Christian tradition has consistently downplayed the importance of women's experience. In turning to images of the Goddess, feminist thealogians are seeking a mode of expression to combat this lack of a theological framework for women's experience.

While this emphasis on a female deity might suggest that feminists are merely offering a reversal of the traditional God with its male language and male cultural forms, this need not be the case. This becomes clear when the nature of God/ess is approached from a non-realist perspective. It seems to me that one of the most important thealogical insights involves the lack of interest in the Goddess as a being whose existence could be proved. It is precisely this realist understanding of divinity that is rejected by many thealogians. The American thealogian Starhawk makes this rejection explicit:

> When I say Goddess I am not talking about a being somewhere outside of this world nor am I proposing a new belief system. I am talking about choosing an attitude: choosing to take this living world, the people and creatures in it, as the ultimate meaning and purpose of life, to see the world, the earth and our lives as sacred.[6]

This avowedly non-realist approach to thealogical language does not presuppose that theological language is only meaningful if it corresponds to some existent reality or an entity separate from human existence. Rather, it is a way of considering this world, a way of endowing this world with meaning.

---

5.   It should be noted that this is not the only approach open to thealogy—as someone influenced by the writings of Don Cupitt, I find it the most interesting.

6.   Starhawk, *Dreaming the Dark* (London: Unwin Hyman, 1990), p.11.

At this point it is appropriate to address Melissa Raphael's critique of a non-realist interpretation of thealogy.[7] While I accept to a large extent some of Raphael's comments on my earlier work in this area[8]—particularly concerning my rather naïve claim that all Goddess—women are non-realist—I want to challenge some of her claims about the way in which the language of the Goddess is used. At times Raphael's understanding of this seems too simplistic and straightforwardly realist. At one point, Raphael refers to Monica Sjöö's experience of the Goddess when flying back from a conference in California. Sjöö writes that 'the night I was flying back to London was the full moon of June 23, and for a while I could see Her in the dark sky above the clouds, the radiant Queen of the Night'.[9] Raphael sees such language as clearly referring to the Goddess as a separately existent reality. Yet it does not seem to me that such language is self-evidently realist. As a non-realist, I can feel equally moved by such language, and might on occasion even *use* such language. But this does not mean that I think of the Goddess *as* the moon, or of the moon *as* a revelation of some Goddess who exists separately from this world, its processes and cycles. Poetry and expressive language have an important role to play in shaping religious forms; perhaps more so than factual, referential language.[10] Acknowledging this significantly alters one's understanding of the focus of religious language.

Having said this, Raphael's comments and my own responses suggest that the distinction made between realist and non-realist interpretations of Goddess (or God for that matter) are not wholly adequate. Where does realism end and non-realism begin? It seems that a thealogical approach not only challenges certain dualistic interpretations of reality,[11] but also the attempt to fit certain approaches to religious language into different philosophical camps. Thealogy challenges the very way in

---

7. Cf. Melissa Raphael, 'Monotheism in Contemporary Goddess Religion: A Betrayal of Early Thealogical Non-Realism?' , pp. 139-49 (140-50) in this volume.

8. Cf. Beverley Clack, 'The Denial of Dualism: Theological Reflections on the Sexual and the Spiritual', *Feminist Theology* 10 (1995), pp. 102-115.

9. Monica Sjöö, 'My Journeys in USA and Canada: '94 International Goddess Festival and British Columbia Travels', *Goddessing Regenerated* 5 (1996), p. 27, cited by Melissa Raphael, 'Monotheism in Contemporary Feminist Goddess Religion', p. 145.

10. Cf. I.T. Ramsey, *Religious Language* (London: SCM Press, 1957) for precisely this expressivist account of the nature of religious language.

11. So the distinction between physical/spiritual, the world/God, body/soul.

which we consider the universe and our place within it, and that challenge may also have the effect of breaking down the barriers between people who might have thought of themselves as realist or non-realist. Perhaps the Goddess is telling us that such distinctions do not do justice to the complex way in which religious language works.[12]

Consideration of the complex way in which religious language works may lead to a reappraisal of the way in which we consider the notion of God/ess. Rather than seek for one, monolithic account of the concept of God and the meaning of life, the kind of thealogy I am advocating suggests a more open and dynamic discussion of divinity and that which it represents. While I am calling this non-realist—and will do for the remainder of this article—I am hopeful that in the future such labelling will be unnecessary. In order to explore the implications of this approach, it is useful to consider one area of concern for Christian philosophical theology. In defining the nature of God, one of the key theological issues concerns the relationship between unity and diversity, an understanding that has a considerable impact upon the structure and content of academic debates.

Unity and Diversity

One of the key concepts employed by Christian theology in its attempt to define the nature of God has been that of the Trinity: God is One in three persons. It is this doctrine that expresses the Christian understanding of the complex relationship between unity and diversity, the One and the Many. In holding to the triune God, Christian theology has (at least traditionally) argued that these apparent polarities can be held together in the being of God. As John Macquarrie puts it, God 'embraces diversity in unity; [God] is both transcendent and immanent; [God] is dynamic and yet has stability'.[13]

However, when the history of Christian doctrine is surveyed it is difficult to escape the conclusion that the One has been exalted at the expense of the Many; the transcendent God has been exalted above the idea of divine immanence. Indeed, unity—not only in the Godhead but also in the context of defining Christian beliefs—has dominated theological discourse. This is hardly surprising; in worshipping a God who

---

12. I hope in the future to work with Melissa Raphael on precisely this point.

13. J. Macquarrie, *Principles of Christian Theology* (London: SCM Press, 1977), p. 192.

is celebrated as One in Three, maintaining that unity *is* the key issue in a context which views monotheism as superior to polytheism. The One God embraces the three persons. In seeking to explain this 'mystery', some—notably Arius—found to their cost that diversity is antithetical to unity. In order to achieve unity, the diverse must be brought together. But in that act of bringing together, diversity cannot but be lost.

In addition to shaping the monotheism of Christianity, the notion of the Trinity has had a corresponding impact upon the shape of theological methodology. The overriding concern of theological discourse has been that one's theological language should correspond to the divine reality revealed in Jesus Christ. Once it is believed that this correspondence has been attained, one dominant concept of God can be imposed at the expense of all others. A similar effect, though grounded not in revelation but in human reason, is found in the concept of God offered by philosophical theism. There is one definition of God which, theists claim, corresponds to the divine reality. So, God is defined as omnipotent, omniscient, immutable, impassible. To challenge such a definition is to court controversy.[14]

A thealogy that starts from the premise that the meaning of theological language is not based in its supposed correspondence to a divine being, suggests a rather different way forward. Rather than emphasize one, overarching paradigm for the idea of divinity into which all other models must fit, thealogians suggest an openness to diversity and plurality in framing theological discourse. As Carol Christ argues, the image of the Goddess offers a framework against which women can explore their experience of what it means to be a woman.[15] How individual women employ this image is their concern. Whether they wish to use imagery drawn from Greek mythology, from other historical religions, or to create their own images is entirely up to them. The important point to grasp is that there is no one, correct interpretation of this image: the Goddess is 'the many-named queen of all',[16] and it is in that

---

14. This is true not only for non-realists like Cupitt who suggest a different approach to issues of truth, but also to realist accounts of the suffering God. In offering critiques of such a position, critics such as R.E Creel, *Divine Impassibility* (Cambridge: Cambridge University Press, 1986) attempt to reassert the notion of impassibility.

15. Cf. C. Christ and J. Plaskow (eds.), *Womanspirit Rising: A Feminist Reader in Religion* (New York: Harper & Row, 1979), p. 281.

16. Christine Downing, *The Goddess* (New York: Crossroad), p. 73.

plurality of meaning that the strength of this image lies. This might seem chaotic and disturbing. Questions of how we are to judge between rival claims might arise, and it may be that the non-realist coherence model for 'truth' will have to be adopted. Yet as Christine Downing points out when arguing for the use of many goddesses in shaping one's life:

> Living more than one myth does not mean that one is schizophrenic; rather it is what keeps mythic identification from stultification or inflation.[17]

If such a model for God/ess were adopted, the effect upon theological debate would be considerable. Diversity of opinion is not to be feared, but welcomed in a context where discussion and connection are the most important values. In an increasingly global and pluralistic world, such a method is increasingly attractive.

Thealogy and Immortality

In challenging preconceptions concerning the meaning of 'God', thealogians are doing more than simply offering an openness in theological discourse; connections are being made between ideas of God and their effect on human relationships. The idea of immortality provides a useful illustration of the effect of such an approach.

Fundamental to the notion of immortality is the belief that it is possible to transcend the physical self and the physical world. Dualist accounts of the self are built upon this desire for transcendence. For Plato, this meant that at death the soul could escape the prison of the body and return to the world of ideas or forms. For Descartes, the essential self was identified with the mind. This concept of the lonely self, trapped in the physical world, is mirrored in the concept of a God who lies beyond the physical, who is radically independent, self-sustaining, in need of no other for 'his' existence. The spiritual is opposed to the physical, mind to matter. In order to attain transcendence of the physical, to be like God, the life of the flesh must be overcome.

Ecofeminists have highlighted the connection between the ideal of self-transcendence and the patriarchal attempt to dominate the physical realm. According to Ynestra King, the masculinist attempt to dominate the physical world has a corresponding impact on male/female rela-

17. Downing, *The Goddess*, p. 53.

tions. Woman is identified with the natural world, and, like nature, she must be overcome.[18] Transcendence is equated with dominance and finds its logical conclusion in hierarchy. Taken to its extreme in the little known writings of Otto Weininger, this supposed connection between woman and nature is used to support the claim that woman is not and cannot be immortal.[19] In expounding this idea, Weininger writes:

> That the woman has no craving for perpetual life is too apparent; there is nothing in her of the eternal which man tries to interpose and must interpose between his real self and his projected, empirical self.[20]

Surprisingly, in light of the misogynistic nature of his work, Weininger may be on to something! In a recent television programme, six elderly women from the Hen Co-operative described their experience of the ageing process.[21] Their views on death were particularly interesting. A common theme ran through their discussions; life was viewed as cyclical. We are all part of the cycle of life, and death is part of the wheel of life, death and rebirth. But not rebirth in the sense of new life in a heavenly realm; it is enough to be part of nature and reclaimed by the great natural processes.

Rosemary Ruether develops this theme in her book *Gaia and God*. Like the women of the Hen Co-op, she wants to offer an alternative account of immortality. Rather than think of this as involving an escape from the natural world, she suggests that we think of it in a more ecological way. We should see ourselves as part of the great cycle of the natural world. She writes:

> Like humans, the animals and plants are living centers of organic life who exist for a season. Then each of our roots shrivels, the organic structures that sustain our life fail, and we die. The cutting of the life center also means that our bodies disintegrate into organic matter, to enter the cycle of decomposition and recomposition as other entities.[22]

18. Cf. Ynestra King, 'The Ecology of Feminism and the Feminism of Ecology', in M.H. MacKinnon and M. McIntyre (eds.), *Readings in Ecology and Feminist Theology* (Kansas City: Sheed & Ward 1995), pp. 150-60.

19. Cf. O. Weininger, *Sex and Character* (London: Heineman, 1910).

20. Weininger, *Sex and Character*, p. 284.

21. 'Growing Old Disgracefully' (BBC2) 7 August 1996.

22. R. Radford Ruether, *Gaia and God: An Eco-Feminist Theology of Earth Healing* (London: SCM Press, 1992), p. 252.

This is a form of immortality, for 'the material substance of our bodies live on in plants and animals'.[23] There is, however, no conscious survival for the self. This loss of self may seem frightening, but Ruether argues that this must be accepted if we are to become more aware of our oneness with the physical world. There is no escape from this world, and, rather than seek Weininger's transcendence of the physical, we should embrace mortality joyfully, finding our kinship with all of creation.

While Ruether is a Christian feminist, it is interesting to note that the language she uses resonates with the image of the triune Goddess. Under this account of deity, God/ess is not outside the life-cycle, but embodies it. The ageing process is given dramatic form in the Goddess described as virgin (or young woman), mother (or mature woman) and crone (or wise/old woman). Rather than seek to find our home beyond the stars, the image of the Goddess divinizes mortality. Life and death are part of the same process, and in accepting this we accept our place as beings in and of this world.

A thealogical approach to death is, of course, not without its own set of problems. The cyclical understanding of life and death makes sense if one is able to achieve a long life and die contented! I remember the peaceful death of my 83-year-old godmother with joy; her life was complete, she had loved and been loved. There was even the sense that she had decided that her time had come. It is difficult to see how the death of an infant or a teenager could be approached with the same sense of 'rightness'. So does death pose an insurmountable problem for the thealogian? It could be argued that at least Christianity offers the prospect of an eternal future beyond the grave. I am not convinced, however, that death is any more a problem for feminist thealogians than it is for Christian theologians. Within Christian theology and the philosophy of religion questions have been raised as to the coherence of the belief in life after death,[24] and its desirability for pursuing the moral or religious life.[25] Indeed, it could be argued that rejecting the notion of justice *after* death might empower us to strive for justice in *this* life. As

---

23. Ruether, *Gaia and God*, p. 252.

24. See, for example, D.Z. Phillips, *Death and Immortality* (Basingstoke: Macmillan, 1970).

25. See Simone Weil's views in *Waiting for God* (London: Fontana, 1959), p. 115: 'To empty ourselves of our false divinity, to deny ourselves, to give up being the centre of the world in imagination...'

the Christian Aid slogan so evocatively put it: 'We believe in life *before* death', and a thealogical model seems well-suited to aiding that commitment to life.

Conclusion

My aim in this article has been to suggest a possible way forward for a post-Christian feminist theology. In so doing, I have suggested the way in which a non-realist thealogy might challenge preconceived notions of methodology, emphasizing openness of debate and diversity of opinion. In suggesting an alternative account of immortality, the effect of holding a different account of the meaning of God/ess can be seen. As we prepare for the twenty-first century, feminist theology is about to come into its own. In seeking new understandings between ourselves, others and the earth, new kinds of theology can emerge. When Nietzsche declared the death of God at the end of the nineteenth century, he recognized the excitement but also the anxiety of such a vision; in entering the twenty-first century feminists face a similar challenge:

> At last the horizon seems to us again free...at last our ships can put out again, no matter what the danger, every daring venture of knowledge is again permitted, the sea, *our sea* again lies there open before us, perhaps there has never yet been such an open sea.[26]

26. *The Gay Science* 343 (1887), quoted in R. Hollingdale, *A Nietzsche Reader* (Harmondsworth: Penguin Books, 1977), pp. 209-10.

CHRISTIAN MANLINESS UNMANNED: SOME PROBLEMS
AND CHALLENGES IN THE STUDY OF MASCULINITY AND RELIGION
IN NINETEENTH- AND TWENTIETH-CENTURY WESTERN SOCIETY

Sean Gill

Religion, Gender and the Crisis of Contemporary Masculinity

According to the founder and icon of the boy scout movement Lord
Baden-Powell, in his book *Rovering to Success* published in 1922, God
made men to be men. Clearly for Baden-Powell, as one of the last great
exemplars of Victorian values, the relationship between religion and
gender was as close as it was conceptually transparent. Whether men
lived up to this God-given ideal of masculinity was another matter
though, for he went on to warn his readers that 'we badly need some
training for our lads if we are to keep up manliness in our race instead
of lapsing into a nation of soft, sloppy, cigarette suckers'.[1] As a field of
study, the subject of religion and masculinity is a relatively recent one
that sets out to explore the two relationships implied in Baden-Powell's
text. First, it seeks to elucidate the ways in which religious doctrines,
symbols and practices function in the creation and maintenance of ideas
about masculinity, as in Baden-Powell's assertion that God made men
to be men. Second, it examines how social constructions of gender
influence theological and doctrinal formulations; Baden-Powell obviously already had a clearly defined ideal of what constituted acceptable
male behaviour which in his view many of his contemporaries were far
from attaining.

It is not hard to account for the recent growth of interest in these
issues. Surveying recent work in gender studies in his study *Men,*

---

1. Quoted in A. Warren, 'Popular Manliness: Baden Powell, Scouting and the
Development of Manly Character', in J.A. Mangan and J. Walvin (eds.), *Manliness
and Morality: Middle-Class Masculinity in Britain and America 1800–1940*
(Manchester: Manchester University Press, 1987), pp. 199-219 (203).

Masculinity and Pastoral Care, Mark Pryce concludes that much of the literature talks of a crisis in masculinity and male identity. There is, he continues, 'a profound dissatisfaction among some men with the ways of being a man which are open to them', whilst 'others speak of confusion amongst men as traditional masculine identity no longer seems socially acceptable or feels secure'.[2] According to the title of a recent BBC series, it is a bad time to be male. Masculine identity has, it seems, become anxiously self-reflexive.

Numerous explanations have been advanced to account for the malaise of modern manhood.[3] Economic and technological change, it is argued, has destroyed most forms of traditional employment dependent upon male brawn rather than on intellectual ability, leaving a disaffected underclass with no employment prospects and rendering the traditional model of the male breadwinner obsolete. The feminist movement, and changes in the relationship between the sexes at work and in the home, have also been held responsible for the crisis in male self-identity. Feminism has also advanced a devastating critique of the evils of patriarchy for which men are held responsible—evils which extend not only to the oppression of women but to the possible destruction of all life on earth. In this view the rape of women and the violation of the planet are both aspects of the same masculine pathology.[4] Women have also made demands upon men to improve their performance as fathers, not only by sharing more in the burdens of parenthood, but by being more emotionally involved in the upbringing of their children.[5] Criticisms of this kind are aimed at the very heart of traditional understandings of what it is to be a man. As Roger Horrocks

2. M. Pryce, *Men, Masculinity and Pastoral Care* (Contact Pastoral Monographs, 3; Edinburgh: Contact Pastoral Limited Trust, 1993), p. 6.

3. There are good general accounts of this theme in M. Kimmel and M. Mesner (eds.), *Men's Lives* (New York: Macmillan, 1989); and D. Morgan, *Discovering Men* (London: Routledge, 1992).

4. From among an ever growing literature see J. Plant, 'Towards a New World: An Introduction', in J. Plant (ed.), *Healing the Wounds: The Promise of Ecofeminism* (London: The Merlin Press, 1989), pp. 1-4; A. Primavesi, *From Apocalypse to Genesis: Ecology, Feminism and Christianity* (Minneapolis: Fortress Press, 1991), pp. 24-43; R. Ruether, 'Ecofeminism: Symbolic and Social Connections of the Oppression of Women and the Domination of Nature', in C. Adams (ed.), *Ecofeminism and the Sacred* (New York: Continuum, 1993), pp. 13-23.

5. For a recent discussion of this question see P. Moss (ed.), *Father Figures: Fathers in the Families of the 1990s* (Edinburgh: HMSO, 1995).

puts it, patriarchal masculinity cripples men. Its message to them, he suggests, is 'conceal your weakness, your tears, your fear of death, your love for others... Dominate others, then you can fool everyone, especially yourself, that you feel powerful.'[6]

In a climate of such agonized self-questioning, it is not surprising that, whereas to date, nearly all of the most fruitful scholarship in the field of religion and gender has concentrated upon the impact of patriarchy upon women's lives, attention is now focusing upon its effects upon men. As with feminist historical and theological studies, the intention is both to unmask those forms of past religious thought and praxis that have contributed to the pathological nature of contemporary masculinity, and to explore what spiritual resources may yet exist within the Christian tradition for its creative reconfiguration. However, if this is to be done successfully there are a number of methodological problems that need to be taken into account.

Conceptual and Methodological Problems in the Study of Christianity and Masculinity

Undoubtedly the most serious obstacle standing in the way of such research has been the androcentric nature of much traditional scholarship, which has problematized the feminine while treating the category of maleness as normative. This has meant that while the overwhelming bulk of historical writing has concerned the activities and preoccupations of men as agents in the past, there has been little if any appreciation that masculinity itself might be problematic. It makes little sense, for example, to consider the ways in which Augustine's sense of selfhood as a man in a patriarchal society and his conception of the majesty and power of God might be inter-related, if the relationship between the two, although flawed on the human side, is ultimately accepted as one of ontological congruence. By contrast, the fact that within the Christian tradition femininity has been conceptualized as the disruptive other has quite rightly been the spur to an immense amount of fruitful re-envisioning of the past.[7]

Yet even if we succeed in posing new questions of the Christian

6.   R. Horrocks, *Masculinity in Crisis: Myths, Fantasies and Realities* (London: Macmillan, 1994), p. 25.

7.   For the relative neglect by scholars of masculinity as a problematic gender construct, and the reasons for this, see Morgan, *Discovering Men*, pp. 26-30.

tradition, other difficulties arise. If we accept a social constructionist perpective and realize that gender is not a biologically determined or God-given category, but the product of social practices, then it follows that the ideal of masculinity is a context specific one that changes over time. But when we begin to ground our discussion of the relationship between Christianity and masculinity in a particular social context we are then faced with the further problem of deciding to what extent both religion and gender operate as independent variables. Clearly as western society has become more secular and more pluralist, the role of Christianity in sustaining the gendered ordering of the public realm, and in providing models of appropriate male behaviour, is far less easy to identify than in the more distant past.

Perhaps even more of a challenge is the task of locating the formation of gender within the complex interplay of class, race, sexual orientation and nationality. To talk, for example, of a putative crisis of masculinity within advanced capitalist societies conceals as much as it reveals, since its impact upon white or black working-class males or upon white-collar workers has been very different from that experienced by those engaged in professional and managerial jobs. In seeking to understand the dynamics of gender relations in past societies, historians have found it helpful to employ the concept of hegemonic masculinity to describe the attempts to impose a normative model of male conduct upon all sections of society in order to sustain the power of particular social or racial groups. Yet it is important to be aware that such ideological formulations are by their very nature unstable, contradictory and contested. For instance, the role of Protestant Christianity in the creation of what Max Weber called a new masculine model of 'worldly asceticism' suited to the needs of the capitalist economy, should not obscure the fact that this ideal clashed head on with the very different mores of popular male culture.[8] We need to study masculinities rather than masculinity if we are to make sense of gender construction.

We must also be aware of the dangers of studying masculinity in isolation. As R.W. Connell has argued, 'masculinity and femininity are inherently relational concepts', and this is true both in terms of cultural dynamics and of the distribution of power in any given society.[9] So far, it has been the case that the majority of studies of the relationship

8. M. Weber, *The Protestant Ethic and the Rise of Capitalism* (ed. A. Giddens; London: George Allen & Unwin, 1976), pp. 153-54.

9. R.W. Connell, *Masculinities* (Oxford: Polity Press, 1995), p. 44.

between religion and masculinity in the formative period of nineteenth-century English capitalism have concentrated upon single-sex male environments such as public schools and the armed forces.[10] In the rest of this article I shall try to adopt a contextualized and relational approach to two important nineteenth-century theological issues which can shed light on the links between Christianity and masculinity: the ideal of Christian manliness, and the depiction of Christ. In doing so I shall focus largely, but not exclusively, upon the writings of one of the most influential nineteenth-century writers on masculinity, the novelist and Christian Socialist, Thomas Hughes.

The Ambiguities of Muscular Christianity

1857 saw the publication of what has come to be regarded as one of the classic expositions of the Victorian ideal of heroic Christian masculinity, Thomas Hughes's novel *Tom Brown's Schooldays.* Closely associated with the ethos of the newly emergent English public school, the ideal of muscular Christianity exalted an anti-intellectual credo of schoolboy athleticism and adult male toughness perfectly attuned to the ethos of Victorian imperialism.[11] In one sense Hughes's commendation of the virtues of what he calls manfulness or manliness provides a good example of the way in which the gendered polarities operating within mid-Victorian society perpetuated an ideal of masculine power over and against what most Victorian Christians would have regarded as the more feminine virtues of gentleness and compassion. Thus at one point in the novel he delivers a panegyric upon the necessity of conflict waged in a righteous cause:

> After all, what would life be without fighting, I should like to know? From the cradle to the grave, fighting, rightly understood is the business,

---

10. Examples of this genre include J. Mangan, *Athleticism in the Victorian and Edwardian Public School: The Emergence and Consolidation of an Educational Ideology* (Cambridge: Cambridge University Press, 1981); and J. Springhall, *Youth, Empire and Society: British Youth Movements, 1883–1940* (London: Croom Helm, 1977). An oustanding exception is L. Davidoff and C. Hall, *Family Fortunes: Men and Women of the English Middle Class, 1780–1850* (London: Hutchinson, 1987).

11. For the cult of Victorian manliness see D. Newsome, *Godliness and Good Learning* (London: Cassell, 1961); and N. Vance, *The Sinews of the Spirit: The Ideal of Christian Manliness in Victorian Literature and Religious Thought* (Cambridge: Cambridge University Press, 1985).

the real, highest, honestest business of every son of man. Every one who is worth his salt has his enemies, who must be beaten, be they evil thoughts and habits in himself or spiritual wickedness in high places, or Russians, or border-ruffians, or Bill, Tom, or Harry, who will not let him live in quiet till he has thrashed them.

And he goes on to reject an alternative Christian model of masculinity exemplified by the pacifism associated with the Quakers as impracticable.[12] Such a passage can be read as a perfect example of the new enthusiasm for Christian militarism which Olive Anderson has suggested derived from the cult of the pious soldier martyr such as Sir Henry Havelock who died at the relief of Lucknow during the Indian mutiny, and which was to reach its apotheosis in the death of General Gordon at Khartoum in 1885.[13]

Nor was Hughes alone in emphasizing the tougher, more masculine, aspects of the Christian faith, for there was widespread unease at the time that it was appealing far more successfully to women than to men. As the Reverend S.S. Pugh complained in his *Christian Manliness: A Book of Examples and Principles for Young Men* published by the Religious tract Society in 1867,

> The Christian life has often been strangely and mischievously misapprehended as to this, so that men have come to think of it as a state of dreary sentimentalism, fit only for women, or for soft and effeminate men, not calling forth or giving room for the exercise of the sterner and stronger virtues.[14]

Hughes's fellow Christian Socialist, the Anglican clergyman F.D. Maurice, was similarly anxious to repudiate what he called 'the passive or feminine character which has often been ascribed to the Sermon on the Mount', and which, he went on, had 'been thought to discourage all the qualities which have been most conspicuous in heroes who have struggled for freedom'.[15]

Norman Vance has argued, however, that Hughes had serious

---

12. T. Hughes, *Tom Brown's Schooldays* (Oxford: Oxford University Press, 1989), pp. 282-83.

13. O. Anderson, 'The Growth of Christian Militarism in mid-Victorian Britain', *The Journal of Ecclesiastical History* 86 (1971), pp. 46-72.

14. S. Pugh, *Christian Manliness: A Book of Examples and Principles for Young Men* (London: The Religious Tract Society, 1867), p. 95.

15. F.D. Maurice, *Social Morality: Twenty-one Lectures Delivered in the University of Cambridge* (London: Macmillan, 1969), p. 461.

reservations about the label 'muscular Christianity' which came to be associated with his writings, and he suggests that the term manliness is a more appropriate way of describing the synthesis of moral and physical virtues that he sought to promote.[16] More recently this view has been challenged by Donald Hall, who prefers the more traditional epithet 'muscular Christianity' commenting on 'the consistent, even insistent, use of the ideologically charged and aggressively poised male body' in the work of writers such as Hughes and Charles Kingsley.[17] Such differences of interpretation arise in no small part from the ambiguities towards gender differentiation that exist within Hughes's writing, for it is certainly possible to find there a very different attitude towards masculinity and femininity from the one which we have so far been discussing. It is important to recognize, for example, that Hughes sought to stress that the courage implied in his ideal of Christian manliness was primarily not physical but moral. His ideal of heroism turns out to owe a great deal more to the Pauline ideal of spiritual warfare against the world, the flesh and the devil than to any imperialist or neo-Darwinian vision of human competitiveness and aggression. This meant that in practice it was open to women as well as to men to embody it. Thus in the novel, although the father of the hero's school friend Arthur is the epitome of Hughes's ideal of Christian manliness as an Anglican clergyman working for little recognition in an economically depressed working-class parish, his wife shares fully in the hardships of his life and ministry. Finally, both together face the ultimate test of courage when called upon to visit the sick of the parish during an epidemic of typhus to which they both succumb but from which only she recovers.[18]

As Hughes was well aware this was no mere fictionalized account. Women were taking an increasingly active part in the life of the Victorian churches, particularly in the fields of philanthropy and overseas missions.[19] In so doing they were exhibiting many of the qualities of courage, organizational flair and intellect which were supposedly the particular characteristics associated with masculinity. Hughes indeed

---

16. Vance, *Sinews*, p. 2.

17. D. Hall (ed.), *Muscular Christianity: Embodying the Victorian Age* (Cambridge: Cambridge University Press, 1994), p. 9.

18. Hughes, *Schooldays*, pp. 238-41.

19. F. Prochaska, *Women and Philanthropy in Nineteenth-Century England* (Oxford: Clarendon Press, 1980).

recognized such qualities in his own wife, writing to his close friend the future Marquess of Ripon that he felt sure that his wife Fanny could 'be a wonderful parsoness'—a task that he regarded as 'the work which was Christ's special work on earth'.[20] Yet the increasing participation of women in the life of the church—what has been described as the feminization of Victorian Christianity[21]—ran counter to the polarities of contemporary thinking about gender, and neither Hughes nor his fellow proponents of Christian manliness were able to resolve the contradictions that this dualism entailed. For example, Charles Kingsley dismissed the ideal of muscular Christianity associated with his novels as 'a clever expression, spoken in jest, by I know not whom', but then went on to offer his own definition of what he called 'a healthy and manful Christianity, one which does not exalt the feminine virtues to the exclusion of the masculine'.[22]

In Hughes's case the unresolved tension between inclusive and exclusive conceptions of gender is nowhere more evident than in the conclusion to his novel *Tom Brown at Oxford*, written as a sequel to his earlier best seller. Tom has been saved from the vices and frivolities of life by the love of a good woman, Mary Porter. When he laments that in marrying her he has unwittingly tied to himself 'a brave, generous, pitying angel', she indignantly rejects the appeal to Coventry Patmore's image of woman as the Angel in the House insisting that she has made a free moral choice to share his hardships. When Tom enthuses that 'life should be all bright and beautiful to a woman', she replies by asking if women have different souls from men, and if not why they should not share their highest hopes. Yet ultimately Hughes returns to a much more conventional view of the relationship between men and women:

> Cannot a woman feel the wrongs that are going on in the world? Cannot she long to see them set right, and pray that they might be set right? We are not meant to sit in fine silks, and look pretty, and spend money, any more than you are meant to make it, and cry peace where there is no peace. If a woman cannot do much herself, she can honour and love a man who can.

20. L. Wolf, *The Life of the First Marquess of Ripon* (2 vols.; London: John Murray, 1921), I, p. 153.

21. A. Douglas, *The Feminization of American Culture* (New York: Avon Books, 1978).

22. C. Kingsley, *Four Sermons Preached before the University of Cambridge* (London: Macmillan, 1865), p. 5.

To which he replies that she has made him 'feel what it is that a man wants, what is the help that is meet for him'.[23]

There are several reasons why Hughes's construction of an ideal of Christian manhood was an unstable one. For one thing, it was a class based ideal whose applicability to working-class culture was far from obvious. Above all it depended upon an unambiguous understanding of the feminine against which it could be defined. Yet as Hughes was well aware, the role of Christianity in the lives of Victorian middle-class women was far from simple. If it limited them by the stereotypes of pious passive femininity that it promoted, it also empowered them to undertake much more dynamic public roles.[24] By appealing to what were ultimately transcendent values beyond the structures of patriarchal society, Christianity destabilized the category of the feminine even as it attempted to define it, thereby calling into question any attempt to arrive at a coherent notion of Christian masculinity.

Ecce Homo: Victorian Masculinity and the Jesus of History

Nowhere are these strains more evident than in the numerous attempts that were made in the mid-Victorian era to produce a convincing human portrait of Christ with which both men and women could identify. Hughes's contribution to the genre, significantly entitled *The Manliness of Christ*, appeared in 1879. In it he laboured to provide what turned out to be mutually incompatible solutions to two problems. As we have seen, a number of prominent Victorian Christians were expressing alarm that Christianity, by being increasingly identified with the sup- posedly feminine virtues, was ceasing to appeal to men. Thus Hughes refers in the introduction to his work to the lack of success of branches of the YMCA in reaching the young:

> Their tone and influence are said to lack manliness, and the want of manliness is attributed to their avowed profession of Christianity. If you pursue the inquiry, you will often come upon a distinct belief that this weakness is inherent in our English religion; that our Christianity does and must appeal habitually and mainly to men's fears—to that in them

---

23. T. Hughes, *Tom Brown at Oxford* (3 vols.; London: MacMillan, 1861), III, pp. 307-308.

24. G. Malmgreen, (ed.), *Religion in the Lives of English Women, 1760–1930* (London: Croom Helm, 1986), pp. 6-7.

which is timid and shrinking, rather than to that which is courageous and outspoken.[25]

At the same time, the numbers of increasingly active women in the church had also to be able to identify with Christ in a Protestant Christian culture which found no place for the cult of the Virgin Mary and of female saints. Where this did not occur the risk of alienation from orthodox Christian symbolism was a real one. As Florence Nightingale argued, women would never really be liberated until the day when 'there shall arise a woman, who will resume, in her own soul, all the sufferings of her race, and that woman will be the Saviour of her race'.[26] Hughes therefore attempts to portray a Christ who combines the highest qualities of both masculinity and femininity—a man at once of 'absolutely unshaken steadfastness' and at the same time 'this most tender and sensitive of the sons of men—with fibres answering to every touch and breath of human sympathy', a classic definition of the Victorian ideal of female gentleness.[27] The same hypostatic union of gendered opposites is also evident in the concluding peroration of *Tom Brown's Schooldays*, where the rhetoric of muscular Christianity sits uneasily beside that of submissive Christian femininity:

> Such stages have got to be gone through, I believe, by all young and brave souls who must win their way through hero-worship, to the worship of Him who is the King and Lord of heroes. For it is only through our mysterious human relationships, through the love and tenderness and purity of mothers and sisters and wives, through the strength and courage and wisdom of fathers and brothers and teachers, that we can come to the knowledge of Him, in whom alone the love, and the tenderness, and the purity, and the strength, and the courage, and the wisdom of all these dwell for ever and ever in perfect fulness.[28]

How far such rhetorical strategies were successful is another matter given the Victorian rejection of any behaviour by men deemed to be inappropriately feminine as effeminate. The *Westminster Review*, for example, dealt gingerly with the gender implications of Hughes's life of Christ, commenting that the spirit of Christ was not the spirit of an athlete, whilst hastening to add that 'we are far from saying that Jesus

---

25. T. Hughes *The Manliness of Christ* (London: Macmillan, 1879), p. 2.

26. Quoted in S. Gill, *Women and the Church of England from the Eighteenth Century to the Present* (London: SPCK, 1994), p. 140.

27. Hughes, *Manliness*, p. 143.

28. Hughes, *Schooldays*, p. 376.

was not manly'.[29] As the leading exponent of the American social gospel movement, Walter Rauschenbusch put it, 'there was nothing mushy, nothing sweetly effeminate about Jesus'. He was, he reassured his readers, 'a man's man'.[30]

One possible resolution of these difficulties lay in the appeal to the notion of chivalry, that interplay of masculine strength and feminine weakness that served to reinforce both ideals. As the Reverend Pugh explained to his readership of young men, Christ's gentleness was of a particular kind, and in following his example 'a man who is strong, who in fidelity and courage and self-reliance and self-mastery can keep the even tenor of his ways, can afford to be gentle without fearing to be suspected of weakness'.[31] Hughes's fellow novelist and Christian Socialist Charles Kingsley agreed, describing Christ's example of self-sacrifice as 'the true prowess, the true valour, the true chivalry, the true glory, the true manhood' to which we should all aspire'.[32] The appeal of chivalry to Hughes was equally strong. His grandmother knew and entertained the novelist Sir Walter Scott, one of the most influential figures in the development of the Victorian enthusiasm for the middle ages, and Hughes was an avid reader of his works. On one occasion, he recalled, while a student at Oxford he read selections from the novels to a 'broken-down old jockey' in an endeavour to get him to abandon the public house—though the result of this somewhat unusual form of temperance campaigning is not recorded.[33] Hughes's depiction of Christ as a man of 'most exquisite temper and courtesy' in his dealings with both rich and poor alike owes a great deal to the ideals of knighthood seen through the rose-tinted spectacles of Victorian neo-mediaevalism.[34]

29. *The Westminster Review* 57 (1880), p. 547.

30. Quoted in S. Curtis, 'The Son of Man and God the Father: The Social Gospel and Victorian Masculinity', in M. Clynes and C. Griffin (eds.), *Meanings for Manhood: Constructions of Masculinity in Victorian America* (Chicago: Chicago University Press, 1990), pp. 67-83 (72).

31. Pugh, *Manliness*, p. 123.

32. Kingsley, *Four Sermons*, p. 20.

33. E.C. Mack and W.H. Armytage, *Thomas Hughes: The Life of the Author of Tom Brown's Schooldays* (London: Ernest Benn, 1952), p. 116.

34. Hughes, *Manliness*, p.123. The theme of Victorian neo-mediaevalism is well covered in M. Girouard, *The Return to Camelot: Chivalry and the English Gentleman* (New Haven: Yale University Press, 1981).

The Legacy of Christian Manliness

In one sense it might be argued that little has survived of the context and assumptions that inform Hughes's wrestling with the problems of Christianity and masculinity. The ideal of heroic male chivalry did not, after all, survive the brutal realities of the Somme battlefields, and when D.H. Lawrence sought to engage with the Jesus of history in the 1920s, the result would have been unintelligible and deeply offensive to Hughes and his contemporaries. In revolt against what he regarded as the stifling and emasculating conventions of Victorian society, Lawrence rejected what he felt to be the infantilism and the dualism of flesh and spirit implied in conventional portrayals of Christ, substituting for them an image of the risen Lord as 'a full man, in full flesh and soul' who marries and has children.[35] Lawrence's rejection of the traditional image of Christ as an inadequate model for masculinity has in fact striking resemblances to the work of one of the gurus of the contemporary men's movement, Robert Bly. In Bly's *Iron John* Christ is also a problematic model of maleness on account of both his lack of sexuality and his weakness. Whilst he is commended for his machismo at the point where 'he goes wild in the temple and starts whipping the money-lenders', Bly argues that a new and more vigorous Christ is needed to which modern men can relate—'a religious figure, but a hairy one, in touch with God and sexuality, with spirit and earth'.[36] Bly, and the new men's movement with which he is associated, reveal a deeply ambiguous response to feminism, accusing it of being partly responsible for the emasculation of men. One can find similar concerns voiced in fundamentalist Christian groups, such as the American men's movement Promise Keepers, whose appeal to a Christ at once new man and old is designed to reassert traditional ideals of male headship which they fear are being undermined by both feminism and liberalism.[37] As Albert

35. D.H. Lawrence, 'The Risen Lord', in W. Roberts and H. Moore (eds.), *Phoenix II, Uncollected, Unpublished and Other Prose Works by D.H. Lawrence* (London: Heinmann, 1968), pp. 571-77 (575). This essay was first published in 1929 and took up themes which had appeared in his more extended treatment of Christ, *The Man Who Died* (1925).

36. R. Bly, *Iron John: A Book About Men* (Reading, MA: Addison-Wesley Publishing, 1990), p. 249.

37. A. Dyson, 'Carnal Knowledge: Men and Sexuality', in M. Percy (ed.), *Sexuality and Spirituality in Perspective* (London: Darton, Longman and Todd, 1997), pp. 76-85 (83).

Schweitzer remarked in his great critical survey of the Victorian quest for the historical Jesus, 'There is no historical task which so reveals a man's true self as the writing of a Life of Jesus'.[38] In our day, no less than in Hughes's, the search to find and express that self remains both anguished and contentious.

Similarly it would be hard to maintain that we have solved the other problems of gender that made the Victorians so uneasy. The recent tormented debates within the Church of England over the ordination of women reveal, among many other things, a great deal about our contemporary confusions and anxieties in this respect. Thus some opponents of the measure appealed to what were essentially Victorian notions of polarized and God-given gender identities. For instance, V.A. Demant, then Regius Professor of Moral and Pastoral Theology at Oxford, could argue that the divine Logos is in some sense inherently masculine because:

> Maleness is associated with law, order, civilisation, logos, clock time, and what Freud called the 'super-ego'. Femaleness is associated with nature, instinct, biological time, feeling, eros, and what Freud called the 'id'.[39]

Yet even among those in favour of change, there were deep differences as to whether women's ordination was being advocated on the grounds of the unitary nature of masculinity and femininity in which reason, creativity and compassion were the common characteristics of both, or whether appeal was being made to specifically feminine qualities that men lacked and that women would bring to the Church's ministry. What debates such as these suggest is that while we would do well to engage in what Foucault has termed the archaeology of knowledge, and thereby to uncover the origins of much of our contemporary thinking about masculinity, much more is at stake.[40] No more than Thomas Hughes have we found answers to the troubling questions about Christianity and male identity with which his contemporaries would no doubt have said that he grappled so manfully.

---

38. A. Schweitzer, *The Quest of the Historical Jesus* (London: A. & C. Black, 3rd English edn, 1954), p. 4.

39. Quoted in Gill, *Women and the Church of England*, p. 248.

40. M. Foucault, *L'archéologie du savoir* (Paris: Editions Gallimard, 1969).

SEX SLAVES: RETHINKING 'COMPLEMENTARITY' AFTER 1 CORINTHIANS 7. 3-4[*]

Gerard Loughlin

> After I became a prostitute, I had to deal with penises of every imagin-
> able shape and size. Some large, others quite shrivelled and pendulous of
> testicle. Some blue-veined and reeking of Stilton, some miserly. Some
> crabbed, enchanted, dusted with pearls like the great minarets of the Taj
> Mahal, jesting penises, ringed as the tail of a racoon, fervent, crested,
> impossible to live with, marigold-scented. More and more I became
> grateful I didn't have to own one of these appendages.[1]

Thus begins the narration of modern saint number 271 in Tama
Janowitz's *Slaves of New York* (1986), a collection of stories about
male egos and the women who service them, the slaves who tidy the
men's apartments, cook their food and tend their vanities in return for
habitation and—sometimes—protection from other slave owners. These
women are interchangeable, functions without identities. Thus in one
story, the narrator tells us that first you must 'dispose of his wife'. You
lobotomize Mrs Springsteen with an ice pick and send her on her way
to Hollywood, then dress in her 'nightie' and lie in bed, 'looking up at
the ceiling', waiting for the return of the 'boss'.

> Bruce strips down to his Jockey shorts and gets into bed with you. 'Good
> night, honeybunch', he says. In the morning he still doesn't seem to
> realize there's been a change of personnel.[2]

* I would like to thank the following for their comments on an earlier version
of this essay: Tina Beattie, Gavin D'Costa, Sean Gill, Ursula King, Ann Loades,
Esther Reed, Deborah Sawyer and Elisabeth Stuart. Needless to say, none of them
are responsible for its persisting errors.

1. Tama Janowitz, *Slaves of New York* (London: Pan Books, 1987 [1986]), p. 1.
James Ivory's film of the book, with the same title, was released in 1989. While
scripted by Janowitz, and retaining the conceit of slavery, the film finally opts for
romance rather than the sense of quiet despair that pervades Janowitz's stories.

2. Janowitz, *Slaves*, p. 37.

He never does, and nor does anyone else; and this is not surprising, for as he tells you, "There's only one thing I'm interested in'. 'Me'? you say. Bruce looks startled. 'My music', he says'.[3] Though you have sex with Bruce—'he likes you to pretend to fight him off'[4]—you are never more than an adjunct to his ego, an object in his world.

Matters are slightly different for modern saint number 271. She has a 'boss', a writer, a 'double Ph.D. candidate in philosophy and American literature at the University of Massachusetts', for whom she keeps house, though not very well, fetches food and otherwise cossets; working the streets—'crouched in dark alleys, giggling in hotel rooms or the back seats of limousines'[5]—while he lies on his bed reading Kant or Heidegger, or 'dreamily eating' whatever she brings him.[6] But he is also her friend, Bob, with whom she has long and intense conversations. 'When I was near Bob, with his long graceful hands, his silky moustache, his interesting theories of life and death, I felt that for the first time in my life I had arrived at a place where I was growing intellectually as well as emotionally'.[7] On the nights when she cannot sleep, feeling herself 'adrift in a sea of seminal fluid', he softly ties up her arm and injects her with a 'little heroin', or if none is available, 'a little something else'.[8] Bob is also her pimp, though somewhat inadequate as her protector on the streets.

> Sometimes I wished Bob was more aggressive as a pimp. There were moments on the street when I felt frightened; there were a lot of terminal cases out there, and often I was in situations that could have become dangerous. Bob felt that it was important that I accept anyone who wanted me... Still, I could have used more help from him than I got. But then Bob would arrive at the hospital, bringing me flowers and pastrami on rye and I realized that for me to change pimps and choose a more aggressive one, one who would be out there hustling for me and carrying a knife, would be to embrace a lifestyle that was genuinely alien to me, despite my middle-class upbringing.[9]

We may presume that Janowitz does not intend her readers to admire and emulate the modern saint; on the contrary, we are to discern in her

3. Janowitz, *Slaves*, p. 40.
4. Janowitz, *Slaves*, p. 38.
5. Janowitz, *Slaves*, p. 6.
6. Janowitz, *Slaves*, p. 5.
7. Janowitz, *Slaves*, p. 3.
8. Janowitz, *Slaves*, p. 2.
9. Janowitz, *Slaves*, p. 3.

a distressing internalization of the slave condition; complete abjection. 'My clients', she tells us, 'had a chunk of their body they wanted to give away; for a price I was there to receive it. Crimes, sins, night-mares, hunks of hair: it was surprising how many of them had some-thing to dispose of'.[10] But it is she who gives herself away, handing herself over to anyone who wants her, who needs her; dispossessing herself, so that 'now at night, cruising the great long avenues of the city, dust and grit tossed feverishly in the massive canyons between the skyscrapers, it often occurs to me that I am no more and no less'.[11] But above all she hands herself over to Bob, to his fantasizing of her as 'madonna and whore'.[12]

> I could have written a book about my experiences out on the street, but all my thoughts are handed over to Bob, who lies on the bed dreamily eating whatever I bring him—a hamburger from McDonald's, crab soufflé from a French restaurant in the theater district, a platter of rumaki with hot peanut sauce in an easy carry-out container from an Indonesian restaurant open until 1.00 a.m., plates of macaroni tender and creamy as the sauce that oozes out from between the legs of my clientele.[13]

This modern saint, refusing no one who wants her, thinks of herself as 'like a social worker for lepers',[14] or like a nun in the convents she used to read about as a child. Since 'there are no convents for Jewish girls', she has created her own in the cloisters of New York, in the canyons between the skyscrapers, in the back seats of limousines; places of holy devotion, where the poor are tended, their bodies caressed and pleasured. Afterwards she returns to Bob, her confessor, who dreamily consumes the stories of her abasement along with his hamburger or soufflé.

But the modern saint's devotions are not pure, since she exacts a price for her body. She does not give herself away for nothing: dollars are exchanged for flesh. This modern saint makes money in order to buy the things that money can buy. 'Even saints have human flaws'.[15] She does not give her body as a pure gift, without recompense or return. Yet it is her willingness to give herself away, to make her body

10. Janowitz, *Slaves*, p. 2.
11. Janowitz, *Slaves*, p. 5.
12. Janowitz, *Slaves*, p. 3.
13. Janowitz, *Slaves*, pp. 5-6.
14. Janowitz, *Slaves*, p. 2.
15. Janowitz, *Slaves*, p. 3.

available for the want of others, that permits the conceit of saintliness. Christians may recoil from this idea of saintly prostitution—this prodigality of the body—yet is this not the very practice that St Paul enjoined upon those Corinthians who burned for want of sexual gratification?[16]

Bodily Dispossession

St Paul advised the Corinthians that while lack of sexual congress is a good, its want should not lead to fornication, and therefore every man should have a wife and every woman a husband.

> Let the husband render unto the wife due benevolence: and likewise also the wife unto the husband. The wife hath not power of her own body, but the husband: and likewise also the husband hath not power of his own body, but the wife (1 Cor. 7.3-4).

Husband and wife are to be as slaves to one another, each giving away his or her body to the other, for his or her use, each ready to receive what the other gives and to give what the other wants. This dispossession of one's body includes giving up, at least for a time and by consent, one's claim on the body of the other, in order to give oneself to 'fasting and prayer', before coming together again in order to avoid 'incontinency' (1 Cor.7.5). Such radical dispossession is possible for husband and wife because in Christ they already stand within a yet more radical relation of dispossession. They are already the recipients of a body totally given away, given over to the satisfaction of their want, their lack and desire; a body that will receive anything they give it, and accept anyone who wants it. This is the body of Christ.

In 1 Cor. 7.3-4 Paul does not describe husband and wife as each other's 'slave', but in the context of the chapter and the letter, it is a warranted interpretation. It is quite likely that the Corinthian disputes in which Paul intervened were influenced by Stoic and Cynic teachings on marriage, and that in 7.3-4 Paul advocates a moderate Stoicism that sees marriage as the mutual sharing of power over the body of one's spouse, as against a stricter Cynicism that advocated celibacy and sexual renunciation within marriage ('It is well for a man not to touch a woman'—1 Cor. 7.1). Marriage as slavery was a common enough

---

16. For a brief overview of Paul and his anxious—'even alarmist'—teaching on the body and its sex, in particular in 1 Cor. 7, see Peter Brown, *The Body and Society: Men, Women and Sexual Renunciation in Early Christianity* (London: Faber & Faber, 1989 [1988]), pp. 44-57.

conceit in philosophical discourses of the time, not least in Stoic and Cynic teachings, and this may have led some Corinthians to understand marriage between a Christian and an unbeliever as the latter's enslavement of the former; which Paul denies in 7.15—'in such a case the brother or sister is not bound'. However, Paul does not so much deny as subvert the Stoic-Cynic construal of marriage as slavery. In 7.17-24 he insists that one's material circumstances do not affect one's relationship to Christ, who spiritually frees the slave and enslaves the free. Thus here I am proposing to fold Paul's notion of enslavement to Christ (7.22)—which again is arguably influenced by Stoic teaching—back onto his idea of marriage as mutual 'ownership' (7.3-4), while stressing the dispossession—the real freedom born of spiritual enslavement—that such 'ownership' requires if it is to be indeed mutual and non-coercive: the paradoxical disowning of one's ownership.[17]

Husband and wife are able to give themselves to one another, to be one another's sex slave, because they are already the slaves of Christ—'bought with a price' (1 Cor. 6.20, 7.23)—and thus no longer the slaves of this world. For Paul—as for most of the Christian tradition—one is never the owner of oneself, but always the slave of other powers. It is really only with the project of Enlightenment—and subsequent modernity—that Christians have been tempted to suppose autonomy a possibility for themselves. For Paul there is no real possibility of freedom from slavery; rather it is a matter of becoming the slave of that master whose service *is* freedom. In Christian marriage, as Paul imagines it, husband and wife are completely the slaves of Christ, in body and spirit, to be trained in the practice of dispossession, which is the very price by which they have been purchased. They own one another only to the extent that they are owned by a third, whose ownership constitutes the relationship of dispossession between them. They

17. For the historical background to this rhetorico-theological interpretation see Will Deming, *Paul on Marriage and Celibacy: The Hellenistic Background of 1 Corinthians 7* (Society for New Testament Studies Monograph Series, 83; Cambridge: Cambridge University Press, 1995), pp. 108-73. The metaphor of 'slavery', while deployed in church and theology at a symbolic, imaginary or phantasmatic level, nevertheless raises the question of actual slavery, and the rectitude of 'playing' at it when many people had (and have) no choice about doing so. See further I.A.H. Combes, *The Metaphor of Slavery in the Writings of the Early Church: From the New Testament to the Beginning of the Fifth Century* (*Journal for the Study of the New Testament*, Supplement Series, 156; Sheffield: Sheffield Academic Press, 1998).

become the slaves of a slave, and must act as he does; giving themselves away in the way that he disposes of himself.

> Know ye not that your body is the temple of the Holy Ghost which is in you, which ye have of God, and ye are not your own? For ye are bought with a price: therefore glorify God in your body, and in your spirit, which are God's (1 Cor. 6.19-20).

Thus Paul, at his most radical, imagines marriage as a partnership between sex slaves, where each disposes of his or her body for the use of the other, in imitation of their mutual master, who is the slave of all: a body entirely dispossessed for the want of the other. Thus the modern saint of Tama Janowitz's story is already performing, however imperfectly, the Pauline ideal; imperfectly because her body is purchased for a price which is not that of a reciprocal dispossession. Her sexual relationships are not married ones in the Pauline sense, but fornicatory. However, this observation does not so much call into question her saintliness as invite the suggestion that her sex slavery opens unto the possibility of a yet more radical invention of 'marriage' than Paul ostensibly envisaged. But before elaborating that suggestion I want to consider a problem raised earlier, namely that Janowitz's modern saint is not proffered for admiration but rejection, as a satiric example of women's subjugation to male want in modern society. Thus the condition of the modern saint is precisely that which is to be overcome; which is also the project envisaged by several feminist critiques of the Pauline conceptuality.

After Slavery

Elizabeth Stuart has questioned the idea that Paul understood Christian marriage as a relationship of 'mutuality between husband and wife', and has done so by drawing attention to the use of slavery in his theology. She argues that in the Pauline texts marriage is understood as an asymmetric slave relationship, in which the wife is always subordinate to the husband, notwithstanding that Paul imagines an equal reciprocity between the two partners.

> In Paul the language of mutual authority obscures notions of ownership in which the wife will always be disadvantaged because of the web of power relations she has to exist in, which cannot be conveniently unspun in a marriage bed.[18]

18. Elizabeth Stuart, *Just Good Friends: Towards a Lesbian and Gay Theology*

Stuart insists that the Pauline ideal of reciprocal sex slavery precludes mutual love and respect because it involves the having of power over another, which in itself is objectionable, but which moreover can never be truly reciprocal between husband and wife in a society where men have power over women. Furthermore, as Stuart reminds her readers, women's authority over their own bodies has been 'the first and most symbolic and controversial aim of the feminist movement'.[19] Thus she concludes that the idea of reciprocal slavery is 'simply an unacceptable one to those who take the pain and struggle of women seriously'.[20]

A similar conclusion is reached by Adrian Thatcher, who, having noted the integration of marriage and slavery in the Pauline texts, argues that once the institution of slavery has been repudiated, so must the theology of marriage built upon it. 'It is inadmissible to appeal to biblical teaching on marriage while at the same time rejecting slavery since marriage and slavery are as indissolubly linked as a man and a woman are linked in marriage'.[21] There is certainly no question today of the church not repudiating slavery: the use of people as objects. But it might still be suggested that Stuart and Thatcher's criticisms of the Pauline texts pay insufficient attention to the way in which those texts start to turn or subvert the idea of slavery away from violent power toward pacific charity. If Christ's dispossession is made the model of true slavery, its repetition within a mutual relationship constitutes an economy in which power is constantly circulating, given away in order to return, and only returning because given away. But for this suggestion to be at all persuasive one must first repudiate the notions—neither of which Paul nor much of the Christian tradition would accept—that one can be the self-sufficient author of one's life, and that a contrary ideal can make no headway against a persistent social order.

Thus even if it is the case that men have power over women in society, this is not a sufficient reason for holding to an ideal that gives equal power to both men and women; though it is a power that neither

---

of Relationships (London: Mowbray, 1995), pp. 125-26. Stuart also suggests that the understanding of marriage in Hosea is one of slavery: 'the woman whom the jealous but faithful husband passionately pursues is an object to be shamed, humiliated, starved and seduced, reduced to proper passivity' (p. 125).

19. Stuart, *Just Good Friends*, p. 123.

20. Stuart, *Just Good Friends*, p. 126.

21. Adrian Thatcher, *Liberating Sex: A Christian Sexual Theology* (London: SPCK, 1993), p. 16.

possess. The church itself is constituted as the witness to the promise of a hoped for future which is the 'impossible' contrary of all known societies. Thus the ideal nature of the Pauline conception can be a problem only for those who have no such hope, and do not pray for the coming of such a future. One might therefore suggest that the practice of the ideal—as construed above—should not wait upon the reform of society, but be practised in order to hasten that reform.

The Pauline ideal contests Enlightenment notions of autonomy, of powers rightly possessed, and thus does put certain questions to women's right to author their own bodies—as also to men's control of their own and other bodies. However, the Pauline ideal does not so much deny women—or men—authority over their own bodies, as relocate that authority within the slavery of Christ, so that—again—one comes to self-possession through dispossession, to having through being had, to getting through giving. In order to see further how this may be so, I turn to Karl Barth, but in the context of another recent critique of Christianity as inadmissible slavery.

In *After Christianity* (1996), Daphne Hampson seeks to articulate what comes after the demise of Christianity and goes after Christianity in order to hasten its demise. Following Simone de Beauvoir, she argues that under patriarchy 'woman' is constructed as the other of 'man', that is as the 'slave' of the 'master'. In western societies women become slaves by internalizing an image or images of woman projected by men, and the chief means for projecting such images—and presumably internalizing them—has been and is religion: the 'over-arching framework through which men have projected their understanding of reality'.[22] Hampson discerns a threefold construction of woman as 'other' in western religion: 'woman as ideal, woman as slut, and woman as complement to the male'.[23] I shall attend to the third of these three images since it most closely resembles the Pauline concept of reciprocal slavery, and most clearly articulates Hampson's own definition of sex slavery as the systematic projection of the 'other' by the 'same'; of 'woman' by men.

For Hampson, 'woman as slave is socialized to conform' to a male construct of 'the feminine', understood as the '"complement" of the male and never *vice versa*'.[24] The feminine is constructed as that which

22. Daphne Hampson, *After Christianity* (London: SCM Press, 1996), p. 169.
23. Hampson, *After Christianity*, p. 173.
24. Hampson, *After Christianity*, p. 192.

man is not: gentle, receptive, humble, nurturing and obedient. While this image is normally projected onto women, real or imaginary, it is also applied to social groups such as the church in relation to Christ or God, and can even be applied to men. This mobility of the feminine allows men to explore what they envisage as the 'female or maternal', but their exploration does not lead them to respect women, because while the image is adulated, actual women are despised. More importantly, the male projection of the feminine denies women the possibility of developing their own subjectivity, their own image of femininity.[25] 'Woman' is made according to the imagination of men.

Hampson's critique is chiefly aimed at ideological constructions of the feminine in various Christian traditions, especially that of Catholicism, for which she appears to have a particular *animus*, not least because of the 'astonishing' extent to which 'Catholicism has distorted its symbolism…in order to construct a place for the feminine'.[26] Hampson has much less to say about the idea of complementarity itself, beyond noting some of the ways in which it 'quickly translates into giving woman an inferior position to the male'.[27] This seems to suggest the possibility of a genuine 'complementarity', which Hampson would seem to understand as a radical equality between man and woman, for she writes that the 'patriarchal imagination substitutes for woman as the equal of man, a male projection of "woman".'[28] But Hampson does not discuss the difference that is man and woman, and the relation between them, which is surely the burden of the idea of complementarity. Hampson supposes that there are significant differences between men and women,[29] and moreover that woman has her own essential identity, which needs to be set free from the 'suppression' of patriarchy.[30]

> It need not follow from the fact that there are manifestly differences [between men and women] that we should set up dualisms around gender (or anything else) which consign some members of humanity to some-

25. Hampson, *After Christianity*, pp. 192-93.

26. Hampson, *After Christianity*, p. 193. Hampson's admission that she 'grew up within Protestantism' (p. 203) may account for this curious criticism.

27. Hampson, *After Christianity*, p. 200.

28. Hampson, *After Christianity*, p. 206.

29. 'There is every indication…that women tend to be more religious or spiritually inclined than men' (Hampson, *After Christianity*, p. 205).

30. Hampson, *After Christianity*, p. 206.

thing less than the status of being a full person. It could be possible simply to allow other persons to be themselves![31]

Yet it is of course the idea of an already existing but suppressed self, an essential identity as man or woman, which has been the subject of much criticism in recent feminist theory,[32] and which much Christian anthropology would want to question. For such anthropology, the self is called into being by God in Christ, and formed through the practices of that calling. The self is not that which, already made, awaits its release from oppressive structures, but that which has to be formed, over time, through the ministry of certain practices. This is to understand the self as a project; as the disciplining of a soul.[33] The question is then what self is one to be? How is one to be man or woman in Christ? It is precisely this question that the notion of complementarity addresses by setting before us, as it were, an image of the finished product.

Gender Anxieties

Karl Barth—to take a theologian whom Hampson briefly discusses and dismisses[34]—sets before us a picture of man and woman as produced or constructed in Christ. What is of fundamental importance for Barth in his picture is the non-negotiable sexual difference of man and woman. Each one of us is either male *or* female, while at the same time being oriented to the sex we are not.

> [S]ince man has been created by God as male or female, and stands before God in this Either-Or, everything that God wills and requires of him is contained by implication in this situation, and the question of good and evil in his conduct is measured by it... We remember that the

31. Hampson, *After Christianity*, pp. 207-208.

32. See Naomi Schor and Elizabeth Weed (eds.), *The Essential Difference* (Bloomington: Indiana University Press, 1994).

33. See further Rowan D. Williams, 'Interiority and Epiphany: A Reading in New Testament Ethics', *Modern Theology* 13 (1997), pp. 29-51. The idea that the Christian self or soul is formed in and through a slave relationship, raises the question of subject/ion as addressed in Hegel, Nietzsche and Foucault. See further Judith Butler, *The Psychic Life of Power: Theories in Subjection* (Stanford: Stanford University Press, 1997). In advance of a larger project, it may be suggested that the Christian subject is produced in and through subjection to Christ, who however is always already subject to his disciple(s); and this is what it means to be born again of the Spirit.

34. Hampson, *After Christianity*, p. 195.

'male *or* female' is immediately to be completed by the 'male *and* female'. Rightly understood, the 'and' is already contained in the 'or'...For how is it possible to characterise man except in his distinctive relation to woman, or woman except in her distinctive relation to man? But just because in the being of both it is so deeply a question of being in relation to the other, of duality rather than unity, the first principle must be stated independently that, in obedience to God, man will be male or female.[35]

Of course for Barth there is a sense in which the call to be man or woman before God is a call to be what one is already and always, a call to realize an underlying and essential self. But for Barth this self is not known other than in our response to the call of God to become what we are already; the self is realized only through a process of becoming. Barth rejects 'every phenomenology or typology of the sexes', and indeed pours scorn on ideas of the feminine such as are to be found—as Hampson argues—in Protestant as well as Catholic Christianity.[36] Furthermore, Barth—writing in the late 1940s and early 50s—is aware that women are increasingly seeking to determine their own identities.

The question what specific activity woman will claim and make her own as woman ought certainly to be posed in each particular case as it arises, not in the light of traditional preconceptions, but honestly in relation to what is aimed at in the future. Above all, woman herself ought not to allow the uncalled-for illusions of man, and his attempts to dictate what is suitable for her and what is not, to deter her from continually and seriously putting this question to herself.[37]

Barth insists that however woman constructs her own identity, she 'must always and in all circumstances be woman;...she must feel and conduct herself as such and not as man;...the command of the Lord, which is for all eternity, directs both man and woman to their own proper sacred place and forbids all attempts to violate this order'.[38] Yet

35. Karl Barth, *Church Dogmatics*, III/4 (trans. A.T. Mackay *et al.*; Edinburgh: T. & T. Clark, 1961), p. 149.

36. Barth, *Church Dogmatics*, III/4, pp. 152-53.

37. Barth, *Church Dogmatics*, III/4, p. 155. Barth praises Simone de Beauvoir's *Le deuxième sexe* (1949), noting that 'the description of the way in which man has made and still makes himself master of woman, the presentation of the myth with which he invests her in this process and for this purpose, and the unmasking of this myth, are all worthy of attention especially on the part of men and not least of Christian theologians' (*Church Dogmatics* III/4, p. 162).

38. Barth, *Church Dogmatics*, III/4, p. 156.

this concern, which Barth might be thought to share with some femi-nists such as Luce Irigaray, betrays a certain anxiety regarding an implicit typology of the sexes. He wonders if Schleiermacher, as a male, should have 'defined religion as the feeling of sheer dependence', and wonders even more about Schleiermacher's 'impossible wish' to have been born a woman.[39] Whatever man and woman are to become under God, they are not to deny or seek to overcome their fundamental difference from one another as male and female.

> That God created man as male and female, and therefore as His image and the likeness of the covenant of grace, of the relationship between Himself and His people, between Christ and His community, is some-thing which can never lead to a neutral It, nor found a purely external, incidental and transient sexuality, but rather an inward, essential and lasting order of being as He and She, valid for all time and also for eternity.[40]

Thus while Barth allows for variability and new possibilities in the meaning of masculine and feminine—such that what it means to be a man or woman in society is always to be determined anew by each individual man or woman—he nevertheless insists on an underlying stability of sexual identity and orientation. 'All the other conditions of masculine and feminine being may be disputable, but it is invio-lable...that man is directed to woman and woman to man'.[41] For Barth, man and woman are mutually constituting of one another, and this 'complementarity' (though it is not a term Barth uses) replaces all other typologies of the sexes.[42] But Barth is unable to maintain the distinction

---

39. Barth, *Church Dogmatics*, III/4, p. 155. 'What are we to think when in the year 1804 we find him writing to a woman friend: "Women are more fortunate than we in that their business affairs take up only a part of their thoughts while the long-ing of the heart, the beautiful inward life of the imagination, always dominates the greater part... Wherever I look, it always seems to me that the nature of women is nobler and their life happier, and if ever I toy with an impossible wish, it is to be a woman"'. It may be suggested that Barth's anxiety concerning Schleiermacher's masculinity betrays a deeper cultural anxiety which is, according to Mark Breiten-berg, constituted by and constitutive of western patriarchal society. See Mark Breitenberg, *Anxious Masculinity in Early Modern England* (Cambridge Studies in Renaissance Literature and Culture, 10; Cambridge: Cambridge University Press, 1996).

40. Barth, *Church Dogmatics*, III/4, p. 158.

41. Barth, *Church Dogmatics*, III/4, p. 163.

42. Barth, *Church Dogmatics*, III/4, p. 164.

between inviolable sexualities and otherwise disputable conditions of 'masculine and feminine being'. Most obviously, the rigid polarity of male and female precludes homosexuality as a possible condition of masculine and feminine existence. It is rather the 'physical, psychological and social sickness, the phenomenon of perversion, decadence and decay', which emerges when God's fundamental ordinance is refused. While Barth allows that homosexuality, in its early stages, 'may have an appearance of particular beauty and spirituality, and even be redolent of sanctity', he nevertheless insists that it is—as St Paul suggests (Rom. 1.25)—a form of idolatry, in which the person—man or woman— thinks that he or she alone constitutes true humanity, having no need of the other sex, who is thus despised. The homosexual fails to recognize that 'as a man he can only be genuinely human with woman, or as a woman with man'.[43] The argument is of course no argument at all, but a mere prejudice, and unacceptable to those Christian traditions that value segregated sororal and fraternal communities, the formation of which Barth describes as 'obviously disobedience' and incipiently homosexual.[44]

It may be suggested that Barth's argument arises from his thinking through of Paul's remark about idolatry in relation to Barth's own— though unacknowledged and culturally constructed—fear of homosexuality, not least for the threat that it poses to Barth's insistent anxiety concerning sexual boundaries, such that Schleiermacher's theology— which both fascinated and repelled Barth—might be thought a symptom of Schleiermacher's wish to be a woman. That disputable genderings of male and females bodies are not disavowed but everywhere present in Barth's thought is even more obvious when he turns to consider the 'order' of man to woman. Here everything that Hampson and others have said about complementarity is confirmed.

Man and woman are equal but not equivalent: man comes first and woman second, subordinate to the superordinate male.[45] 'Properly speaking, the business of woman, her task and function, is to actualise the fellowship in which man can only precede her, stimulating, leading and inspiring.'[46] And when the man fails to act as he ought, it is no business of the woman to do likewise. For if 'there is a way of bringing

43. Barth, *Church Dogmatics*, III/4, p. 166.
44. Barth, *Church Dogmatics*, III/4, pp. 165-66.
45. Barth, *Church Dogmatics*, III/4, p. 169.
46. Barth, *Church Dogmatics*, III/4, p. 171.

man to repentance, it is the way of the woman who refuses to let herself be corrupted and made disobedient by his disobedience, but who in spite of his disobedience maintains her place in the order all the more firmly'.[47] It is a matter of keeping 'order', and, for the obedient man, of being 'strong'. 'He is strong to the extent that he accepts as his own affair service to this order and in this order. He is strong as he is vigilant for the interests of both sexes.' Woman, on the other hand, is to be 'mature', that is 'to take up the position which falls to her in accordance with this order, desiring nothing better than that this order should be in force'.[48]

While Barth opened the possibility of rethinking woman in theology—and thus man also, and moreover of women rethinking woman— he himself was unable to resist the culture of his day, which, more grievously, he presented as the minimal command of God, the 'order' that must be kept irrespective of what individual men and women hear as God's address to them. This 'order' is pernicious, as Hampson and others allege. Not only must women conform to the command of God and man, but if man fails in his obedience, woman's only redress is to be yet more obedient to her calling, namely obedient to the disobedient man; whereas if she fails, the man must chastise her for it. But it is not for this that we should read Barth today, which only confirms Hampson's critique of Christianity, but rather for what Hampson neglects, namely Barth's prior insistence that the address of God is a word of freedom to us, which calls into question the norms, orders and frameworks, the phenomenologies and typologies, that our cultures would impose on us. If Barth's own attempt to delineate this freeing of our bodies merely reproduced a cultural order that we must now disdain, he nevertheless first maintained the power of the Word to open for us a space in which our bodily relations can be remade as tangible, fleshly promises of God's beatitude. For Barth—after Paul—this freedom is possible only as a certain form of obedience, a certain kind of slavery.[49] Thus in the last part of this essay I want to consider a

47. Barth, *Church Dogmatics*, III/4, p. 172.
48. Barth, *Church Dogmatics*, III/4, p. 177.
49. 'Barth presupposes that there is initially not-much-to-speak-of in the creature—all is owed to the positing work of the Holy Spirit. The creature becomes interesting as a subject only when he or she stands under the divine call or injunction and responds appropriately. But from this initial restriction of what we might think of as creaturely entitlements or faculties, there opens up a great domain of

different conception of complementarity, one more suited—I suggest—
to Barth's space of obediential freedom than Barth's own, one that
takes further the idea of mutual sex slavery in Christ. Needless to say, it
is as much a cultural product as Barth's own rendering of God's sexual
order, but unlike Barth, it seeks to acknowledge the always unstable
and culturally contingent meaning of such an order, of 'man' and
'woman', 'masculine' and 'feminine', and to locate this contingency as
a final undecidability in the bodily relationship of gifted dispossession
that Christ makes possible, as disclosed in the Pauline text.

Undecidable Bodies

The Slovenian philosopher, Slavoj Zizek, has ventured an understanding of complementarity based on his reading of quantum mechanics,
and in particular of Heisenberg's 'uncertainty principle'. On certain
readings of the principle, one cannot measure the mass *and* momentum
of a particle simultaneously: one can measure only one or the other. It is
a case of epistemological uncertainty. Zizek, however, insists on a
'stronger' reading of the principle, which accords an ontological status
to the uncertainty of the particle's mass and momentum: it has mass *or*
momentum, but not both. Thus uncertainty is a fundamental property of
the particle itself, and this ontological uncertainty constitutes a form of
oppositional complementarity: 'two complementary properties do not
complement each other, they are mutually exclusive'.[50] This form of
complementarity is like those pictures which can be seen in one of two
ways—either as a vase or as two faces, either as a duck or as a rabbit—
but which cannot be read in both ways at the same time. Both images
are as it were present, but at any one time only one can be realized;
mass and momentum are potentially mutual, but actually exclusive in
the particle.

Zizek suggests that the counterpart to quantum complementarity in
the human condition is a 'situation in which the subject is forced to

freedom in Christ—life in a dynamic and open space (which is how he envisages
the church)'. Ben Quash, 'Von Balthasar and the Dialogue with Karl Barth', *New
Blackfriars* 79 (1998), pp. 45-55 (52). On Barth's obediential freedom more generally see Nigel Biggar, *The Hastening That Waits: Karl Barth's Ethics* (Oxford:
Clarendon Press, 1993).

50. Slavoj Zizek, *The Indivisible Remainder: An Essay on Schelling and
Related Matters* (London: Verso, 1996), p. 211.

choose and to accept a certain fundamental loss or impossibility'.[51] Thus, for example, a person who would be virtuous in certain ways—who would be forgetful of self and give without thought of return—must not so consciously seek, otherwise he or she will remember him or herself and receive a restitution in the knowledge of his or her generosity. A true gift or act of humility is accomplished only through ignorance of its actuality. Knowledge of the act—*in* the act—is impossible: if one knows what one is doing in such an act, one doesn't so act.[52]

Another example of this logic of complementarity is the relationship between an action and knowledge of its circumstances. We think that the more we know about the circumstances, the easier it will be for us to act; but the more we know the harder it becomes. With full knowledge, action becomes impossible. We must simply act. Zizek suggests that this condition is analogous to religious belief.

> [T]he decision to believe never results from a careful weighing of *pro* and *contra*, that is, one can never say: 'I believe in Christ because, after careful consideration, I came to the conclusion that reasons for prevail'—it is only the act, the decision to believe, that renders the reasons to believe truly comprehensible.[53]

This is why, of course, the Gospels tell us stories of people who choose to follow Jesus for no reason. Another example that Zizek offers—the 'most pathetic'—is that of love: 'the decision to love somebody is free (compulsory love is no love), yet this decision can never be a present and conscious one (I can never say to myself: 'Now I will decide to fall in love with this person...')—all I can do in the present is to ascertain that *the decision has already been taken* and that I am caught in the inexorable necessity of love'.[54] In order to act there is always something we must either not know or forget, and forget that we have forgotten.

This then is what is here meant by complementarity: the condition of forgetfulness for action, the very condition that is necessary for the Pauline idea of marriage as mutual dispossession or slavery. In order to

51. Zizek, *The Indivisible Remainder*, p. 211.
52. See further Jacques Derrida, *Given Time: I Counterfeit Money* (trans. Peggy Kamuf; Chicago: University of Chicago Press, 1992); and Gerard Loughlin, *Telling God's Story: Bible, Church and Narrative Theology* (Cambridge: Cambridge University Press, 1996), pp. 226-29.
53. Zizek, *The Indivisible Remainder*, p. 212.
54. Zizek, *The Indivisible Remainder*, p. 213.

turn the idea of slavery away from one of abject compliance with the will of another, one must choose to give oneself away to the other, and to do this utterly, as a pure gift of self without thought of reciprocation. But at the same time one must not know that this is what one is doing, even as one disposes of oneself. It is in this sense that one becomes the 'complement' of another; not in the sense that one is the other half that makes a whole, understood in an entirely biologistic manner, according to a certain cultural biology,[55] but in the sense that one's body is an unknown gift to the other, given as an utter gratuity, an absolute grace, to the point that in the relationship one can no longer say who gives and who receives, or even, whose body is whose.

No doubt this reading of the Pauline text has taken us far beyond its warrant, especially if—as may be suggested—we understand 'marriage' not in terms of a preceding legality, but precisely in terms of an undecidable complementarity, of that mutual sex slavery that I have read in the Pauline text. On such an account, real marriages may well exist in other than legally constituted unions, and such unions be not the confirmation but the undertaking of such slavery. Furthermore, it may be suggested—following moves not argued here, but attempted elsewhere[56]—that within the Christian symbolic, as already in Paul, the mapping of gender relations onto actual bodies is always contingent or pragmatic, so that the relation of 'husband' to 'wife' is applicable not only to heterosexual couples, but to all those bodies in Christ who seek to exercise their sexuality in the order of the gift.[57]

There is, however, another way in which I have perhaps exceeded the text, and contradicted the Zizeckian notion of complementarity. This is the way in which I have too easily spoken of the slave-body-become-

55. For an account tracing the working of such a cultural biology in the theology of Hans Urs von Balthasar see Gerard Loughlin, 'Sexing the Trinity', *New Blackfriars* 79 (1998), pp. 18-25.

56. See Gerard Loughlin, 'Baptismal Fluid', *Scottish Journal of Theology* 51.3 (1998), pp. 261-70.

57. Indeed it may be suggested that once the church imagined its relation to Christ as that of a bride to her groom, the church had—if only phantasmatically and only for men—instituted same-sex marriage. Thus the contemporary theology of same-sex unions merely seeks to actualize what has already been thought, from the first, though disavowed until now. On same-sex unions see the following articles by David McCarthy Matzko, 'Homosexuality and the Practices of Marriage', *Modern Theology* 13 (1997), pp. 371-97; and 'The Relationship of Bodies: A Nuptial Hermeneutics of Same Sex Unions', *Theology and Sexuality* 8 (1998), pp. 96-112.

gift as a realizable possibility. Does not the very fact of mutuality in the married relationship preclude the possibility of the pure gift of the body? Even as I give myself to the other, do I not know that I receive his body in return? Even if I forget—a forgetting that must surely seem impossible—that I am giving myself to the other, how can I forget that he is giving himself to me in return for myself to him? Thus we might think that it is only outside of marriage as mutual sex slavery that there can be true slavery in the sense of absolute gift; and thus it is only somebody like Tama Janowitz's modern saint who approaches the condition of true bodily dispossession. Admittedly, Janowitz's modern saint is a prostitute: she gives her body not gratuitously, as a grace poured out, but in return for money. Thus we might think that it is only the person who gives his body away without any thought of return, who simply makes his body available for the pleasure of others, who most truly achieves saintly slavery: a profitless prostitute.

In a sense it is such a person that Paul already invites us to imagine, since his married couples are not only mutual sex slaves, but enjoined to copulate without desire for each other's flesh.[58] Paul urges celibacy, but allows sex in marriage for the weak; but married sex is disciplined sex. It is sex without want, for marriage puts out the flames of desire. It was a commonplace of Greco-Roman culture that sexual desire was a kind of burning that heated the flesh. While such warmth was good for the body, too much was dangerous, and medical opinion warned against excessive passion, which it conceived as illness. Paul seems to have followed medical opinion in this regard, if for different reasons; but his cure would have perplexed contemporary physicians as it offends today, because for Paul 'it is better to marry than to burn' (1 Cor. 7.9). Marriage is not just an appropriate context for sexual desire, it is its remedy. This view would have seemed preposterous to many in the ancient world, since a certain amount of heat, of burning desire, was necessary for procreation; but procreation was not one of Paul's concerns. His concern was to eliminate fornication, which polluted the Christian body, individual and social, and which resulted from sexual desire. Marriage eliminates both.

> For this is the will of God, even your sanctification, that ye should abstain from fornication: that every one of you should know how to pos-

---

58. For the following argument see Dale B. Martin, *The Corinthian Body* (New Haven: Yale University Press, 1995), pp. 198-228.

sess his vessel in sanctification and honour; not in the lust of concupiscence [the passion of desire], even as the Gentiles which know not God (1 Thess. 4.3-5).

If Paul's thought now seems bizarre, it did so also in his own day, when desire was considered the motive for sex, and marriage its constraint and discipline, rather than its extermination. Yet, as Dale B. Martin has argued, this seems to be Paul's view, that sex in marriage is a prophylaxis against desire.[59] The idea of sex without desire was not unique to Paul, but upheld as an ideal by later Christians such as Clement of Alexandria and Augustine of Hippo, who pictured paradisal sex—the kind of copulation that Adam and Eve might have enjoyed in Eden if they had not first eaten the fruit—as passionless sex, the flesh aroused by the will rather than by lust.[60] But this passionless, lustless sex, is not only paradisal, it is prostituted sex, undertaken not from sexual desire, but as an act of the will. Just as Augustine pictures the unfallen Adam, so the prostitute, or the porn star, 'without feeling the allurement of passion goading him on', wills his flesh to perform, 'in tranquillity of mind and with no impairment of his body's integrity'.[61]

The idea of sex without desire, copulation without passion, is so strange that Dale B. Martin, who strenuously advocates this reading of Paul, suggests that Paul must nevertheless have had some concept of sexual motivation in order to explain why people had sex at all. Martin suggests that this may be an occasion when 'modern categories' fail us, and 'we need to invent or appropriate some other term to convey this necessary urge for sex without invoking Paul's rejected category of desire'. However, the best Martin can suggest is 'inclination'.[62] In Christian marriage there is to be no sexual desire, only the operation of sexual inclination. But this, as Martin acknowledges, leaves Paul's

59. Martin, *Corinthian Body*, p. 217.
60. Martin, *Corinthian Body*, p. 215.
61. Augustine, *The City of God* 14.26. For an illustration of the Augustinian ideal—the ever obedient penis—see the performance of Dirk Diggler's (Mark Wahlberg) member in Paul Thomas Anderson's film *Boogie Nights* (USA 1997). Augustine imagines paradisal or edenic sex as purely instrumental, which is to say, as *perverse* sex, since it is precisely such sex—practised in pornography, prostitution and Pauline marriage—that the Law prohibits. The story of the Fall is then a phantasmatic narrative that institutes passionless instrumental sex (procreative/ recreative/cultic) as that which is lost and subsequently forbidden. See Slavoj Zizek, *The Plague of Fantasies* (London: Verso, 1997), pp. 13-16.
62. Martin, *Corinthian Body*, p. 216.

otherwise unnamed category almost incomprehensible. In line with the reading so far advanced of 1 Cor. 7.3-4, we may better think not so much of inclination, as of inoculation. Against the temptation of the prostitute's body, union with which pollutes the body of Christ (1 Cor. 6.15-16), Paul advocates a form of prostituted sex within the Christic body, as the poison that cures. If one allows that the prostitute, in his or her professional capacity, has sex without desire, then the Christian couple who have sexual intercourse without passion, copulate as prostitutes. They give themselves to one another not in order to fulfil their own want, but to satisfy the need of the other, thereby practising a desire for the other which is not born of any lack, but in imitation of that charitable excess which is God's alone; a giving to the other, for the other, without thought of return, other than to receive back again what was first given, in order to give again. And of course the giving of the body is an almost perfect analogue for this grace of God, since just as God's gift never leaves her hand—God is the gift of God—so the giver of the body is one with the body given.

It is in the married relationship—understood as a relationship of mutual sex slavery—that one receives, as a gift, the possibility of giving oneself; just as in giving oneself in the relationship one bestows the gift of giving to the other. It is in dispossessing oneself of one's body that one makes it possible for the other to approach, to dispossess himself, knowing that what he receives in return is in part the ability of such dispossession. The giving of oneself is itself a gift that one receives in the very act of so giving, just as in giving, the other receives the gift they return to you, and so on, infinitely. And because this gift of self is possible only as it is received, it is never purely in one's gift, but rather a movement that always precedes one, in which one is caught and moved, always already underway. It is like a current in the sea that moves the swimmer's body even before she recognizes that her motion is not the result of her strokes, of her arms embracing the swell of the sea, but of the sea embracing her. Thus we may think Paul's married prostitution a radical instant of the logic of complementarity in Zizek's sense: the impossibility of fully knowing what one is doing in the act of doing it. Is one giving *or* receiving? Is one giving *and* receiving? Is one 'man' *or* 'woman', or 'man' *and* 'woman'?

HAS FEMINIST THEOLOGY A VIABLE LONG-TERM FUTURE?

Ruth Page

Where is feminist theology going? Has it a future? There will no doubt continue to be the unearthing of the hidden women of history, but will a distinctive theology continue? I mean here Christian feminist theology, concerned with God in creation and reconciliation, as opposed to many versions of Goddess theology or thealogy, which, I would argue, is a separate issue. To make an analogy; biologists consider that a new species has arrived when it can no longer mate with what it came from. Much goddess writing, such as Starhawk's *The Spiral Dance*, with its animism, seems to be beyond mating with the traditional theological agenda, and is not my concern here.[1] It might be possible to argue that Rosemary Ruether, in *Gaia and God*, approaches at least an intermediate species,[2] but again I am concerned only with theology that wishes to be clearly both feminist and Christian.

Such theology has inherited patriarchal expressions of the Christian faith which it aims at overturning. Yet I wish to propose that the ultimate aim of feminist theology is to work towards its own demise as a distinct discipline. The final desirable state of affairs is one in which there is no need of feminist theology because its insights and emphases have been incorporated into the way theology is done; at least by a significant number of theologians of both genders. The pattern I have in mind to describe the process is Hegel's progression of thesis, antithesis and synthesis.

The thesis is the status quo. Marx applied the notion to historical situations and we could say that the thesis in this case is the historical situation of male power to define, to make priorities and order in its

1. Starhawk, *The Spiral Dance: A Rebirth of the Ancient Religion of the Great Goddess* (San Francisco: Harper & Row, 1979).
2. Rosemary Radford Ruether, *Gaia and God: An Eco-Feminist Theology of Earth Healing* (London: SCM Press, 1992).

own image in church and theology. But, Hegel and Marx argued, any status quo will have aspects that are intolerable to some, so it will itself give rise to its own opposition, the antithesis, when enough alternative power has developed to oppose the thesis. At present most feminist theology is in the antithesis mode, insisting on its own distinctive character and exploring the implications of its own perspective. But the third moment in Hegel's scheme is the synthesis, which is an *Aufhebung*, a transcendence of the other two, retaining the best from the two earlier stages, or at least, and more realistically, what is capable of survival from the first moments.

I am not championing Hegel's as the only, or even the best, view of the historical process. It is far too schematic for that, and probably, from a postmodern view, too crude. Yet it does have the virtue of seeing history in terms of a progression, and there are a number of places where the pattern fits, or is suggestive. I propose that one of these is the emergence, existence and projected demise of feminist theology.

I recognize that here I am also making a defence of the position I have taken up myself. I came naturally to the synthesis out of my particular history. I became interested in theology only some years after women were ordained in my church, and while I have shared in the putdown of the sex as a whole I have not had the struggle some women have known. It may be, then, that my experience is more like that of women in the future who do not have to fight for recognition. I would say that writing theology elicits all I have to give, and there is more to me than being a woman. In fact the writing of this paper was triggered by some feminist environmental theology whose major concern remained the status of women and not the state of non-human nature. It is one of the characteristics of the antithesis that it creates blinkers.

I have never called myself a feminist theologian, and I have been angry when my books have been reviewed as if I were—on the presumption that a book of theology written by a woman must be feminist. This is a new brand of domination, not willed by feminists, and probably the result of an overly neat desire for categorization, which reads in terms of the presumed category, and not in terms of the actual writer. It does tend to happen that as feminist theology becomes something like the norm for what women theologians write, the rest of us are either ignored or assimilated to the norm by some male theologians.

Yet I am a woman, and there are certainly moments when I am making what appears to be a feminist point in my books. Most recently, for instance, I have argued that 'acts of God' have been construed along not merely male, but positively virile, lines; where God descends to sort things out, like a sheriff in a run-down frontier town. Against that model of divine activity I want to argue that the making and maintaining of relationships is as much an action as anything with more panache, and is attributable to God.[3] Most women would instinctively agree—but so would many men, and this crossover of response between women and men is another reason for moving on to the synthesis as the transcendence of our separate positions. It is quite possible to envision an account of God's action in relating coming from a theology written by a man.

Women are supposed to be particularly good at discerning what is going on in a relationship, and working to maintain it. My own experience and observation would certainly bear that out. But increasingly, in student seminars and in life generally, I find men are more aware of the importance of relationships. of what makes for a good relationship, and so on. They can hardly be denied this advance because this is 'women's ground', for that would deny the interconnectedness women describe as the ideal. So women who write as if 'relationship' were the preserve of women alone are both being overtaken by events, and are denying the very matter they hold most important. It may seem that surrendering a monopoly on understanding relationships, and their outcomes in theology, diminishes the ground staked out for feminist theology. But I would argue that it is a succes story when feminist theology is no longer needed to insist on such matters. And to the extent that relationship still is not valued by men, it is more important that they should come to value it than that women should congratulate themselves on its possession.

Certainly the position of the antithesis was required historically to make coherent and audible the opposition in theology to the status quo. A critical mass was needed since individual voices tend to be submerged. Power games are, regrettably, required if one is to be heard. There are indeed still reasons for maintaining the antithesis at the present in everything from the glass ceiling for women academics or the denial of ordination in some churches, to the continued appearance of unreconstructed theology. But the difference I am proposing would lie in perceiving the antithesis as, in Hegelian terms, a moment, part of a

3. Ruth Page, *God and the Web of Creation* (London: SCM Press, 1996).

process that leads somewhere and does not end at the establishment of feminist theology. I recognize that for those who have made, or wish to make, their reputations as feminist theologians that may be a difficult vision. But if female investment in a certain perspective that comforts us leads to resistance to change, then we are no better than our brothers.

Another objection to this vision for feminist theology to work for its own ending in an enlarged theology, could be that it resembles too much a servant's role—serving the good of theology as a whole—rather than the specialized good of women and their theologians. And women have always been too easily relegated to servant status. Would this not confirm men in their suspicions of female inadequacy? Can it be imagined that men would work towards the ending of their own theologies? (Yet on the contrary, one could say that even if they do not, that is not an adequate reason for women not to. We do not have to take any of our patterns of being from past male practice).

But I would argue that all liberation theologies are in a category of their own in this matter. There is a real sense in which liberation theologies of all kinds—including feminist theology, in so far as it is also one of liberation—who want real emancipation, will envisage a state of affairs where they are no longer needed as the voice of the oppressed group, and where the oppressors themselves are liberated. There is a limited precedent here in the theology of South Africa. There the theology of struggle was itself an antithesis to the theology of apartheid. And in many ways the struggle is not yet over: the move from one Hegelian moment to another is not a clean break but something more like the removal of a monopoly. But now in South Africa people are working at a theology of reconstruction, though it was not until the elections of 1996 were in view that people even began to envisage such a shift of paradigm. But we can already envisage a theology inclusive of male and female insights, so reconstruction is already a possibility for us.

To believe this is to believe that people and their theology can change. I think Daphne Hampson, for instance, makes out her case against Christian theology from the point of view that it cannot change, and that any move away from the patriarchal past will be a move away from Christianity. But that, I believe, is more convenient for her critique than an accurate account of all theology. Certainly it is in many ways a highly traditional subject, but it does have a history of response to changed conditions or ways of thinking, and it does have to address current situations. Perhaps one could say that there is an enduring theological agenda, but the way of working with it changes, and if theology can change to accommodate feminist thinking it can change to accommodate the coming together of male and female perspectives.

Finally then, when I say that feminist theology should be working towards its own demise, I mean that it should express a consciousness of its own interim nature, and of the pressures which keep it in the antithesis while a synthesis would be preferable. At the same time more women should be writing more general theology, so that that comes to be expected. They will remain the women they are in the process. Women are various and men are various; where we agree or disagree cannot be contained on simplified gender lines, and each person is, in any case, more than a woman or a man. And if the aim of a liberation theology is to free not only the oppressed but also the oppressors, then women will bring that about better by working with men where possible than by working against them.

FEMINIST THEOLOGY—OUT OF THE GHETTO?

Linda Woodhead

As the essays in this volume reveal, feminist theology is at a crucial point in its development. Whilst its roots stretch back to the nineteenth century, it is only since the 1970s that feminist theology has flourished, found a place in the academy, and produced a body of literature so sizeable that it can be treated as a discipline it its own right. Yet it would be premature to conclude that feminist theology has reached maturity; erroneous to assume that its methods, tasks and boundaries and now clearly set; and mistaken to imagine that it should now settle to the comfortable task of consolidation. On the contrary, feminist theology now stands at a cross-roads, faced with choices of the most far-reaching consequence for its future shape. My argument in what follows is that the most significant of these choices concerns feminist theology's willingness to move more decisively into dialogue with the Christian tradition, with other disciplines and audiences, and to free itself from an isolation that threatens its future.

Before developing this argument, I need to make two important clarifications. First, in speaking of feminist theology as isolated and ghetto-bound, I do not necessarily imply a criticism. Existence within the ghetto is rarely a simple matter of choice, but is forced upon those who need a space in which to flourish in the face of threatening and hegemonic forces. The analogy is immediately applicable to a feminist theology struggling to carve a space for itself in the world of mainstream academic theology in the 1970s and 1980s. Ignored, marginalized or ridiculed by many 'malestream' theologians, feminist theology seems to have been left with little choice but to carve out a protected space in order to survive. Today, however, I will suggest that this situation is changing and needs to change as the power balance between feminist theology and other disciplines also begins to shift.

Secondly, I should make it clear that I do not assume that feminist theology is a unified and homogenous discipline whose spokespersons all think the same way, adopt the same methodologies and reach the same conclusions. Indeed, a central purpose of the argument that follows is to distinguish between 'Feminist Theology' in a narrower sense and 'feminist theology' in a broader sense (using upper or lower case to make the distinction clear). By the former I intend that enterprise which attempts to speak of God and the world in relation to God in a way which is true to women's experience, and which exists in critical relationship with the older discipline of Christian theology.[1] It is this enterprise of Feminist Theology that I shall accuse of being most dangerously isolated. By contrast, I find in feminist theology in the broader sense evidence for the move outside the ghetto, which I commend. In this broader sense, I understand feminist theology to encompass all those scholarly enterprises that are centrally concerned with the topics of both gender and religion (particularly the Christian religion), and which are engaged with a number of other disciplines in both the humanities and social sciences.

Feminist Theology and Mainstream Theology

Nowhere is the isolation of Feminist Theology seen more clearly than in its relation to mainstream academic theology. Though rarely remarked upon, the lack of constructive engagement between these closely related disciplines is striking. It is plainest, perhaps, on the side of mainstream theology, where a lack of interest in feminism or Feminist Theology has been evident since the 1970s. With few exceptions, this lack of engagement has been clearest in the neo-orthodox tradition of theology which continues to take inspiration from Karl Barth, and which has recently been vivified by various forms of postmodern philosophy and social theory, but has also been evident in the liberal and radical wings of Christian theology.

On the other side of the equation, Feminist Theology's engagement with mainstream theology has been both more sustained and more complex. On the one hand, Feminist Theology has drawn heavily upon some elements of such theology from its very inception. Even after her

---

1. For a fuller description of such 'canonical' Feminist Theology, and for evidence of its shared assumptions and procedures, see my article 'Spiritualizing the Sacred: A Critique of Feminist Theology', *Modern Theology* 13 (1997), pp. 191-212.

break with the church and with Christianity, for example, Mary Daly continued to draw extensively on a theological heritage not only in order to criticize it, but also in order to formulate new options for women. In *Pure Lust*, for example, her dependence upon a Thomistic tradition of moral theology was powerfully apparent, as was the influence of Paul Tillich on her formulations of a spirituality fit for feminists.[2] Similarly, Rosemary Radford Ruether's enormously influential *Sexism and God-Talk* is structured around standard themes of Christian systematic theology, and draws heavily on aspects of post-war liberal and liberation theology in both its method and conclusions.[3]

How then, if Feminist Theology draws so extensively on mainstream theology, can I claim that it has become isolated from the mainstream theological tradition? My answer is that Feminist Theology's indebtedness tends to fall short of a truly constructive engagement with the tradition, since it is generally overwhelmingly critical and deconstructive. And even where Feminist Theology does owe clear debts to the tradition, these debts are generally left unacknowledged and unexplored. (To push this point a little further, I would say that, despite its important emphasis on the importance of contextualization, much feminist theology has tended to be surprisingly blind to its own cultural, intellectual and sociological situatedness.) Furthermore, when I accuse Feminist Theology of being isolated from the Christian tradition, I have in mind its lack of engagement not only with theology of the postwar period, but with theological traditions of almost two millennia. Again, whilst there are examples of critical, deconstructive engagement on the part of Feminist Theologians with, for example, Tertullian, Jerome, Augustine, Aquinas, Luther, Calvin and Barth, examples of critically constructive engagement are much rarer.

While it would be going too far to claim that Feminist Theology never engages constructively with the tradition, it would thus be hard to deny that it displays little sense of continuity or loyalty to this tradition, and generally signals a much greater willingness to attribute authority to contemporary women's experience than to that of past generations of Christians. This is understandable, of course, in the case of post-Christian Feminist Theologians like Mary Daly or Daphne Hampson

2. Mary Daly, *Pure Lust: Elemental Feminist Philosophy* (London: The Women's Press, 1984).

3. Rosemary Radford Ruether, *Sexism and God-Talk: Toward a Feminist Theology* (London: SCM Press, 1983).

who are explicit in their rejection of the tradition on feminist grounds. The isolation from the tradition seems less explicable, however, in the case of Feminist Theologians who still claim to be engaged in Christian theology, and it may be one reason (though of course not the only one) for mainstream theology's continued refusal to take Feminist Theology seriously. While for the most part I think that mainstream theology's lack of engagement with Feminist Theology is due more to culpable ignorance than palpable prejudice, I can also see that for those who seriously wish to think through the doctrine of the Trinity in the late twentieth century, or to offer a theory of the atonement, or to reflect upon the nature of the risen Christ, much Feminist Theology has little to offer. At its worst, Feminist Theology can be crudely dismissive of such topics and concerned only with the material and political conditions of contemporary women's lives, or with a vague and amorphous expressive spirituality. Whilst this may be an understandable reaction to the marginalization of women and gender in mainstream theology, it does little to address it, and is, I believe, a prime factor in the contemporary ghettoization of Feminist Theology.

Feminist Theology and other Academic Disciplines

If Feminist Theology exists in isolation from much mainstream theology, what of its relationship to other disciplines? In the academy the most obvious dialogue partners next to theology are, of course, feminism and women's studies. In many ways, however, these latter have tended to treat feminist theology in much the same way as mainstream theology: by ignoring it and failing to engage with it in either a constructive or a critical way. Feminist Theology, as Tina Beattie demonstrates so well in her essay in this collection, is the Cinderella who is not invited to the feminists' ball—and yet the Feminist Theologians seem neither to notice or care that they are excluded from the action. If anything, Feminist Theology seems to be even more isolated from secular feminism than from mainstream theology, for while some theologians have at least made nods in the direction of Feminist Theology, very few feminist theorists have even gone this far, Luce Irigaray's brief engagement with Elisabeth Schüssler Fiorenza being an isolated and much celebrated exception.[4]

4.   Luce Irigaray, 'Equal to Whom?', in *The Essential Differences* (eds. N. Schor and E. Weed; Indianapolis: Indiana University Press, 1994), pp. 63-81.

Looking at the relationship from the other side, Feminist Theology has demonstrated a rather more active engagement with feminism than vice versa. Even here, however, the engagement has been somewhat selective (again mirroring Feminist Theology's relationship with mainstream theology). Obviously, Feminist Theology owes a deep intellectual debt to feminism, and the rise of Feminist Theology from the 1970s seems to have been directly stimulated by second-wave feminism. This debt is clear in the way in which Feminist Theology has tended to employ some of the conceptuality of such early feminism, including its emphasis on the importance of liberation, its granting of authority to the private and the experiential as well as the political, and its critique of traditional religious thought and institutions as 'patriarchal'. Yet here again—as in relation to mainstream theology—Feminist Theology's indebtedness is qualified. It is qualified above all by the fact that Feminist Theology has been slow to engage with the new forms of feminism that have appeared since the 1980s, including those which question essentialist understandings of women and women's experience, which radicalize our understanding of gender by viewing it as constructed and/or performed, which highlight the role of language and power interests in these processes, and which in some instances signal a revival of interest in the sacred.

It is in this lack of engagement with more recent feminist theory I find yet another instance of Feminist Theology's isolation—along with some new and encouraging signs of a breakout from the ghetto. One notable example of the latter is Mary McClintock Fulkerson's *Changing the Subject: Women's Discourses and Feminist Theology*, a book which, while committed to the Feminist Theological enterprise, is newly aware of the danger of reliance on essentialized notions of women's experience, and of the limitations of a Feminist Theology nurtured in academic institutions and reflective only of the interests of white, middle-class academics.[5] McClintock's response is to move beyond the academy to listen to the voices of Christian women in several churches, and to construct a theology informed by their discourses rather than by a postulated 'women's experience' which is liable to be construed as much in terms of the interests of the Feminist Theologians who write about it as by the actual lives of real women.

Fulkerson's book offers a good illustration of what can be gained by

5. Mary McClintock Fulkerson, *Changing the Subject: Women's Discourses and Feminist Theology* (Minneapolis: Fortress Press, 1994).

Feminist Theology's move from an enforced isolation to a more confident dialogue with other disciplines. Fulkerson learns not only from feminism and women's studies, but from social scientific approaches to the study of religion, and weaves these several approaches together in a new methodology appropriate to her task. What is particularly encouraging in this example is that her move from the ghetto involves no surrender of Feminist Theological concerns and interests, nor a craven acceptance of all that secular feminism has to offer. On the contrary, Fulkerson has much to teach secular feminism—particularly about its ideological blindness to the importance of religion in many women's lives, and to the potentially empowering effects of such religion. (Ironically, it seems possible that Feminist Theology may in the end turn out to be more willing to break out of the ghetto of disciplinary confinement than a secular feminism which continues to be almost uniformly blind to the importance of religion and illiterate in matters of theology.)

The encouraging openness to other disciplines revealed by Fulkerson's work is also evident in several other areas of recent feminist theology understood in its broadest sense. Most striking, perhaps, has been the enormously fruitful engagement with historical studies of Christian life, thought, and institutions. While this engagement has important roots in Feminist Theology and its early critique of Christianity (as in Ruether's edited collection *Religion and Sexism: Images of Woman in the Jewish and Christian Traditions*),[6] it has since tended to break free of such explicit theological commitments, as well as from secular feminism's uncritical assumption that all religion is necessarily patriarchal and oppressive. Some of the most interesting historical studies of recent times have grown from these seeds, including Caroline Walker Bynum's studies of the mediaeval period, and Lyndal Roper's studies of the Reformation. Far from existing in disciplinary isolation, such works represent significant achievements within the discipline of history as well as feminist theology.

A similarly fruitful move from the ghetto may be seen in feminist theology's relation to sociological and cultural studies of women in the Christian churches today. Whilst, as Fulkerson points out, many previous assertions about women's experience (including women's religious experience) were made without any empirical grounding, a number of

6. Rosemary Radford Ruether (ed.), *Religion and Sexism: Images of Woman in the Jewish and Christian Traditions* (New York: Simon and Schuster, 1974).

recent studies offer more responsible accounts of Christian women's beliefs, interests, values and discourses. Early examples like Nancy Ammerman's *Bible Believers* (a study of American fundamentalism) included material on the place and agency of women in such groups, while a number of recent studies like R. Marie Griffith's, *God's Daughters: Evangelical Women and the Power of Submission*, have focused exclusively on women in Christian organizations.[7] The interesting conclusion of such studies is that even in communities with powerful patriarchal discourses of support for the family and the subordination of women, women still use their religion to exercise responsible agency and to achieve control over parts of their lives that might otherwise be deemed chaotic and controlled by others.

Finally, this discussion of feminist theology's relation with history and the social sciences leads directly to consideration of its relation with biblical studies. As several articles in this volume indicate, this has been another area of extraordinary fruitfulness consequent upon the ability of feminist theology to move from the ghetto into fruitful dialogue with other disciplines and approaches. It would not, I think, be an exaggeration to say that biblical studies has been revolutionized by the influence of feminist approaches, which have in turn become permeable to new literary, social, historical and cultural approaches to the text. Utilizing various creative combinations of such approaches, feminist theological studies have served to shed fresh light on both Old and New Testaments, and seem to have much to offer the future development of Feminist Theology.

Feminist Theology, the Churches, and Women outside the Academy

One further area to which my argument that Feminist Theology needs to break out of the ghetto could be extended is that of its audience. Is Feminist Theology isolated in the sense that it speaks only to itself and addresses only other Feminist Theologians within the academic community? The difficulty in answering these questions lies in the dearth of research on the readership and influence of Feminist Theology, but my hunch would be that Feminist Theology is probably somewhat

7. Nancy Tatom Ammerman, *Bible Believers: Fundamentalists in the Modern World* (New Brunswick: Rutgers University Press, 1987); R. Marie Griffith, *God's Daughters: Evangelical Women and the Power of Submission* (California: University of California Press, 1997).

less isolated in these respects than most other academic disciplines—including mainstream theology. My only evidence on this matter comes from publishers who have told me that Feminist Theology has been one of the best selling sectors of religious publishing, as well as from my observation that women outside the academy often have some familiarity with Feminist Theology and that talks on Feminist Theology tend to draw wider audiences than those on other theological topics. It is also notable that most Feminist Theologians seem to assume a general as well as a scholarly audience, and to write in a fashion appropriate to such a readership (paradoxically Fulkerson and other feminist theologians more influenced by contemporary disciplines often adopt a less accessible style).

In terms of audience then, Feminist Theology may have moved out of the ghetto some time ago—and to have helped pull academic theology along with it in the process. Yet it is precisely in this area that Feminist Theology has faced some of its harshest criticisms, particularly from women in north America who accuse it of being bound to the lifeworlds of white, educated, middle-class women. Womanist theologians have articulated these criticisms most clearly, and in a number of cases have developed alternative theologies which aim to do greater justice to the experience of women of colour. In the United Kingdom these criticisms may have a little less bite, black religion being a less well established sector of the Christian scene, yet the criticism that the experience of women of different social classes who actually people the churches has been ignored by Feminist Theology could almost certainly be made to stick.

In response to such criticisms, I would agree that it is wrong for Feminist Theologians to tell us what 'women's experience' is without having researched such experience, just as it is wrong for Feminist Theologians to tell women (as they sometimes have) that we cannot (or do not) believe such and such a doctrine. Just as secular feminism has often made women feel guilty for having husbands, so Feminist Theology has often made women feel guilty for believing in the incarnation or the resurrection, or for valuing the church. Yet, as we have seen above, the movement of feminist theology from the ghetto has already begun to correct some of these excesses, both by taking social scientific modes of research more seriously, and by learning from secular feminism the importance of standpoint in the construction of knowledge. It is interesting to speculate that a deeper engagement with the Christian tradition might also help Feminist Theology reach wider audiences of women—most notably those in the churches who view Bible and tradition more positively, and who wish to engage with them in ways which are responsible both to faith and to feminism.

Will Feminist Theology disappear? Even in the wholly positive sense that Ruth Page intends in her essay above, I do not believe that it will or that it should. I have, however, tried to show why I believe it to be at a crucial stage in its development, and to be faced with a challenge that it must meet in order to survive. The challenge is to come out of isolation into greater openness with the Christian tradition, with other disciplines, and with wider audiences. I have pointed to several examples of feminist theology already taking one or more of these steps, and achieving remarkable results in the process. I have also tried to show that this need not involve the disappearance of Feminist Theology, but its rebirth. As the essays collected in this book reveal so well, the diversity of the discipline at the present moment should be viewed not as a sign of dissolution, but of the vitality which can accompany the move from the ghetto.

INDEX OF AUTHORS